T0358527

The Interdependent Organization

A Path to a More Sustainable Enterprise

Rexford H. Draman

THE
INTERDEPENDENT
ORGANIZATION

The Path to a More Sustainable Enterprise

Routledge
Taylor & Francis Group

LONDON AND NEW YORK

First published 2016 by Greenleaf Publishing Limited

Published 2017 by Routledge
2 Park Square, Milton Park, Abingdon, Oxon OX14 4RN
711 Third Avenue, New York, NY 10017, USA

Routledge is an imprint of the Taylor & Francis Group, an informa business

Copyright © 2016 Taylor & Francis

Cover by Sadie Gornall-Jones
Image used under license from Shutterstock.com

British Library Cataloguing in Publication Data:
  A catalogue record for this book is available from the British Library.

  ISBN-13: 978-1-78353-291-9 [pbk]
  ISBN-13: 978-1-78353-292-6 [hbk]

Contents

Acknowledgments

First, I want to say thanks to all of my teachers and mentors over the years. Without your efforts and contributions, I would not have become the person I am today. Among this group there are three individuals that I want to single out because of their direct impact on my academic life and the journey that led to this book. First is Dr. Asterios G. Kefalas. It was his encouragement that led me to enroll in the Systems Ecology course during the first summer of my Ph.D. program. It was in this course where my understanding of business shifted from being an assortment of independent pieces to becoming an interdependent organism with a guiding purpose. This new perspective gave me a new lens through which I could see and understand the interactions and activities of business and organizations. The second is Dr. James F. Cox, who was my major professor and has been a mentor for many years. He introduced me to the systems-based tools and practices contained within the Theory of Constraints and also encouraged me to follow my heart. These gifts provided me a foundation and focus upon which I have built my academic career and the commitment to undertake the journey associated with writing this book. Third, and most important, is my loving wife Marsha. Without her ongoing love, support, and encouragement, the learning journey I have been on that led to the writing and publication of this book would not have been possible. I love you.

Thanks again to all of you.
Rexford Henry Draman, Ph.D.

Introduction

The beginning of a learning journey

It was the summer of 1991 in Athens, Georgia, and both the heat and humidity were higher than normal. I was one of 22 graduate students sweltering in an un-air-conditioned classroom, half-way through a class on Systems Ecology, when my future was forever changed. I went from being a 46-year-old Ph.D. student diligently working to successfully complete my first year of classes in Operations and Strategic Management, to an academic whose new life's goal was to "change the way business is done."

The previous fall I had become a graduate student in the Terry College of Business at the University of Georgia (UGA). I had undertaken this journey hoping to find answers to or an explanation for the frustrations I had experienced during my 15+ years in the business world. These frustrations were focused on what I saw as an unwillingness by most managers, directors, and vice presidents to openly share valuable information and to work cooperatively with others toward a common organizational goal. For the most part, business professionals tended to focus their efforts on their own specific measures or goals which led to a perception of the information and resources they possess as treasures or possibly the spoils from a battle, when simply sharing some insight might have improved our decisions and actions. It seemed as though we were all participating in an undeclared internal conflict with our peers, while the organization was engaged in other battles with its competitors. It was my desire to better understand the *why* behind this type of behavior, which I had experienced in each of the organizations I had worked for, that led me to the Systems Ecology course.

When I think back to that day, I felt like a cartoon character with a light bulb lighting up over his head. The "light bulb" went off when I realized organizations are *living systems.* Organizations are organisms that need interaction and cooperation both internally, between their functions and divisions, and externally, with the various organisms that support and compete with them, in order to effectively grow and prosper. At that moment, I instinctively understood that all organizations, regardless of their structure (for-profit, not-for-profit, NGO, etc.), are no different than any living system. It is the interaction between and among their components that makes them strong and sustainable, not the individual performance or value of an individual piece. Yet, as I thought about all the business classes I had taken throughout my educational journey (BA, MBA, and the first year of my Ph.D. program), I could only identify one class that had contained anything more than a brief mention of this new understanding. I instinctively knew I had to find answers to the two questions I was now facing:

- *Why* do organizations behave this way?
- *What* is a better path forward for future organizations?

While this book is the result of more than 20 years of my life, it is by no means my work alone. The insights and dialogs that follow are the result of discussions and arguments, both passionate and passive, with those I have learned from, worked with, and had conflicts with. I tried to include real-world examples to enable others to begin their own transformational journeys. Finally, I extend a heart-felt *thank you* to the reader for your insight, curiosity, and willingness to look at and consider a new perspective for your organization. Before getting into the details, I want to establish a frame of reference that I hope each of you will keep at the forefront of your minds as you begin this journey.

Foundational insights and assumptions behind our understanding

Before we begin looking into the evolution of organizations and a path towards a more sustainable organizational future, we need to delve into how we as humans make decisions and take actions. Without understanding this, the changes this journey will require an organization to make will be impossible. To begin looking into this phenomenon, I would like to submit two examples of how our best decisions can produce unforeseen negative consequences.

The first example comes from the late 1980s when a small number of larvae from a mollusk native to Russia (zebra mussel) were inadvertently introduced into the Great Lakes when a visiting cargo ship dumped its bilge water. Ten years later, it was estimated that the zebra mussel has cost the power industry in and around the Great Lakes in excess of $3 billion.

In the second example I worked with an associate to provide consulting services to a medium-sized manufacturing company. Prior to our involvement with the company, its largest division, with whom we were working, had been losing about $300,000 a month for close to a year. Drawing on our in-depth understanding of systems-based processes and practices, we introduced a set of new assumptions and measures into the division to guide its production planning and control decisions. Within three months, it was making close to $300,000 a month in profit. This initially stood out as a wonderful demonstration of how easily and effectively we, as humans, can change our behavior (decision-making) when the changes produce desired results. But the story does not end there. More than six months later, the same company had a quality issue and lost one of its major customers, which had a sizable negative impact on overall sales and profits. It was at that time the CFO began speaking up, saying: "I told you these new approaches to our planning and control decisions were not correct." Within a short time the organization had reverted to the old measures and practices. Yes, you guessed it, within the next six months, the company was bankrupt.

These stories and thousands of others like them exist because, without strong discipline and training, we humans do not have the ability to identify and quantify the potential impact from our daily decisions and actions. We tend to rely on our current set of assumptions when we evaluate our daily actions and their potential impact on the future. As such, it is the assumptions and mental models we use on a daily basis that are brought into all of our actions and reactions. While this worked well in the past, when our processes and practices were more stable, with today's ever-increasing rate of change in the level of technology, information, and cultural interactions (interdependence) around the world the reliance on old models will not allow us to effectively transition into the future.

In a more sustainable future we will need a new perspective through which we can look at, evaluate, and develop solutions. That said, I hope these and the other stories throughout the book will jog your memory into reflecting on how we, as individuals, draw on our understanding and assumptions of a situation, our existing level of knowledge, and our unique set of experiences to guide our choices and actions. There is no doubt that the cargo ship captain and the CFO assumed that their decisions and their resulting actions were the correct ones: emptying the bilge and changing the organization's practices. Yet, in hindsight, we see that these actions were incorrect and produced disastrous results.

Every day, every one of us relies on our current level of understanding, experience, and assumptions—many of which we embraced as young children—about the situation we are facing in making decisions and taking action. Sometimes the actions produce wonderful results; sometimes we get disastrous results; and sometimes the results are just so-so. If we do not have a process for evaluating our assumptions, which are the foundational beliefs upon which we build our new knowledge, we are destined to continue taking the same actions and making the same mistakes over and over again. Or, as Karl Popper said, "We are prisoners caught in the framework of our theories; our expectations; our past experiences; our language."[1]

1 Popper, Karl R. 1970. "Normal Science and its Dangers." In *Criticism and the Growth of Knowledge*, edited by I. Lakatos and A. Musgrave. Cambridge, UK: Cambridge University Press, pp. 51-58.

The way out of this prison is to learn how to identify and challenge our currently held assumptions and beliefs. This change enables us to break through that barrier and into an expanded framework of understanding. When this proves to be limiting, we can then expand the framework again. The goal of this book is to provide the reader with the insights needed to make the first breakthrough, and provide them with the foundations of a path forward, to a more organizationally sustainable future.

A brief overview of the coming chapters

The Interdependent Organization effectively presents a deeper understanding of the financial and cultural crossroads we are facing and introduces a systems-based transitional path that can lead individuals, organizations, and societies toward a more holistic and sustainable future.

This book has been divided into three segments. Part I, "The journey to today's crossroads," will provide the reader with the foundational insights and contexts upon which the remaining two segments of the book are built. To this end, the first part involves a historical reflection designed to provide the reader with an expanded understanding of how we got to the situation facing us today. It is this understanding of *how* we got here that is critical when one begins to explain and share these new insights, which challenge commonly held beliefs and practices.

Chapter 1, "More of the same or something different?" starts by taking an in-depth look at today's business through the eyes of economics, the popular business press, and some of the most popular solutions currently being offered. It is my hope that this chapter will help readers understand that we need new solutions rather than the approaches of the past.

Chapter 2, "Foundation for the path forward," focuses on establishing an awareness of how the fundamental shift in our understanding of knowledge creation and the development of the scientific method facilitated the Industrial Revolution. . What emerged throughout the Industrial Revolution can be traced to the application of the scientific method (reductionism) to the development of solutions to the problems businesses and governments were facing. This chapter looks at those problems and the solution(s) that were adopted.

Chapter 3, "The evolution of modern day business," covers the twentieth-century origins and development of modern business practices. This chapter aims to help you recognize the situations that existed and ultimately led to the new approaches that formed the foundational assumptions of today's business practices. By understanding the situation and assumptions on which the processes of today are based, one can more readily see the limitations within them.

Part II presents an in-depth look at the development and evolution of systems thinking, not only within the field of science, but as it has migrated into the field of business and organizational management.

Chapter 4 provides the reader with a look into the history of modern-day systems thinking, which is normally traced back to the 1950s when botanists and biologists such as Ludwig von Bertalanffy began to see the existence of systems and the importance of interdependence.[2] Our investigation follows the growth of this field by considering the work of the cutting-edge thinkers who, over more than 60 years, have expanded Bertalanffy's work across a wide spectrum of the sciences.

Chapter 5 looks into how systems thinking has been brought into the field of business and organizational management. A few of the pioneers in this field were Russell Ackoff, Jay W. Forrester, and Elliott Jaques. It was their pioneering work along with the efforts of many others over the last 50 years that built a broad assortment of proven systems-based business tools and practices. The goal of this second part of the book is to introduce the reader to proven business tools and the foundational assumptions on which they are built. With this knowledge, the reader will be able to look at the business with a different perspective and possibly see a different response to the problems and issues they are facing.

Part III describes *what* a sustainable organization looks like and how it leverages the interdependence within and across its industry and supply chain. In addition, I present my understanding of what an organization's transformational journey would be like. This is followed by an explanation of the transitional efforts that would be required to move an organization from its current position to being ready to begin the transformational journey.

Chapter 6 draws on the content and insight presented in Part II to describe and explain what an interdependent organization is and how it behaves. I have adopted the term—Systems-Based Business Model (S-BBM)—to identify this new perspective.

In Chapter 7 I present what I believe would be the most efficient path for the transitional journey. This 3-step journey starts by bringing change to an organization's operational activities which are the easiest to transition and can produce almost immediate results. These gains build support for the transformation and provide the impetus for the next steps.

Chapter 8 takes an in-depth look at what needs to be accomplished before the organization can begin the transformation. This transition is focused on helping stakeholders and leaders across an organization to move to the new business model, that of a sustainable business, and facilitate their buy-in to the transformational journey.

It is my sincere hope that each of you will enjoy this learning journey and, on reaching the end, have new knowledge and understanding of how to become part of a long-term transformation effort within your organization. In an effort to enhance the readability of this book and increase the breadth of its readership, I have integrated both academic analysis and documentation with real-world stories drawn from a wide spectrum of individuals and organizations. I have taken the liberty to disguise the names and locations of individuals and organizations.

---

2 Bertalanffy, Ludwig von. 1968. *General Systems Theory.* New York, NY: G. Braziller.

Part I
The journey to today's crossroads

1
More of the same or something different?

I am sure we all remember the latest economic crisis that began in 2007. While the economists can argue about the details of whether this downturn met the official criteria to be classified as a depression or only a recession, there is no doubt we all felt and experienced the effects of a shrinking economy. Not only were millions and millions of jobs lost as organizations contracted and/or failed, the anticipated returns on investments, be it the $40K nest egg of a retired tire builder or the $50 million trust fund of an investment banker, were also greatly reduced. Today, in early 2016, the stock market is back and the unemployment levels are approaching pre-downturn levels. Some see the current state of the economy as a signal to breathe a sigh of relief because the worst of this financial downturn is, with any luck, behind us. However, along with a growing number of individuals I am beginning to look back at these repeating cycles as something different—a signal that there is something within the way we manage our organizations and make decisions that is contributing to the frequency and/or magnitude of these downturns. It is my hope that this chapter will help to answer the question posed in the chapter's title: do those who have been entrusted with a managerial position within an organization just continue on the same path, after all that is the path of least resistance, or do we need to begin looking into an alternative route that may well lead to a different result? If we reject the first alternative, then the question becomes which alternative path? This chapter introduces a variety of perspectives and data.

Past economic trends and...?

The first perspective I want to look into is economics. While I agree that a country's economic measures are in the aggregate and, as such, do not single out the well or badly performing organizations, what the aggregate data does provide is an indication of the health of the average business. When these indicators are down businesses, in general, are focused much more on survival and, as such, their decisions and actions will be very different than they are riding the wave of growth.

As we begin looking back at the economic data over the last 100 years there are at least two ways of viewing this data. First is the commonly accepted phenomenon that all economies experience, business cycles. The National Bureau of Economic Research (NBER) in the United States published a table showing the timing and duration of these cycles from the mid-1850s. In Table 1 I have reproduced the NBER information covering 1900 through 2009. The two date columns on the left identify the cycle from peak (highest quarterly performance) to the following trough (lowest quarterly performance) before the next upswing. The following four columns provide additional insight (monthly measures):

- Contraction: months from peak to trough

- Expansion: months from previous trough to this peak

- Cycle measures: months from trough to trough or peak to peak

Table 1 **US business cycle expansions and contractions**

Source: Public Information Office, National Bureau of Economic Research, Inc., Cambridge, MA (www.nber.org/cycles/cyclesmain.html).

Business cycle reference dates		Duration in months		
Peak	**Trough**	**Contraction**	**Expansion**	**Cycle**
(Quarterly dates are in parentheses)		Peak to trough	Previous trough to this peak	Trough from previous trough	Peak from previous peak
June 1899 (III)	December 1900 (IV)	18	24	42	42
September 1902 (IV)	August 1904 (III)	23	21	44	39
May 1907 (II)	June 1908 (II)	13	33	46	56
January 1910 (I)	January 1912 (IV)	24	19	43	32
January 1913 (I)	December 1914 (IV)	23	12	35	36
August 1918 (III)	March 1919 (I)	7	44	51	67
January 1920 (I)	July 1921 (III)	18	10	28	17
May 1923 (II)	July 1924 (III)	14	22	36	40

Business cycle reference dates		Duration in months		
Peak	Trough	Contraction	Expansion	Cycle
October 1926 (III)	November 1927 (IV)	13	27	40	41
August 1929 (III)	March 1933 (I)	43	21	64	34
May 1937 (II)	June 1938 (II)	13	50	63	93
February 1945 (I)	October 1945 (IV)	8	80	88	93
November 1948 (IV)	October 1949 (IV)	11	37	48	45
July 1953 (II)	May 1954 (II)	10	45	55	56
August 1957 (III)	April 1958 (II)	8	39	47	49
April 1960 (II)	February 1961 (I)	10	24	34	32
December 1969 (IV)	November 1970 (IV)	11	106	117	116
November 1973 (IV)	March 1975 (I)	16	36	52	47
January 1980 (I)	July 1980 (III)	6	58	64	74
July 1981 (III)	November 1982 (IV)	16	12	28	18
July 1990 (III)	March 1991 (I)	8	92	100	108
March 2001 (I)	November 2001 (IV)	8	120	128	128
December 2007 (IV)	June 2009 (II)	18	73	91	81
Average, all cycles:		14.7	43.7	58.4	58.4
Average, 1945–2009		10.8	60.2	71.0	70.6

When we take a deeper look at the data we see that the NBER identified 23 unique business cycles (measured from peak to peak) that ranged in duration from 17 months as we moved into the 1920s to the ten year cycle (128 months) that extended from July 1990 to March 2001. There are two points one should recognize when looking at this information. First, one should look at the timing/duration of the different cycles—contraction and expansion. If we take a look at the average duration of the downward (contraction) part of the cycle—from peak to trough—we see that overall it lasts about one year, whereas the upward swing (expansion) of the cycle runs for almost four years (43.7 months). A second perspective concerns the lack of any recognizable patterns in their movement except that they go up and down. The magnitudes and duration of these cycles appear to be random in nature. Yet, if this magnitude of variation appeared on the tracking of my bodily temperature or heart rate, I am sure my doctor would be frantically looking for an explanation.

Another way of viewing economic data is to look at the magnitude of the cycle or, put another way, the impact it had on the overall economic conditions in the country. For that we will have to take a look at a different kind of data—the change in the gross domestic product (overall value of all goods and services produced by the country). This includes personal consumption, governmental purchase and expenditures, private inventories, dollars spent on construction, and the foreign trade balance (imports are subtracted and exports are added), adjusted for inflation. Figure 1 shows the percentage change in the GDP of the U.S. economy by quarter. Once again, I offer this graph as an indicator of the magnitude of impact the business cycle is having on individual businesses and as a surrogate for the intensity of the actions businesses are taking to either survive during the economic downturn or meet the increased demands during the upturns.

Figure 1 **Quarterly growth in real GDP at annual rates, %**

Source: www.economagic.com/em-cgi/charter.exe/var/rgdp-qtrchg+1947+2016+0+0+1+290+545++0 (retrieved November 11, 2016)

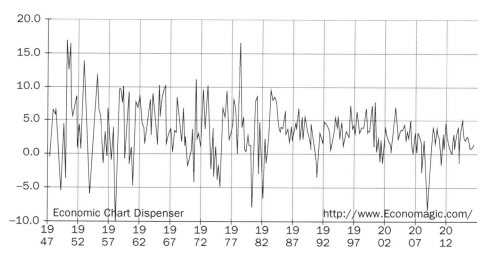

A quick review of the data shows that there have been 16 different occasions since 1947 that the quarterly growth of the U.S. GDP has actually fallen below zero. While this type of data tells us when and to what magnitude the quarter to quarter change occurred, it does not provide any data about what is happening within the economy. The NBER[1] produces reports that dissect and provide additional details behind the summary tables and graphs, but their analysis is focused on the things that occurred during the period (quarter or year) that may have contributed to the adjustment in the GDP. While this is indeed insightful, it does not necessarily point to the causes of the change or provide us with any hard facts that can be used to better oversee and facilitate the economy's ongoing growth.

Before we delve a bit deeper into trying to understand how and why the afore-mentioned shifts in economic performance affect organizational behavior, I think it is important to take a look at the shifts and changes in the field of economics over the last 400+ years.

1 www.nber.org/

To begin, let's take a look at the concept of Mercantilism which was developed during the 1600s when the isolated feudal estates of the Middle Ages were being replaced by more centralized nation-states which had an almost insatiable desire for more wealth to support their growth. At this point in time the economists/philosophers encouraged exports and discouraged imports through the use of tariffs which, if practiced correctly, produced a positive trade balance and funneled more funds to the crown. After all, that was their goal—to facilitate the crown's growth and prosperity.

By the mid-1700s, the physiocrats in France began expressing another economic perspective. They saw the nation's wealth related to the size of the net products it produced. At that point in time the vast majority of the products being produced were agricultural and these were seen as the source of wealth. These economists described the economy's "natural state" as one in which the income flows within and between the different sectors of the economy which did not expand or contract. As for structure, the physiocrats saw the economy as being composed of three different classes: **productive**—farmer and farm workers; **sterile**—industrial laborers, artisans, and merchants; and **proprietor**—who collected the net products as rents. Compared to the Mercantilists in Britain, the economists in France saw the structure and needs of an economy very differently.

These perspectives laid the groundwork for what is commonly referred to as the classical economics that originated in Britain in the late eighteenth century. Adam Smith is commonly seen as the father of classical economics. In 1776, the year of the American Revolution, he published a book entitled *An Inquiry Into the Nature and Causes of the Wealth of Nations*.[2] In this seminal text, Smith lays out a multitude of ideas, but what I want to focus on is his prescription for increasing productivity. At a time when a vast majority of the items being produced were made by hand by craftspeople who started and finished one product at a time, Smith introduced the concept referred to as the division of labor, which broke the overall task down into smaller parts and assigned individuals to perform each part independently. By doing so, productivity was greatly increased and this began the transition from cottage industries to the beginning of manufacturing. This shift to businesses creating products for a market led to the need to expand the market to consume the increased level of output. Both of these shifts required an increase in capital to effectively achieve the objective of increasing productivity and growth. Another major addition from *The Wealth of Nations* to the field of today's economics was included within Book 4, Chapter 2, entitled "Of Restraints upon the Importation from Foreign Countries of such Goods as can be Produced at Home". In this chapter Smith introduces the idea of how an individual "intends only his own gain … is … led by an invisible hand to promote an end which was not part of his intention."[3] In this case, Smith's metaphor was focused on showing his strong support of domestic/

---

2 Smith, Adam. 1776. *An Inquiry into the Nature and Causes of the Wealth of Nations*. London, UK: W Strahan & T Cadell.

3 *Ibid.*, Book 4, Chapter 2.

local industries and comparing that to the importation of foreign-made goods. At that point in time his perspective was that the small, local economies interacting with each other and guided by the self-interest of the owners and the local community would provide a stronger economy than one that drew in imports from other countries. His position was counter to the crown-sponsored transnational organizations, such as the British East India Company and others, which tended to be unresponsive to the needs of local economies. In more recent times the idea of an "invisible hand" has been expanded by those within the neoclassical economic sphere to encompass nearly all aspects of economics.[4]

Another contributor to classical economics was Jean-Baptiste Say. In 1805, he published his book entitled *A Treatise on Political Economy*,[5] which contained insights that eventually became known as Say's Law of Markets. This theory remained part of economic thought for the next 125+ years. Say's Law argued that there could never be a general deficiency in demand nor a general glut of commodities in the whole economy. Simply put, the objective of a businessman, when he produces a product, is to sell the product as soon as possible. After all, the sale creates wages for the worker and income for the businessman. Therefore, the production and sale of good A increases individual wealth and as such demand for goods B and C. Say recognized there could be some imbalances across economic sectors but, over time, businesses will recognize these imbalances and retool and produce products with larger demand.

The nineteenth century saw the rise of the Socialist approach to economics, most notably put forth by Karl Marx. He looked at the traditional approach to labor and its value a bit differently. He started with the currently accepted labor theory of value which defined the value of a product by the labor it took to produce it. He referred to this as the "use value" of the product. Next he pointed out that products are sold at what is called the "exchange value" which is what the customer will pay and more than the "use value". The difference is what capitalists refer to as "profit" and Marx referred to as "surplus value". Marx saw this as the exploitation of the worker.

Shortly after Marx published *Das Kapital* in 1867,[6] a revolution in classical economics took place. Economists abandoned the labor theory of value which had been a tenet of economics for close to 100 years and replaced it with something new: the theory of marginal utility. This shift is commonly referred to as the marginal revolution referring to the shift to marginal utility as the primary measure. This change recognized that an equilibrium of people's preferences established product prices, which included the price of labor, removing any question about capitalism exploiting the worker. This shift in perceptions of economic behavior

4 Basu, Kaushik. 2010. *Beyond the Invisible Hand: Groundwork for a New Economics*. Princeton, NJ: Princeton University Press.
5 Say, Jean-Baptiste. 1805. *A Treatise on Political Economy*. Philadelphia, PA: Lippincott, Grambo & Co.
6 Marx, Karl. 1867. *Das Kapital*. Hamburg, Germany: Vertag von Otto Meissner.

led to the emergence of two very different perspectives to explain economic behavior. Let's take a quick look at both of these:

One of the outputs from this shift was the emergence of Alfred Marshall's work at Cambridge. He saw economics as a path to improving overall material conditions but he recognized that to accomplish this it must be done in conjunction with social and political forces. He added a great deal of insight and rigor to the field. Some of his contributions to the expanding field of economics are: the math and structure enabling the development of supply and demand graphs, the relationship between quantity and price and their effect on supply and demand, the concept of producer and consumer surpluses, and the law of diminishing returns. One of his most lasting impacts on the teaching of economics was his use of diagrams to explain the relationships between variables which he included in his text *Principles*, published in 1890.[7]

John Maynard Keynes also studied at Cambridge and is considered by many as the most influential economist of the twentieth century and one of the founders of modern macroeconomics. Prior to Keynes, the neoclassical economists believed that free markets would provide full employment in the short and medium term as long as the wage demands by the workers were flexible. Keynes argued that aggregate demand established the overall level of economic activity and if the demand was inadequate, the overall economy could see high levels of unemployment. He went on to say that intervention by the state—through spending and monitory controls—was necessary to intervene in the "boom to bust" cycles of economic activity. As the Western economies entered World War II, they begin to adopt Keynes's economic policies. After WWII, the Bretton Woods Agreement introduced economic controls that greatly restricted the influence the speculators and financiers had enjoyed after WWI which eventually contributed to the Great Depression. By 1950, his economic policies had been adopted by most of the developed world and many of the developing nations. Indeed, the cover article of the December 31, 1965 issue of *Time* magazine, entitled "The Economy: We are all Keynesians now," focused on the favorable economic conditions. It described the positive economic conditions of the mid-1960s as having been reached because of "Washington's economic managers' … adherence to Keynes's central theme: the modern capitalist economy does not automatically work at top efficiency, but can be raised to that level by the intervention and influence of the government". It is also of note that the title of the article, "We are all Keynesians now", is attributed to Milton Friedman, who is described as the nation's leading conservative economist.[8]

The second interesting perspective was initially defined by Carl Menger in 1871. His argument for marginal utility was based on the fact that the value of goods varies because they provide differing levels of importance to different people at different times. One of Menger's earliest followers was Friedrich von Hayek who, in

7 Marshall, Alfred. 1880. *Principles of Economics*. London, UK: Macmillan and Co.
8 *Time*. 1965. "We Are All Keynesians Now". *Time*, December 31. Retrieved October 20, 2016 (http://content.time.com/time/magazine/article/0,9171,842353,00.html).

his book entitled *The Road to Serfdom* (1944),[9] argued that within centrally planned economies the individuals charged with determining the distribution of resources cannot have enough information to do it reliably. Thus they will be less effective and efficient than a free market economy. By the late 1940s Milton Friedman had arrived at the University of Chicago and continued the work of Jacob Viners and his criticism of Keynes's approach to economics. Friedman believed that a government policy that is based on the laissez-faire approach to business was more desirable than having government intervening in the actions of business. He strongly supported the virtues of a free market economic system with few controls and minimal intervention. As for monitory policy, he thought that government should establish a hands off/neutral monetary policy that is focused on long-term economic growth and not too concerned about the short-term issues that may arise. Friedman believed that there was a close and stable association between inflation and the supply of money. That said, inflation could be avoided with the proper control and regulation of the growth rate of money within the economy. Put another way, control the amount of money in circulation and you can control the rate of inflation. His economic perspective was embraced by both President Reagan and British Prime Minister Thatcher and has received solid support from political conservatives on both sides of the Atlantic Ocean.

Finally, we have arrived at the latest perspective researchers have taken when looking into the ever-broadening field of economics. Starting in the 1980s a group of systems and economics researchers working at the Santa Fe Institute began viewing economics through the lens of complexity science. The result of this effort is today commonly referred to as complexity economics.

So, what have we learned during this short journey through the last 300+ years within the field of economics? A couple of things should stand out. The first is that the perceptions with which economists have viewed the study of economics, the issues and problems they saw, and the solutions/recommendations they have offered have varied greatly over time.

Second, over the last 150 years a lot of the focus of economic thinkers has been on the issue of how much governmental involvement/control should exist in business. These range from complete governmental control and direction under socialism (Marx and Lenin), to the other extreme where no controls are necessary (Menger, Hayek and Friedman), to somewhere in the middle (Marshall, Keynes and others). While Marx was first, publishing *Das Kapital* in 1867, Menger's response was published in 1871 and Marshall's perspective arrived a few years later in 1882. During that 16 year period the three different foundational beliefs relative to the impact and role of government intervention and control in economic activity were published. Since then, the followers of these three perspectives have continued their debate. One thing I have learned on my journey is that it is very hard for any of us to give up the foundational assumptions we carry—whether they are about family,

---

9 Hayek, Friedrich. 1944. *The Road to Serfdom*. Abingdon-on-Thames, UK: Routledge.

culture, or our understanding of "how the world works". Economists and the field of economics are no different.

In conclusion, what I see when I look at the fields of economics, psychology, and the other "soft sciences" including my peers in the field of business, is that we are all still learning and, for the most part, relying on correlative analysis to support our pre-supposed assumptions/positions/theories. While sometimes correlative analysis may lead us to a correct conclusion, it is not *cause and effect* and, therefore, we cannot get past what it shows. Sometimes this is sufficient but sometimes we assume a strong correlation to be cause and effect when it is not: summer weather does not cause drowning even though they are very strongly correlated. Today, after my many years spent in the "real world" and academia, I think that an economic model most appropriate for today's society, is one that:

- Encompasses the entire globe and all its components and current issues

- Recognizes the interdependence across geographic boundaries and economic levels

- Incorporates the costs and impact linked to the global environmental crisis

- Recognizes the ever-increasing disparity in income and equity ownership

Such a model would downplay our current economic assumption that links the vast majority (all?) of the financial rewards to the investors (financial risk takers) and recognize the existence of interdependence and common goals of the people, communities, and nations around our world. From this perspective, the new economic model would contain a deeper awareness of its impact on the larger whole (providing a more viable path for those less fortunate members of our interdependent world to move forward). While this book cannot address the need or detailed content of economic models, what it does contain is a viable path for businesses to begin moving towards a place that would be more aligned with this new perspective. Before we attempt to draw any conclusions about the current situation, we need to take a look at what the popular business press has been offering as the latest and greatest solution for what ails business.

A look at the popular business press offerings

To begin our journey into what the popular business press has been offering over the last 25 years or more, I identified four lists of the best business books. These lists were put together by: Forbes, Inc, Business Today, and the Business Pundit. I then began to identify and classify the basic focus of each book by what it offered the reader. To that end, I came up with four general categories to describe their structure and content:

- **How to do it**. Describing what the author offers as a successful business process or practice

- **Case study**. Documenting and reviewing the success or failure of businesses

- **Human resources**. Focused "how to" book addressing the human aspects within business

- **New idea**. Offering the reader something new relative to business processes and practices; this category included many foundational books on management from the first half of the twentieth century

After removing the duplicates within each classification, I came up with the following quantities for each category. I have added a few titles within each category to give you some idea of the books included.

How to do it (31):

- *Competing for the Future* (Harvard Business School Press, 1994)

- *Crossing the Chasm* (Harper Business, 1990)

- *The Six Sigma Way* (McGraw Hill, 2000)

- *Competitive Advantage* (Free Press, 1998)

Case studies (25):

- *My Years with General Motors* (Doubleday, 1963)

- *In Search of Excellence* (Harper & Row, 1982)

- *Reengineering the Corporation* (HarperCollins, 1993)

- *Good to Great* (HarperCollins, 2001)

Human resources (11):

- *Seven Habits of Highly Effective People* (Simon &Schuster, 1990)

- *How to Win Friends and Influence People* (Holiday House, 1937)

- The *H R Scorecard* (Harvard Business Review Press, 2001)

- The *H R Value Proposition* (Harvard Business Review Press, 2005)

New way of looking (11):

- *The Tipping Point* (Little Brown, 2000)

- *The Fifth Discipline* (Crown Business, 1990)

- *The Wisdom of Crowds* (Doubleday, 2004)

There are also many books from over 60 years ago: *The Wealth of Nations, The Principles of Scientific Management, The Principles of Management*, to name a few.

While we cannot gain too much insight from this unscientific classification, there are a few facts that are immediately apparent:

- Over two-thirds of these books (How to do it and Case studies categories) were focused on describing the how and why behind current business practice. Most of the books in these categories are tied to the introduction of a new "high potential" process or practice for business and provide the reader with insights and activities that might help them embrace the new process or practice.

- It is pretty evident that the prevailing assumption of the vast majority of "best business book" authors is that people within the organization are not too important. Can this be right? After all, organizations are made up of people and the only way to get the organization to improve its performance over the long term requires its people to begin working together more efficiently and effectively. In a 2014 Gallup poll less than a third of the employees surveyed were engaged with their jobs.[10] It is easy to see there is a great deal of room for improvement in this area.

- The solutions being offered by a vast majority of the popular business press "more of the same". After all, these are the easy ones to write. New solutions, on the other hand, require the author to identify and challenge some or all of the assumptions within an existing practice or process and then work to develop a new solution to that problem or issue.

Impact of past and proposed solutions

Reviewing the trends in economics provides some insight, but to understand more fully how the future might look, it is also important to consider some of the more successful business practices that have been introduced and adopted by business over the last 50 years.

There were two major shifts that began in the 1960s. The first was the development of the corporate structure commonly referred to as a conglomerate. Some of the most memorable U.S. conglomerates of the time were: Ling-Temco-Vaught, Litton Industries, Textron and Teledyne. This corporate structure is a combination of two or more corporations that are engaged in different businesses. The early assumption was that given the low interest rates at the time and short cycles between bull/bear markets, it was possible to purchase a business during the low cycle (bear market) and pay a deflated price for it. As long as the purchased business produced a return that was larger than the interest payment on the loan, then the return on investment (ROI) of the conglomerate was positively impacted and everyone was happy. By the late 1960s, as interest rates began to increase

---

10 Adkins, Amy. 2015. "Majority of U.S. Employees not Engaged despite Gains in 2014". Gallup. Retrieved October 22, 2016 (http://www.gallup.com/poll/181289/majority-employees-not-engaged-despite-gains-2014.aspx).

due to inflation, the overall ROI was negatively impacted and investors became increasingly hostile to the idea of the conglomerate. By the mid-1970s, many of the high-flying conglomerates of the early 1960s had fallen by the wayside and had been split up and sold.

The second shift was the increase in the size and importance of marketing and branding, which began to emerge in the late 1950s and early 1960s. Packaged goods firms such as Procter & Gamble and General Foods began to notice that their competitors were becoming their equals and as such they recognized the need to develop strong product identities that would separate their products from the competition and provide something on which to build customer loyalty. By the 1980s much of the marketing expertise still resided within large firms such as Colgate, Unilever, Coca-Cola, and Pepsi, which made their marketing managers with 5–10 years of experience valuable commodities to the competition and to smaller firms trying to develop a deep understanding of marketing. By the early 1990s the big retailers began to realize that they too could play the branding game and begin to build store loyalty, through the quality level of their products and service. As we look at the markets of today we continually see an explosion of both the number of products being offered and the number of branding messages we are exposed to. In a 2011 *Atlantic* article, Marc de Swaan Arons states that on an average day, the average U.S. customer is exposed to some 3,000 brand messages.[11] He goes on to say that this level of messaging leads to clutter and mixed messages which reduce their effectiveness and increase the level of confusion for the customer.

By the early 1960s computer technology started to play a major role in influencing business and manufacturing in particular. General Motors Research Laboratories had begun to pioneer the use of computer aided design (CAD) to improve the drafting process during the design of autos. The benefits they were seeking to achieve were time-savings associated with using computer technology to revise and correct design drawings. The second benefit from using CAD designs was the growing ability to test the design through simulation. By the mid-1960s they were beginning to see the possibilities of taking the CAD design and using the computer data as input for programming the new numerical controlled (NC) machining tools. By the 1970s, as computer chips became more affordable and computer technology and capabilities continued to expand, there was a rapid adaptation of CAD/CAM within the metal shaping and forming industries. Today, the use of these tools continues to expand with almost seamless integration from the design of a product to the manufacturing processes needed to produce it. This has greatly reduced the level of skills needed in the machine shop where new specialized tools and equipment are used to replace the skilled machinist in the machining and production of parts. All of this adds to the reduction in direct labor and an increase in skill level of the IT team. This change led to a shift in the make-up and amount of labor needed to develop and produce a product.

---

11 Arons, Marc de Swaan. 2011. "How Brands were Born: A Brief History of Modern Marketing". *The Atlantic*, October 2011.

Over the last 25 years or so we have also seen organizations begin to reemphasize a focus on quality by expanding their use of tools such as TQM, 6-sigma, and lean in their production efforts. This shift is in response to customer demand for an improved level of quality in their products. During WWII the Department of Defense required contractors to adopt and use statistical process control (SPC) to ensure the overall level of quality of all military hardware and munitions. As the war effort drew to a close and the firms began transitioning to the production of consumer goods for the expanding home and world market, the requirement for utilizing SPC vanished and since it required extra employees to oversee the SPC efforts, most firms soon reduced and in some instances eliminated it completely. By the mid-to-late 1970s products (other than games and toys) from Japan were beginning to be made available in the U.S. and, in many instances, their quality was much higher than similar products produced domestically. That led to the recognition that U.S. manufacturing needed to reinstate quality into its production organizations. A number of large manufacturing companies made excursions to Japan to try to figure out how they could improve their processes so they could produce products of equal quality. The student becomes the teacher. Since that time the focus on quality in the U.S. has continued to expand.

Another major shift for the general public that began about 25 years ago was the use of the internet. While a few academic and Department of Defense researchers had access to the ARPANET (Advanced Research Projects Agency Network) back in the late 1960s, all it provided was the basics of electronic communications. Organizations had pools of secretaries to prepare the letters, a large purchasing department that monitored inventory and issued purchase orders, a large number of bookkeepers preparing and paying bills, and a number of sales people making calls to current and potential customers. During this time, before the internet, an individual's connectivity was closely linked to their level of personal contact with others. Given the large departments most people worked in at that time, human interaction and staying connected was almost a job requirement. By the 1990s individuals could get access to the World Wide Web through phone modems. Since that time the use of the internet has exploded and brought what has become an unbelievable amount of change to all areas of our life—professional, personal, and private. It has created new professions and careers that did not exist before 1990. Its global interconnection provides an enormous amount of information, with product exposure and outlets that reach around the world. It has allowed businesses and individuals to share, in real time, information and thoughts with others anywhere in the world. In business, this type of almost instant communication, whether it is with customers, suppliers, or employees, helps all organizations stay more aligned and coordinated on the task at hand.

Today, with so much of our communications and cooperation done in cyberspace, we are not able to establish those solid connections and interrelationships at work that were required in the past. While I am not passing judgment on whether this change is good or bad, I believe it is a contributing reason why over 70% of today's employees are "not engaged" or "actively disengaged" at their place of work—according to the 2014 Gallup Poll.[12] I mention this because the viability of all living systems, of which organizations and people are a part, lies in their connections and interdependence. Without these, systems begin to atrophy and lose some of their capability. More on this later, but for now, let us look at some of the changes the internet has brought to businesses of all sizes.

The 1970s saw the beginnings of what is now commonly referred to as the financialization of the U.S. economy. Greta R. Krippner offered the following definition of financialization in her book *Capitalizing on Crisis* (2011): "the growing importance of financial activities as a source of profits in the economy".[13] While I am not going to replicate her well-written argument for this I will provide a few facts and insights from her work. Between the 1950s and 1960s the financial sector's profits ranged between 10 and 15% of the total profits in the U.S. economy. By the 1980s the same sector accounted for approximately 30% of the profits. In early 2001 the sector peaked at over 40% of the economy's profits before the business cycle peaked and it experienced a large drop-off commonly referred to as the dot-com bubble. A point worth noting about the aforementioned numbers is that they do not include the financial profits associated with financial activities within large manufacturing organizations such as GM, GE, Sears, and Ford. Another measure Krippner offers to demonstrate the growth in financial sector profits is the historical ratio within the U.S. economy of financial to non-financial profits. In the past, the value of the profits from the financial sector was around 10% of the value of the profits generated by the non-financial sector. By 2000 the profits from the financial sector were over 70% of the value of the non-financial sector. This means there was a major shift in the type of business generating profits in the U.S. economy. This shift to focusing on revenues from financing instead of from the product side of the business means the priorities and focus within the corporate offices has shifted. This shift makes it harder for organizations to focus on the long term and envision how they will compete in the future. I encourage you to look within your organizations at the decisions and actions taken over the last ten or more years and see if you can detect a difference in their decision-making. When I left my last business position in 1987 I was reacting to some of these changes but at the time I could not verbalize what was going on. I just instinctively knew I could no longer support the company's actions. My decision was to leave and begin this 20 year search for a deeper understanding and a better solution.

By the time the 1990s arrived, the shift to offshoring and outsourcing was expanding greatly. The primary assumption behind moving manufacturing to countries with low wages is that U.S. companies would receive significant savings over the higher domestic labor costs. The difference between these two terms is that offshoring is moving the facility and work while outsourcing is sending the work to outside contractors to perform. While the existence of the internet did not initially

---

12 Adkins (2015).
13 Krippner, Greta. 2011. *Capitalizing on Crisis: The Political Origins of the Rise of Finance.* Cambridge, MA: Harvard University Press.

contribute to the movement towards outsourcing, as the level of connectivity and communications around the world increased, this provided support for the outsourcing argument. For the last twenty or more years this shift has been going on and it was an accepted strategy for any firm that manufactured consumer products. In addition, a vast majority of us have experienced the shift in phone-based customer service to India and other parts of Asia. Some of the stories are good and some of them not so. All of these decisions were based on the assumption that lower wages would lower labor costs and improve profits.

While there was some truth to that twenty years ago, today with the increase in wages across the East and the time delays in getting products from the factory in China to the store in Des Moines, IA, the savings are becoming much harder to find and justify. In 2012 Boston Consulting Group surveyed American manufacturing companies and found that 37% of those with sales over $1 billion were planning on reshoring. What is more important is that, of those firms with sales over $10 billion, 48% were planning and involved in reshoring.[14] I would suggest that the rush to offshore was in many cases justified by an incomplete analysis of the overall impact of such a decision. Part of that oversight was because the organization did not want to get left behind—some form of herd mentality existed instead of in-depth analysis and pushing hard to challenge assumptions and expectations.

In 1993, in response to a 1992 Boston Federal Reserve study that showed bank loan officers gave whites preferential treatment in approving mortgages, the new Clinton administration created new criteria for evaluating bank compliance with the Community Reinvestment Act (CRA). This new criteria also called for the use of "innovative or flexible" lending practices to address the needs of low- and moderate-income borrowers. Then in 1999 the Gramm-Leach-Bliley Act was signed, which expanded the reach of the CRA. At the signing President Clinton said it, "establishes the principles that, as we expand the powers of banks, we will expand the reach of the (Community Reinvestment) Act".[15] As this initiative took hold and began to grow it created a large positive feedback loop within the financial industry which led to its continual expansion. As the industry continued to grow, businesses specializing in effectively doing small pieces of the work continued to expand. By the time we reached the mid-2000s, a year or two before the crash, it was quite easy to get a mortgage. I offer the following personal story as an example of how easy it was. In 2007, I was part of a start-up in Santa Fe, New Mexico. One day, I was out with one of the associates, who happened to be a real estate agent, and we saw a unique piece of property that I expressed an interest in. She said something to the

---

14 Sirkkin, H., M. Zinser, and D. Hohner. 2011. *Made in America, Again: Why Manufacturing will Return to the U.S.* Boston, MA: BCG. Retrieved October 22, 2016 (https://www.bcg.com/documents/file84471.pdf).

15 Clinton, Bill. November 12, 1999. "Statement by President Bill Clinton at the Signing of the Financial Modernization Bill." U.S. Treasury Department Office of Public Affairs (Press release). Retrieved October 12, 2016 (https://www.treasury.gov/press-center/press-releases/Pages/ls241.aspx).

effect "don't worry about getting a mortgage, just fill out the application" and she and her associates would find the funding—even though I had no viable income at the time. While I did not go through with it, I have no doubt they could have found a mortgage for me and it would have soon gone into default.

The question I would like you to reflect on is: did anyone, in the time leading up to the crash, intentionally make a decision or take action with the explicit intent of bringing on the crash? Of course, the answer is a resounding, *no*. Everyone involved in the real estate industry, from the agents to the mortgage brokers to the various CEOs within the industry were all making, what they believed to be, the correct decisions—as guided by the current situation and assumptions. I am also quite sure that as the crisis approached they looked at their past and current actions and thought that they were only doing what everyone else in the industry was doing and if they did not do it someone else would, which would mean losing business. So I ask you: *why* were these well-intentioned people going down the path that would lead to the second largest economic crash in modern history?

I would like to suggest a combination of two basic facts. First, the financial rewards that were tied to making certain types of decisions and taking associated actions were focused on short-term performance. The system, set up by the various mortgage businesses worked to provide its employees with guidelines and incentives that rewarded the desired behavior as they had defined it. Second, the understanding of any possible negative ramifications from these actions was isolated from the action itself. By this I mean that each of the steps in the process was being performed by individual divisions or organizations and no one was responsible for the complete chain of events, which includes the successful repayment of the mortgage. No one was looking at or responsible for the entire chain of activities and as such no one was concerned about any negative ramifications associated with the inability to repay the mortgages. As a result, the world economy suffered a major recession.

So, "How are we doing?"

I guess that depends on who you ask. It is pretty clear to me that if we really understood the how's and why's upon which the economic system is built, we would have effectively applied that knowledge to bring the wild cycles and swings the world has experienced over the last 100 or more years under some control. While I will agree with those that say without variation life would be very boring, these ups and downs indicate the financial uplifting and ruin of many individuals and families. We are working on learning more but we still have a large gap between the two primary perspectives in economics. We must be willing to surface and challenge the assumptions we are hanging on to if we expect to develop a deeper understanding of this very complex system.

When we take a look at business books over the last 50 years a large percentage appear to be the "how-to" and the "lessons learned" types of book. In both of these instances they are sharing insights with the reader based on "what has worked in the past". I believe the reason for that is threefold. First, for the lessons learned book, it is a biography of some form that enables the author to say "here is how I did it" and look at my track record. Second, the currency in academics is research and publications. By identifying and studying businesses that have proven to be successful, the likelihood of being able to put together academic articles and a marketable book or two are very good. Third, more of the same with a slight twist is easy and welcomed by the audience. Selling a similar instead of a new idea is much easier and safer for one's career. Conversely, when we look at books that introduce new ideas, they take much more work. New ideas challenge the currently held assumptions. Newton and Descartes challenged the church as the holder of truth. Fredrick W. Taylor challenged the assumption that workers just work and put together processes to find and develop the one best way to do a job. These are the types of ideas that bring change to our level of understanding, not just a few dollars to the author.

As someone who had a successful business career, returned to school, earned a Ph.D., and practiced within academia for close to 20 years, I have identified two business school-related issues which I believe have contributed to the current situation of business: The first is the make-up of academia within most major schools of business. Let me talk a bit about how/who comprises the vast majority of professorships in business schools. Higher education is structured so that the higher your degree the narrower your focus and area of expertise. Earning a Ph.D. requires a narrow breadth of knowledge but a very deep understanding about a small section within a functional area. It could be as narrow as becoming a true expert in the effective use of technology to monitor shipping between producer and distributor. This narrow focus is good because the most important currency in academia is published research and the narrower the focus the easier it is to publish and the more you publish the more respected you become. The second point about most academics, especially those in business, is that very few of them have any real-world experience in business. A vast majority of the respected, well-published academics went straight through school, from their BS, to an MBA and then to their Ph.D., and then into the research side of academia with a limited time in the classroom. While a number of these faculty are involved in consulting and research within organizations, they have not held managerial positions where they carried the responsibility for the output of work by others.

Yes, you guessed it, the other area where this lack of real-world experience raises its head is in the books they publish and the perspectives they offer. My journey was different. Given my 15 years in manufacturing management, where I held both line and staff positions, I possessed a real-world lens through which I filtered all of the lessons my professors were presenting. Most of the questions I asked and the answers I gave were framed through my real-world experience.

I, like most of you reading this book, have lived through a couple of economic downturns/business cycles and each time they come around we discuss them and their cause among ourselves and others as we try to understand what led to the change. Today, most of us still rely on various descriptions and prescriptions that are used to describe and predict economic behavior. We continue doing what we have done in the past and hope for better results.

At this point in my life I am convinced we need to recognize that we do not have a comprehensive understanding of the macroeconomic system we are all a part of. I am convinced there is a relationship between the models and assumptions we use within our business planning and decision-making processes and the increasing frequency of economic cycles. The trouble is that the results of these decisions and actions are many times delayed years into the future. It is very hard to hypothesize about the impact of an action or decision deep into the future especially when you are being rewarded for the short-term decisions and actions. Let me offer you a beginning answer to the question of "why do we do this?" Since the beginning of the Enlightenment when the scientific approach was put forth (remember Bacon and Newton) scientific discovery has been based on what is commonly called the reductionist (linear/independent) approach—focusing on the kernels of truth and building our understanding from them. Over the last seventy years the recognition of systems, systems thinking, and interdependence has been introduced and it provides a very different perspective through which one can see a very different world. The answers of the past, and the answers most of us are holding come from this linear perspective and they do not recognize or consider the interdependence of things. The answers to the issues we are currently facing require a different perspective, one that recognizes and incorporates the interdependence between the entities that affect our economic system and our thinking. If I am correct, then the next two chapters should begin to provide some specific examples of the reductionist assumptions in some of our most basic business practices. By recognizing and understanding this reality, you will be ready for an introduction to a new perspective.

2
Foundation for the path forward

Introduction

As we begin our investigation into the 150-year journey that is commonly called the Industrial Revolution, we need to keep in mind that this period of rapid and almost continual technological change came on the heels of the Renaissance which is often described as taking place between the fourteenth and seventeenth centuries. As a result of the transition out of the Dark and Middle Ages, the general population began seeing things differently. For example:

- Artists begin to draw in three dimensions (using perspective) using the new found way of representing what they were painting. Notable among them was Tommaso Masaccio (c.1401–1428) who was one of the first and most successful artists of the time using perspective. Raphael is another Renaissance artist who provided dramatic use of the newly found tool of perspective in his art.

- The ultimate authority for knowledge and education began to shift from the church, where it had resided for centuries, to scientists and philosophers who were creating the path to "Truth" through what has become known as the scientific method. People associated with this journey include Bacon, Galileo, Descartes, and Newton. A bit more about these later.

- This time period also saw the foundations of international trade and banking while well-to-do risk takers began to privately fund international ventures that had previously been the sole domain of the Crowns of Europe. The Medici family in Florence, Italy made their wealth as merchants (traders) and subsequently became strong supporters of the Renaissance art in that area.

The shift to science

While there have been many books written about the Renaissance and all the changes that took place during this 300-year period, there is one aspect of this time that is really important because it established some of the foundational assumptions upon which today's business practices are based. That, of course, is the shift towards relying on "science" and a standardized process for the development of truth and understanding. Before taking a deeper look into their contributions, I want you to imagine how the church and the local royalty, many of whom owed their status to recognition from the church, felt when Bacon and the others began to talk about and print books that were searching for "truth". Through a process that started by identifying the simplest of truths and then building knowledge towards a new understanding these new thinkers were challenging the existing paradigm of the entire Western world.

- Francis Bacon (1561–1626) was one of the first of the thinkers to begin questioning the status quo. He demonstrated a very strong commitment to the use of experimentation as a way to find truth. He did this by using two tables in which to document the results of experiments. The first table contained examples where a phenomenon (i.e. heat) was observed. In the second table Bacon would experiment by removing elements until the phenomenon (i.e. heat) was not found and that element would be recognized as the cause of the phenomenon in that circumstance.

- Galileo Galilei (1564–1642) was a mathematician, astronomer, and philosopher extraordinaire. He was a strong supporter of the Copernican system— the sun is the center of the universe—and as a result was brought before the Roman Inquisition in 1615. Galileo was found guilty of heresy, forced to recant his beliefs and was placed under house arrest for the last nine years of his life. All this because he saw the world differently than the church. He was one of the first thinkers to state that the laws of nature are mathematical. This helped set the stage for the eventual separation of science from the fields of philosophy and religion. He performed experiments at different times in different places and from that was able to rely on inductive reasoning to confirm the mathematical laws he was testing.

- René Descartes (1596–1650) was a philosopher and mathematician. While many refer to him as the father of modern philosophy his work in cubic equations and independent variables is said to have had a sizable influence on the young Newton. In his *Discourse on the Method* he put forward a fundamental set of principles as to how one can know truth without any doubt. This search for "truth" was a major focus throughout his lifetime and it help set the stage for the processes and practices we use today.

- Newton (1642–1726) is known as one of the most influential scientists of all time. His *Philosophiae Naturalis Principia Mathematica* (Mathematical

Principles of Natural Philosophy) put forth the laws of motion and universal gravitation, which provided the foundation on which the understanding of physics has been based for 300 years. He also introduced the foundation for classical mechanics (physics). Since its development, Newtonian physics has provided the direction and framework upon which science has evolved.

These thinkers and their many unnamed associates were responsible for introducing a new paradigm to the Western world. Given their efforts, the field of science and the ability to develop a deeper understanding of how things worked led to an explosion in the development of new knowledge. While the major contributor was the separation of science from religion and philosophy, having a well-defined process for the pursuit of new knowledge through the scientific method established the foundation upon which the ever-expanding search for knowledge and understanding was built. This expanded search for knowledge created a climate that has continued to provide support to the growth of educational opportunities. Another major contributor to this growth was the expanded use of movable type printing, which made the written word cheaper as well as easier to duplicate and distribute. This also contributed to increasing the public's understanding and awareness of the evolving changes.

The expansion of trade

As Europe was coming out of the Dark and Middle Ages, trade began to increase. First trade was confined to the region but as travel became easier and states continued to search for more revenues, expanding the reach of their trading activities was one of the simplest solutions. As trading grew, it began to establish the foundation for a new kind of economy. While the Middle Ages saw people trading one commodity for another, as trade began to expand and grow during the Renaissance the use of coins (money) to facilitate the buying and selling of goods became more and more acceptable and a money-based economy was created. For it to work effectively, the establishment of a system of moneychangers and/or bankers was required, who, for a fee, would convert one type of currency into another. As the reach of trade expanded it created a demand for more things that could be sold, which led to an increasing importance of craftspeople who made things, the merchants who purchased and traded things, and the bankers who facilitated the exchange of monies and provided loans for both merchants and craftspeople to build and expand their reach. Some of the more fortunate merchants and bankers grew very wealthy from being involved in the expanding trade markets. As such, many used their wealth to help their cities prosper. They became patrons to their cities and provided resources for new buildings, the developing artists, and even contributed to the expansion of education and universities. The contributions these patrons and others provided allowed many of the city-states to become flourishing educational and cultural centers.

This growth in trade by definition produced an increase in the demand for products being produced at home which encouraged and rewarded any increase in the rate of production. This need for more things to sell focused the attention of many inventors and forward thinkers across Europe to begin the journey towards the mechanization of their human-powered tools to increase production and as such, increase sales and revenue. One of the primary movers in this area was Adam Smith whose book *The Wealth of Nations* introduced the concept commonly referred to as "division of labor". More about him later.

For the purposes of this book, what is most important for us to recognize is that during these turbulent times the new ideas and technologies needed to facilitate the Industrial Revolution were beginning to surface. Before delving into the details of the Industrial Revolution, let's take a quick look at the impact it has had on our world. One of the most commonly accepted techniques for evaluating the magnitude of an economic transformation is to look at the growth in population and the associated growth in per capita income over time. Since 1800, the world's population has increased over sixfold and the average income per person has increased over tenfold. Robert E. Lucas, Jr., a Nobel Prize winner, described this phenomenon: "for the first time in history, the living standards of the masses of ordinary people have begun to undergo sustained growth."[1] This reflects a major change in the rules of wealth distribution that can be attributed to the ongoing growth of commerce, mechanization, individual ownership of organizations and resources, and their individual ingenuity. So let's begin to trace the history of this transformation and see *what* changes it was able to produce and *why*.

The Industrial Revolution: first stage

It is commonly recognized that the Industrial Revolution can be viewed in two stages. The focus of the first stage is the transition from a time when most of the energy provided for doing work came from animals and/or humans to the development of and reliance on mechanical energy. The initial transition focused on taking power from flowing water through the use of water wheels and converting it into the mechanical power associated with a turning shaft. With the development of the steam engine in 1775, we saw the reciprocating power of the steam piston converted into rotary power. With this type of power, producers could more easily be located in close proximity to the natural resources they were processing. They no longer had to locate themselves next to flowing water. So let's take a look at how mechanization and a few other changes impacted the way things were being done.

---

1 Lucas, Robert E. 1998. *The Industrial Revolution: Past and Future. Retrieved* October 22, 2016 (http://www.econ.hku.hk/~cwyuen/seminar/papers/Lucas%20(Kuznets%20Lectures).pdf).

Mechanization of productive activity

Since the Industrial Revolution is commonly thought of as starting in Britain, let's take a look at the conditions that existed in Britain during the early 1700s. For most of the population day-to-day life was focused on surviving in a primarily agricultural environment. While a majority of their time was spent planting and harvesting crops and tending livestock, most people also possessed some other skills needed for survival, such as working with yarn and cloth or basic wood working along with building maintenance knowledge. There were some who, because of their skills or situation, had traded their agricultural subsistence efforts to become more completely involved in the production of fabrics, whether processing wool and cotton fibers into yarn or weaving the yarn into fabric. The other major occupation of the time was working in the coal mines, which provided resources for heating and cooking as well as energy for the growing iron producing and processing industries. For the average person of the time, day-to-day life remained basically unchanged from that of their parents and grandparents. As such, the expectation for most of them was more of the same.

Needless to say, the ability to use flowing water to power the equipment needed to spin fibers into yarn greatly increased the overall output when compared to the old foot treadle machines. During the period 1775–1779, the spinning mule, which combined the earlier processes of the water frame and spinning jenny, was patented. This second step in the mechanization of the yarn-producing segment of fabric production provided a second growth spurt to the fabric-producing region of northern England.

For those individuals involved in the coal-mining industry, their day-to-day work environment was to a large extent limited by the ability of horse-powered machines to accomplish two unique activities. First was to lift the mined coal out of the mines and the second was to keep the pumps pumping to remove the water from the mines. In both cases, the power of the draft horses limited the depth and the amount of coal that could be extracted each day from a mine. Then came a coal-powered steam engine lifting coal and pumping water. Here was a machine that possessed many times more power than draft horses and was not as temperamental. It not only provided a dryer environment within which the miners could work but it also was quicker at removing the coal the miners had mined. The combination of productive gains enabled the miners to follow the veins of coal deeper into the earth and therefore retrieve more coal from each mine. Soon after, the same steam engine technology was being used to provide a more constant and larger volume of air to the iron making and forging industries.

These applications of mechanical energy to the processing of yarn or using steam to power a piston and converting the piston's horizontal movement into rotating energy for pumping and lifting are examples of someone applying a different frame of reference to solving a problem. Remember, over the previous few hundred years thousands and thousands of individuals had relied on traditional practices to perform their day-to-day work and none had had the vision, courage, and/or resources necessary to develop a better way of performing them. Yet, within fifteen years these three industries (fabric, coal mining, and iron production) had been transformed through the application of basic mechanization to their production processes, which resulted in an explosion in their productivity rates.

The easiest way to think of this explosion of uses for this new technology is to look at the explosion of uses for computers or the internet. In the 1950s when computers were initially being developed, the common belief was that only the very largest and richest of institutions could afford or get any benefit from them. As we all know, today our smart phones have more capabilities than the computers of the late 1960s. The steam engine and the development of mechanized processes provided a similar type of explosive growth and development during this time (late 1700s and early 1800s).

The beginnings of corporations

The British, Dutch, and other European Crowns during the Middle Ages and beyond established what many refer to as the first corporations. These Corporations of the Crown, such as the British East India Company (established in 1600) and the Dutch East India Company (established in 1602), were basically tools to export wealth back to the monarchy that had created them. At the time these companies were created to expand the empire and return wealth to the Crown. These early Crown corporations were given the right to levy taxes, wage war, and imprison people all while enjoying a monopoly over trade in the regions where they operated. Thomas Hobbes suggested that these corporations were really just "chips off the old block of sovereignty."[2] After all, having been created by a sovereign, these corporations could also have their charter (the legal document that allowed the corporation to exist) revoked for any reason by the monarch. This is not the situation one would look for in today's world.

By the early 1800s most states in the U.S. provided laws and regulations addressing the formation of state-chartered corporations. They recognized this form of business had certain utility for aggregating capital for large-scale projects which is why many states restricted the parameters within which corporations could operate and a number of states declared that corporations could only be created for *public benefit*. In fact, the Supreme Court of Virginia stated in 1809 that if the objective of an applicant for a corporate charter is "merely private or selfish; if it is detrimental to, or not promote of, the public good, they have no adequate claim upon the legislature for the privileges."[3] Other states put limits on capitalization, levels of debt, land holdings and in some cases the level of profits that could be earned. These statements and limitations highlight how strong many states felt about the roles of corporations and their obligations. At that point in time, you could almost describe corporations as quasi-public institutions that were enabled by the states' elected representatives. This perspective existed through most of the 1800s. In fact,

---

2 Hobbes, Thomas. 1651. *Leviathan*, edited by R. Tuck. Cambridge, UK: Cambridge University Press (1991).
3 Currie's Adm'rs v. Mut. Assurance Soc'y, 14 Va. 315, 347 (1809).

as late as 1900, only 10% of the manufacturing companies in California had a corporate charter. The last one hundred years has seen a radical shift in the overall number and the breadth of purpose for corporate charters.

The United States was not alone in this view of a corporation. During this time the United Kingdom also had limitations covering both the size and purpose of corporations. In 1856, with the passing of the Joint Stock Companies Act, the United Kingdom allowed private individuals to establish a corporation with limited liability by completing a simple administrative procedure. "Corporations" have undergone a significant transformation over the last 200 years: from initially being limited to only those things that provided "public benefit" to today being envisioned as having the same rights as an individual.

The beginnings of economics

Adam Smith's *The Wealth of Nations* included five segments, each focused on an aspect that affected a nation's wealth. The first covered the improvement in labor productivity through the division of labor or labor specialization. The second segment focused on how individuals purpose and use their own "capital" by investing it to receive "revenue" from its use. It is this payment of "revenue" which is one of the three components of the "price" of a commodity. The other two components are "wages of the laborer" and "rent" for the land and resources used in producing and bringing the commodity to market. The third segment focused on the natural interactions between those residing in the towns and in the country. He addresses how these interactions reflect on both the reciprocal gains for the individuals residing in each location (town and country) and the resulting division of labor within each location. The fourth segment looked at how the antiquated governmental restrictions of the day impacted industrial expansion and the country's overall economic growth. In this he attacked both the use of protectionist tariffs and the need for large financial reserves as necessary to ensure a country's economic success. Finally, Smith looked at taxation and expenditures by the state. His four maxims for taxation were: proportionality, transparency, convenience, and efficiency. While today his work is recognized as one of the most important of its time, it did not have as immediate an impact on the way the businesses and organizations viewed their work as some of the mechanization processes had. After all, the ability of a machine can be seen and verified, the adoption of a new idea or mental frame of reference takes a bit longer to understand and embrace.

At this point I want you to take a minute and think about how the business owners of the time (mid to late 1800s) must have felt. They had been born at a time when the business world was going through what can only be called its most radical transition to date. They had seen the impact of:

- Steam power: predictable mechanized power anywhere it was needed

- Labor specialization, which greatly increased the productivity level of each worker

They were beginning to hear about and envision the possibilities in the near future from the:

- Development and use of steel

- Machine tools made of steel: much more productive, longer productive life, and an increase in quality level of their productive output

- Steam-powered ships and trains: faster transportation and increased market reach

- Electrical power of machine tools: more flexible, predictable, and easier to secure at any location than steam power

What a time to be involved in the business world; the opportunities would have seemed to be almost endless.

As technological and economic progress continued, the focus within the Industrial Revolution shifted from the type of power being used to the evolution of new technologies within the manufacturing processes themselves.

The Industrial Revolution: second stage

There is little doubt that the first stage of the Industrial Revolution which lasted from about 1760 until about 1850 brought to the world the recognition and understanding associated with the specialization of labor and the importance of harnessing mechanical power to assist the worker in accomplishing their individual steps in the overall work/conversion process. I dare say that without these two new tools (concepts) in the toolbox of production (creation of value) and commerce (economic exchange), we would still be doing most things by hand. At this point in time, the stage was set for even more rapid change within the business world.

One of the most important innovations of this time that straddled the border between the first and second stage of the Industrial Revolution was the idea of replaceable parts. While Eli Whitney is often listed as being responsible for introducing this idea in the U.S. through his demonstration of interchangeable parts in 1801, he was not able to deliver on this promise until 1825. By that time, both Captain John H. Hall and Simeon North had successfully produced and delivered muskets and pistols with interchangeable parts. A major requirement for achieving this was the development of precision metal-cutting tools. The first of these was the metal lathe. This machine is used to turn and drill metal parts. This was necessary to mass-produce gun barrels that had the exact same diameter. The second was the metal-cutting milling machine. This device enabled the mass-production of flat and contoured metal parts which could include the location and size of holes. With these two machines, organizations now had the tools and processes needed to mass-produce piece parts. While Samuel Colt invented the first revolver in 1836, it was not until 1847 when the Texas Rangers ordered 1,000 of his revolvers that he had enough funds to establish Colt's Patent Firearm Company. The development and growth of the revolver was tied to the development of specialized machine tools that were designed to mass produce the various pieces needed to assemble the revolvers. This was the first real use of the assembly line concept where each step added value to the product and passed it on. Before this technology, the concept of interchangeable parts and assembly lines was merely a dream for the future.

Multitudes of inventions

So, from a technology perspective, what did the second phase of the Industrial Revolution, which lasted from 1850 till the early 1900s, bring to the economic playing field and when did it do this? During the first two decades of the nineteenth century, machine tools made of metal were introduced. The adoption of these new tools provided the user with increased reliability, greater accuracy, and much higher rate of output. As a result, the overall costs associated with the produced parts were reduced while the level of quality was increased.

The other technology that had a sizable impact on the rapid industrial growth of the period was the expanded use of steam-powered transportation. The adaptation of this more predictable power source to ships and the development of steam-powered railroads greatly reduced travel time and increased the reach of all producers and sellers of products.

Arguably one of the most important improvements to the productivity of the second stage of the Industrial Revolution was the development of the process for making steel and the subsequent use of steel in the production of machine tools. For over 3,000 years humans had been making iron by melting iron ore. While the furnaces used to melt the ore have continually been improved, their output, iron, with a carbon content that ranged between 3 and 5%, has remained basically unchanged. Using iron with this level of carbon and other impurities results in an end product that is relatively brittle, wears easily, is not very workable, and is highly susceptible to rust. Good for pots, pans, and cannon balls, but not very good for machines with many moving parts. That said, we can all give thanks to British metallurgist Sir Henry Bessemer. He was the one who, in 1856, developed an efficient process for reducing the carbon content of iron to less than 1%, which resulted in the production of Bessemer steel, a stronger, less brittle, more workable, and more durable cast iron. Shortly thereafter, this process for making steel arrived in the U.S. and Andrew Carnegie began to build his steel empire. This industry grew because it was the primary ingredient in the growth of both the railroad industry, providing tracks and materials for the rail cars, and the building construction industry, providing the structural steel for the skeleton of multi-story buildings. As the steel industry grew and the producers developed more efficient processes, the cost of steel dropped. In 1865, steel cost more than $85 a ton and by the turn of the century it had fallen to as low as $14 a ton. This is an example of the impact mass production can have on the cost of a product.

As was mentioned above, one of the major contributors to the rapid growth in steel production in the United States was its use in the building of railroad lines across the country. Looking at Table 2 we see that rail lines were all but non-existent in 1830, extending an estimated 40 miles. Twenty years later the mileage had increased over 10,000% to more than 8,500 miles. By 1890, when the Bessemer steel process was fully implemented in the U.S. and producing steel at much lower cost, the mileage of rail tracks had increased a further 1,000% to over 163,000 miles.

Table 2 **Extent of railroad coverage in the U.S. (miles)**

Source: United States Census Bureau. *Report on Transportation Business in the United States at the Eleventh Census 1890*, p. 4.

Region	1830	1840	1850	1860	1870	1880	1890
New England	30	513	2,596	3,644	4,326	5,888	6,718
East		1,484	3,740	11,927	18,292	28,155	40,826
South	10	737	2,082	7,908	10,610	14,458	27,833
Midwest			46	4,951	11,031	22,213	35,580
South Central		21	107	250	331	1,621	5,154
West				239	4,578	15,466	47,451
Total U.S.	40	2,755	8,571	28,920	49,168	87,801	163,562

This rapid growth in rail coverage across the country increased the reliability and affordability of transporting people and products to almost any location. One of the early hurdles to expanding rail service across the country was having a bridge across the Mississippi River. In the early 1870s, Andrew Carnegie was the first to undertake and complete a steel structure of this size and magnitude. It provided the critical link to tie the rail lines from the eastern half of the U.S. to those already in place in the west. The development of the country-wide rail transportation system had a large impact on the demand for goods and the ability of producers to supply their offerings. In addition, the growth of these two industries demonstrates their interdependence. A concept we need to hold on to.

A third industry we need to take a brief look at that began its life in the mid-1800s was the petroleum industry—which was founded and grew on the refining of crude oil into lubricants and kerosene for lamps. It is important to remember that, before the development of kerosene for lamps, when the sun set there were no lights in houses or outside other than from a candle or torch. In the late 1860s John D. Rockefeller was one of many entrepreneurs in northern Ohio who were engaged in refining oil into kerosene. At the same time Cornelius Vanderbilt, a railroad entrepreneur, was in a desperate need to expand the level of commercial shipping on his trains to help him cover expansion expenses. Vanderbilt gave Rockefeller what today might be seen as an unrefusable offer—a large reduction in the per unit shipping cost if he doubled his shipping commitment to the railroad. The easiest way for Rockefeller to expand his refinery capacity and shipping needs was to establish Standard Oil and buy up his biggest rivals. This marked the beginning of what became the largest oil company in the United States.

As we can see from Figure 2, the production and refining of oil in the U.S. expanded at a growth rate that parallels the growth in rail miles. During this time the growth of these industries reflects the transition from small, almost craft-based businesses to the manufacturing of mass-produced products. The growth of these industries provided a model for business to follow in the future.

Figure 2 **Growth of the U.S. oil industry**

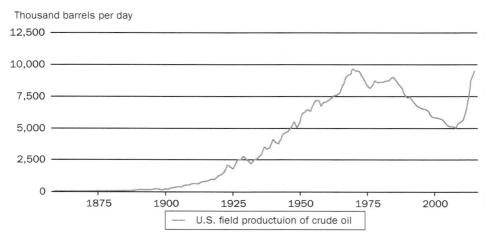

Source: U.S. Energy Information Administration

Retrieved from: https://www.eia.gov/dnav/pet/hist/LeafHandler.ashx?n=PET&s=MCRFPUS2&f=A

All three of these industries started as small businesses that were focused on providing their product, be it steel, rail transportation or kerosene oil, to a small geographical region. While they were initially one of many providers, their owners had a better vision for the future and the ability to do what was needed, for example: raise funds, identify new markets, and see the next step needed to grow and outperform their regional rivals. As they grew they bought out their rivals and proceeded, full speed ahead, into the future. The fourth industry that contributed to the foundation for today's business model was led by Henry Ford. He became one of these titans of industry at the beginning of the twentieth century. His focus was on producing an inexpensive automobile that the average person could afford. He accomplished this through the development and use of the assembly-line process and increased vertical integration. He also recognized that paying his workers a livable wage was good for his business because, with it, they could afford to buy his Model T.

Improvements in agriculture

Improvements in agricultural productivity also occurred during the same time frame. It was close to the turn of the century when Eli Whitney patented the cotton gin—a machine used to clean cotton by removing the seeds. Since this was a very labor-intensive process, the adoption and use of this machine greatly improved productivity on cotton-producing farms and plantations. While the gin was initially powered by a hand-turned crank, as the production of cotton grew, adapting the gin to more predictable power sources—horse and then the steam engine—soon followed. It was reported that in 1793, the year the cotton gin was invented, the south produced less than 200,000 pounds of cotton. By 1810, a mere 17 years later, the country produced approximately 93 million pounds of cotton. Any product with this kind of increase in demand will attract an ever-expanding number of investors and participants who want to make their fortune in this growth industry. Needless to say, a lot of these new participants were farmers who had previously been involved in the production of food crops. Then in the mid-1830s both the corn planter and the grain reaper (a machine that cuts grain crops) were developed. These tools, like the cotton gin, reduced the amount of manual labor needed to plant and harvest crops which increased the overall productivity of the farm worker. With the increased production of cotton in the south, there was now a need to address the production process of converting cotton fabric into clothing and cloth goods. While the spinning and weaving processes had begun their journey into mechanization by 1769, converting the cloth into clothes and other products was still done by hand. Then in 1845, Elian Howe developed the first American sewing machine. While the first machine relied on manual power, it was only ten years later that Isaac Singer patented the sewing machine motor. This mechanization increased the daily productivity of the seamstress and established the foundation for today's garment industry.

The introduction of electricity

Prior to the development of the technology to distribute electricity, cities and entrepreneurs relied on telodynamic (cables in motion), pneumatic (pressurized air), and hydraulic (pressurized liquid) systems to transmit power to users across a distance. Needless to say none of these technologies was particularly effective. As the technology of using electricity to turn motors and power lights grew, the search turned to developing the mechanisms needed to distribute electricity over distance. In 1878, at the Paris Exposition, electric arc lighting was installed to demonstrate the technology of electric street lighting. In 1879, the California Electric Company began supplying power from its central plant to customers for lighting. Between 1880 and 1881 the Brush Electric Company built power generation and transmission lines to bring arc lighting to most of the major cities in the U.S. With lines for lighting being strung, it was a small step to using electricity to power motors in production machinery.

With all these changes in both products and processes associated with new and expanding industries, the most obvious question to ask is "what was the impact of these changes on the economy and people of the United States?" Figure 3 presents the growth in gross domestic product per capita from 1800 to 2008. Looking at the time between 1800 and 1904, you notice that the annual growth rate of the U.S. GDP per capita for was 1.5%.

Figure 3 **U.S. real annual GDP per capita ($ 2004), 1800–2008**

Source: The Market Oracle (http://www.marketoracle.co.uk/Article11110.html)

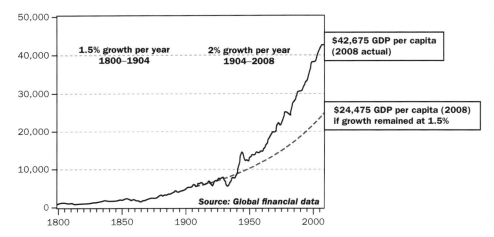

This growth rate is quite impressive given that between 1873 and 1879 the U.S. was in what is commonly referred to as the "Long Depression" during which time ten states and over 18,000 businesses went bankrupt. During 9 of the following 21 years the country was technically in a recession. This says a lot about the power of the technological innovations that were put in place during the first 100 years of the second phase of the Industrial Revolution. While these mechanical tools were an important contributor to economic growth and development during this time, there were also a variety of changes to the business tools and practices of the time that contributed to the rapid expansion of business. Before we take an in-depth look at the changes that brought about the increase in GDP (from 1.5 to 2%) during the twentieth century, let's continue our look into how organizations and management changed during the nineteenth century.

The evolution of organizational structures

Until the late nineteenth century most businesses, with the exception of steel, railroad, and oil, were based on the craftsman model. They were relatively small and usually managed by the owner who had leveraged his skill as a craftsman into a business. Their customer base may have reached across the town or possibly a country, but seldom much further. The primary determinant of success for this type of business could be tied to the ability of the owner/manager to oversee the successful production and delivery of goods for the customer. Founding and managing such a business required three basic characteristics:

- The requisite skills needed to oversee the production and sales of a limited variety of products

- The ability to obtain (save or borrow) and manage a limited amount of assets such as: inventory, production tools and equipment

- The people skills needed to hire, train, and oversee the work of subordinates

Given the limited size and scope of most businesses at the time, they were able to rely on very simple planning and cash management systems. This approach to management was also facilitated by the composition of business costs. At that time, most of the costs a business had were either material or labor, both of which are truly variable. They varied directly with the number of units produced. If you did not make any units on one day, you did not have any variable costs. The other costs, such as rent and loan repayment, were small and as such not too difficult to manage. Finally, the owner's profit—their reward for their efforts—were the funds that were left. This model had prevailed for centuries and most of the shopkeepers/craftspeople of the time had little need to change. After all, the model fit their business environment. As businesses began to grow and the number of employees exceeded those that had a familial relationship with the owner/manager, most managers relied on the military style of leadership which had been around for hundreds of years. The person in charge calls the shots and the subordinates do as they are told. This approach had worked for armies for centuries and there was no pressing need to change. However, the practices and processes that had been the most common in the nineteenth century were about to change.

A quick look at management thought up to 1900

As the mechanization of the factories in Britain grew in the early 1800s, the issues associated with *how* the workers should be treated became more pressing. While a vast majority of the contemporary writers supported the new "factory system" and what may be called traditional "top down" management that reflected the practices within the military, a few individuals spoke up against this. The first was Robert Owens, who was repulsed by the working conditions and poor treatment of the factory workers. He proposed a bill that would limit employing children under 10 years of age, restricting them to no more than 10½ hours a day. And we think we have it bad. Charles Babbage saw the economic advantage of the shift to manufacturing but thought the practices could be improved. He suggested a process for improving how work gets done by observing and identifying steps/actions that are not necessary. He also said that the businesses should include "profit sharing" as a way of investing the workers into the manufacturing processes. During this time the field of economics contributed the foundational understanding of pricing and resource allocation. Finally, from those involved in the manufacturing of cotton gins, guns and a few basic products came the beginnings of the transition to mass production/assembly lines which drove the growth during the next 60 or so years.

The beginning of the twentieth century brought about another shift in business. Up until 1903, all businesses, large or small, were single-industry organizations. All this changed when DuPont, which produced gunpowder, purchased a bullet-making company. This created the first multi-division business which introduced a new set of problems for management to deal with. The issues faced and their solutions set the stage for what many refer to as the modern-day business, which will be dealt with in the next chapter.

3

The evolution of "modern-day" business

Bringing together the Industrial Revolution and the beginning of modern business

During the last twenty years of the 1800s, the business environment began to change rapidly. The growing success of the steel, railroad, and petroleum industries (the first large businesses) heralded a movement towards industrialization: the investment of large amounts of capital to finance the transformation of production processes from what had been a very manual approach to one that relied more and more on mechanization. The increase in the amount of capital that was needed to make this transition brought with it an increase in the level of financial risk associated with the business. As a result, the owners and investors began to recognize the need for better, more precise methods to predict and control costs and outputs. Before this shift, most organizations were expansions of the craftsman model and the owner/craftsman's profits were what he had in his pocket at the end of the month. This approach to management was no longer capable of providing answers to the questions being asked by the new managers of these more industrialized businesses. Finding more effective processes and practices became a major focus of managers and engineers during this time of rapid expansion and growth.[1] There were three major shifts over the next 20 or so years that facilitated modern-day business. Let's take a look at each of them independently.

---

1 Epstein, M.J. 1978. *The Effect of Scientific Management on the Development of the Standard Cost System.* New York, NY: Arno Press; Rabinbach, A. 1990. *The Human Motor: Energy, Fatigue and the Origins of Modernity.* New York: Basic Books; Schor, J. 1990.

The beginnings of modern business (late 1800–1920s)

The advent of scientific management

The first of the aforementioned issues facing business was addressed by Frederick W. Taylor, who in 1895 presented a paper at the American Society of Mechanical Engineers entitled "A Piece Rate System: Being a Step toward Partial Solution of the Labor Problem".[2] In this paper he first presented his ideas about how to solve the wage problem facing businesses. At the time, the management alternatives were centered on piece-rate and day-rate systems, both of which were remnants of the artisan model and were failing miserably when applied in an industrial environment. Taylor's solution was based on two interdependent parts. The first was an engineered standard process for determining how much output a worker could produce. This required the completion of an engineered time standard that measured the "engineered process" for accomplishing the work. Once this was established, it was linked to the second key to Taylor's model, a differential piece rate. This differential rate paid a low rate per piece for low output and a higher rate for higher output.[3]

Taylor's work was strongly supported by the works of Frank and Lillian Gilbreth, which focused on defining the "one best way" to perform work, defined as physical labor.[4] This was accomplished through the development of a set of basic movements called "therbligs," and scientifically establishing an associated standard time for performing each one. With these defined, industrial engineers could then combine the needed basic movements into the appropriate series of movements needed to accomplish the task being analyzed. Since each of these small movements had a scientifically established time associated with it, the summation of the individual task times produced the "total task time" for the work being done.

As the first decade of the twentieth century passed, the Eastern Rate Case was heard. In this case, the proponents of scientific management models testified that, given their experiences, the railroads could expect to see a 300% increase in per worker output from the adoption of scientific management methods. With this

The Overworked American. New York: Perseus Books Group; Karsten, L. 1996. "Writing and the Advent of Scientific Management: The Case of Time and Motion Studies". *Scandinavian Journal of Management* 12(1): 41-55, cited in Kreitner, R. 2001. *Management,* 8th edn. Boston, MA: Houghton Mifflin Company.

2 Taylor, Frederick Winslow. 1895. "A Piece Rate System: Being a Step toward Partial Solution of the Labor Problem". Presented at the Detroit Meeting of the American Society of Mechanical Engineers.

3 Taylor, Frederick Winslow. 1911. "Principles of Scientific Management" in *Scientific Management,* edited by F. Taylor. New York: Harper (1947); Epstein (1978).

4 Bateman, T.S. and C.P. Zeithaml. 1990. *Management: Function and Strategy.* Homewood, IL: Irwin Publishing.

in the court records, scientific management was well on the way to being readily adopted by businesses across the country.[5]

As they began implementing the scientific management model, managers could, for the first time, establish a reasonable estimate of the time necessary to perform a task and, thereby, calculate a standard cost for the worker's output. They also gained a scientifically based and mathematically accurate approach for predicting the process output. Achieving what appeared to be scientific predictability was a wonderful development for the practice of management. The widespread adoption of scientific management led to publication of Taylor's book, *The Principles of Scientific Management*, in 1911.[6]

The implementation of scientific management had a positive impact on the predictability and performance of workers, and provided managers with the ability to accurately plan the costs and expected outputs of a given process. The amazing result of Taylor's work was that process improvements, on average, increased productivity by 400%.[7] This increased productivity, which reduced the overall labor costs of the products being produced and led to growth in both sales and profits, became the "go to" measure for managers. As a result, managers became more focused on improving productivity and much less worried about the human side— needs and expectations of the employees. After all there were plenty of available workers outside the plant that were willing to do what they were told. Even today, productivity is high on the list of measures used when evaluating the performance of a business or an economy.

This unfortunate side-effect also contributed to the growing divide between management and workers. After all, if management and engineers were charged with establishing the "one best way" for doing work, the assumption must be that they possessed some additional intelligence—something more than that of the average worker. As such, workers were not expected to question how they accomplished their tasks and assignments, but were expected to trust management to develop the "correct" way. In many cases, this perception created and/or expanded the divide between the workers and those responsible for providing their direction (managers and engineers). As such, the cooperation between these two groups was greatly reduced. It was almost 30 years before the human resources movement would attempt to refocus management on the whole employee and some would say their efforts have not had the effect on management that is needed.[8]

5 Caldari, K. 2007. "Alfred Marshall's Critical Analysis of Scientific Management". *European Journal of the History of Economic Thought* 14(1): 55-78, in Capra, F. 1996. *The Web of Life*. New York: Anchor Books.

6 Taylor (1911).

7 Kreitner, R. and A. Kinicki. 2001. *Organizational Behavior*, 5th ed. Boston, MA: McGraw Hill; Schmerhorn, J. 2002. *Management*, 7th edn. New York: John Wiley & Sons; Daft, R. 2004. *Management*, 7th edn. Mason, OH: Thompson Southwestern.

8 Daft, R. 2004. *Management*, 7th edn. Mason, OH: Thompson Southwestern.

The birth of cost accounting

The second major innovation associated with the rise of industrialization was the idea of allocating "overhead costs" to products. In 1903, DuPont, which at the time only produced gunpowder, became the first multi-divisional business when it purchased a company that made bullets. With this purchase, the senior management team faced a level of complexity that no other set of company executives had ever faced: how do you distribute and pay for the business's overhead costs (management, engineering, etc.) between the two divisions? Before this, when businesses only produced one product/product line, all the costs associated with the business (both fixed and variable) had to be covered by the business. With two divisions to oversee and evaluate, DuPont's senior management team were the first group of corporate executives that had a need to evaluate the performance of two or more business unit managers. In an effort to resolve this issue, DuPont called on its engineers to develop an approach that would *fairly distribute* the various overhead costs across the two divisions. The solution they came up with was to allocate the company's total overhead costs between the two divisions based on the percentage of total *direct labor* that belonged to each division.[9]

In practical terms, this new approach meant that each division would be responsible for covering its percentage of DuPont's total overhead costs based on the division's percentage of DuPont's total direct labor expenses. At the time, this made perfect sense. After all, they were concerned about three categories of costs: materials, direct labor, and overhead costs. Of these three costs, direct labor was the largest component and the overhead costs were the smallest at less than 10%. Given this mix of costs and their desire to allocate the overhead fairly, it made logical sense to allocate the smallest amount (overhead) by the amount of the largest component (direct labor). At the time, this approach was seen as a *good proxy* for an accurate measure which they could not actually calculate. This approach was adopted by Alfred Sloan at General Motors, which was beginning to face the same issues as DuPont. These two organizations continued to collaborate to develop and refine the mechanisms of cost accounting.[10]

As with any model that addresses the core problem of a system, cost accounting enabled its practitioners (managers) to develop a new and deeper understanding of the financial side of their business, which led to the beginning of a whole new set of questions that could be asked and answered with cost accounting. Although the developers of cost accounting noted that its results were a close approximation and

9 Johnson, H.T. 1975. "Management Accounting in an Early Integrated Industrial: E. I. duPont de Nemours Powder Company, 1903-1912". *The Business History Review* 49(2): 184-204; Johnson, H.T. 1981. "Toward a New Understanding of Nineteenth-Century Cost Accounting". *The Accounting Review* 56(3): 510-518.

10 Johnson, H.T. and R. Kaplan. 1984. *Relevance Lost: the Rise and Fall of Cost Accounting.* Boston, MA: Harvard Business School Press; Mcnair, C.J., W. Mosconi and T.F. Norris. 1989. *Beyond the Bottom Line: Measuring World-Class Performance.* Homewood, IL: Dow Jones–Irwin.

not an exact representation of the true costs, organizations and managers became so enticed with the new insights and the level of detail provided that they began to accept the answers produced by the new tool as being both mathematically correct and an accurate representation of the true costs and values within the business.

Over the next generation, cost accounting provided managers with the means to more easily calculate and compare the efficiency and productivity (as defined by the model) of the organization's various departments and functions. It also provided businesses with the ability to establish a product cost that included both direct and indirect costs. With the newfound ability to accurately measure and calculate the performance of various business components as well as to calculate an accurate product cost, managers had a much better understanding of the how's and why's behind the performance of their businesses. The increased visibility and understanding that was provided by cost accounting was as revolutionary to the development of management as the thermometer was to conducting chemical experiments. It was the spark that allowed its practitioners to evolve from alchemy to chemistry.[11]

There is no doubt that the development of both cost accounting and scientific management addressed the root cause of the major problems facing managers before the turn of the century, which was the ability to link the predictable amount of output produced to the wages paid, along with a structured approach to measuring and managing performance across the various functions of an organization—obtaining more visibility and control of their businesses to offset the increases in capitalization and risks. With the adoption of these new tools, the owner/manager of the business possessed a set of scientifically based practices that addressed their core issues—understanding non-direct costs, the predictability of output, and determining a fair wage. Resolving these issues allowed business to transition from what had been a craftsman paradigm to the paradigm of a business. Looking back at the development of business, it is clear that the adoption and use of these two linked solutions had a significant impact on the organization's decision-making and productivity.

As the use of cost accounting and the practices associated with scientific management grew over this period of time, their users were continually enhancing associated tools and techniques. The focus behind these improvements was the desire to provide managers with an ever-increasing level of understanding regarding the internal workings of their businesses, as well as the ability to produce ever more refined methods of quantitative measurement, allowing them to predict, monitor, and control the outputs from their money-making business machine.

These tools had such a significant effect for the simple reason that, as a model for organizational systems, they addressed the core problem being faced by organizations as they began to transition into what would be considered modern business. After all, throughout the history of organizations and societies, whenever a new model or framework is introduced that addresses a core problem, the resultant shift in perspective leads to revolutionary improvements: Newton's *Principia* in both math and physics, the thermometer in chemistry, quantum mechanics in

11 Jaques, Elliott. 2002. *Social Power and the CEO*. Santa Barbara, CA: Praeger.

physics, etc. This is the definition of a true paradigm shift. Just remember, paradigm shifts are not forever.

The inclusion of government and labor with business

The third change was the inclusion of government and labor into the practice of business. This was particularly apparent in the United States. To understand the changes, we need to look at what had happened and what caused this shift. The period of industrialization created a phenomenal transformation in the processes, tools, and practices businesses relied on to produce, distribute, and market their offerings. Not only were they much more productive, they had much more effective transportation and communications tools which began to more closely tie the suppliers of parts to the producer and ultimately to the consumer of the finished goods. Needless to say growth during the last part of the 1800s and the first few years of the twentieth century was phenomenal. It was the time when the Rockefellers, Carnegies, and other captains of industry were, without concern, reaping the benefits from the growing industries and organizations they had built. Additionally, the U.S. was continuing the isolationist path laid out by Washington 150 years ago when he warned against becoming entangled in European wars. Up to this point the U.S. Government had placed very few controls over the practice of business; it was a time when selfish men with blind ambition ruled. Revenues were not taxed and what you made is what you had. While it was not completely the "wild west" it was not too far from it. Figure 4 depicts the interrelationship or lack thereof, between the three major entities—government, business, and labor—whose actions and reactions contributed to the economic conditions in the country.

Figure 4 **Relationship between government, business, and labor**

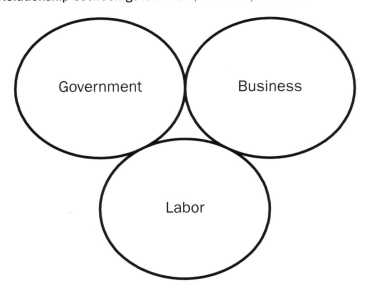

As you can see there was very little interaction between these three elements. The logical explanation for this lack of interaction resides in past practices. From the Middle Ages forward, any economic exchanges outside those authorized and/or run by the Crowns of Europe were individual exchanges between neighbors that leveraged the expertise or extra produce one family had and the other needed. By the mid-to-late 1800s the entity of "business," led by the aforementioned titans of industry, had grown exponentially in size and impact on the country's economy. Business's initial relationship with the labor segment was very much one-way: we have the jobs and here are the rules—take it or leave it. By the late 1800s labor had begun to organize and exercise some of strength against what they saw as the heavy hand of business. By the time WW I arrived the conflicts between labor and business, some of which at times were violent, had reached a point where the government was drawn into the disagreement with the goal of calming the issue to facilitate the economy's progress.

In August 1914, the heir to the Austria-Hungarian throne was assassinated. This was the crisis that led to World War I. Within a couple of months, Bethlehem Steel had reached out to the British Government and secured an order to supply them with millions of artillery shells and ten submarines. This was the beginning of many U.S. companies taking advantage of the war in Europe to expand their sales and profits even though the U.S. Government had a non-entanglement policy towards Europe.

As the war in Europe began, the U.S. economy was in a recession. The war changed that. For the next three years, until it entered the war in 1917, the U.S. was one of the primary suppliers of armaments for the Allied Powers (Great Britain, France, Russia, Italy) and as such experienced an economic boom that lasted through the end of the war (a total of 44 months). Given the great increase in demand for war munitions, the U.S. economy responded by investing capital into producing the needed tools of war. This was of great benefit when the U.S. finally entered the war in 1917; we knew how to increase our productive capacity to meet the added demand of the U.S. armies to the existing demand of the Allied armies. Once the U.S. entered the war it authorized massive federal spending to shift more capacity from civilian goods to the tools of war. As you can imagine, this growth in economic activity had a positive impact on the unemployment level, reducing it from 7.9% to 1.4%. The U.S. labor force grew during this time by over 1 million people. With the focus on producing more and more war materials, there was a large decline in the volume of civilian goods and the country began to experience price increases (inflation). This added to the existing labor unrest across the country and by 1917 workers began demanding change by holding hundreds of strikes across the country. This led to the establishment of the National War Labor Board that worked with the American Federation of Labor to develop new regulations. The changes included increased wages, reduced hours, and the recognized right to organize and collectively bargain with management. Needless to say, the third change set the stage for the expansion of unions in response to the abuses of workers across the growing industrialized nation.

To assist in overseeing and guiding this massive economic effort, the government established the War Industries Board to set price and production controls. In addition, it created both a Food Administration and a Fuel Administration to centrally manage the production and distribution of these resources and outputs. This level of government involvement and control in the country's economic system was unprecedented and, as such, this change introduced a new model, based on interdependence between the three entities (government, business, and labor), that has continued today. The other important contributor to this change was the fact that by the time the war was over the United States had shifted its position in the financial world. Prior to WW I the U.S. was a net debtor in the international capital markets, yet by the time the war was over it had become a creditor nation and was well on its way to becoming the world's banker. This transition for the U.S. was facilitated by investing large amounts internationally, especially in Latin America. The emergence of New York as a financial center was under way and, in the not too distant future, it surpassed London to become the world's leading financial center. Supporting this growth was a national perspective focused on staying within our borders and not becoming involved with the issues of other countries. While the U.S. had joined the war with its European allies against the Central Powers, once the war was over, it was quick to leave its commitment to Europe.

The Great Depression and Dust Bowl

It was just after World War I came to an end that the U.S. experienced a short-lived recession extending from August 1918 until March 1919. This was followed by a second, deeper recession that began in January 1920 and lasted 18 months. The following upturn led the U.S. economy into what is commonly referred to as the Roaring Twenties when growth and excesses were quite common. During this time, we saw a large number of rural Americans emigrate to the cities in search of a more prosperous life working in a factory instead of relying on agriculture for their livelihood. It was during this time the businesses and stock markets, which were relatively unregulated, moved at the whims of those that had large amounts of investments in the markets. As long as things were going up and there was money to be made, people were attracted to the activity.

By the time 1929 arrived things were starting to look a little questionable. In March there was a small run on a bank that lasted two days. In addition, a variety of industries such as construction, steel, and automobiles were experiencing sluggishness and declining sales. In addition, consumers were extending their credit because it was easy to come by. Between June and September 1929 the Dow gained more than 20% which kindled more faith in the system. On September 20, the London Stock Exchange officially crashed when a top investor was jailed for fraud and forgery. The Dow reached its peak of 381.17 on September 3 and it was downhill from there. By the time that Black Tuesday arrived on October 29 the Dow had been reduced to 230.07 which reflected a 39.9% drop from its high seven weeks earlier. The market continued its downward journey for another 43 months, which included reaching its lowest level of the twentieth century of 41.22 on July 8, 1932. One of the economic results of the depression was the passage of the Smoot-Hawley Tariff Act of 1930. This act was enacted in an effort to protect American jobs and agriculture from foreign competition. Senator Reed Smoot made clear that he believed the depression was a result of the ruthless destruction of life and property during the war and the inability of countries to adjust purchasing power to productive capacity during the industrial growth (roaring twenties) after the war. Looking back on the act, many economists do not believe this act achieved its objective of reducing the length and magnitude of the depression.

Another factor that impacted the American economy during this time was what is commonly referred to as the Dust Bowl and its effect on agriculture and the migration of people. The extreme droughts crossing the U.S. and Canadian prairies, combined with the deep-plowing of the topsoil on the plains and the failure of the farmers to use dryland farming techniques led to the dramatic impact associated with the droughts of 1934, 1936, and 1939–1940. These droughts and the extreme winds led to days and days of blinding dust being blown across the plains, reaching Chicago and eventually New York, Boston, and DC. This natural phenomenon led to the relocation of some 3.5 million people out of the plains states.

Patrick Allitt recounts how fellow historian Donald Worster responded after his mid-1970s return visit to some of the counties that received substantial damage during the Dust Bowl era. He described that period as "an example of human folly, environmental mismanagement, and economic shortsightedness". He went on to say that the actions that led to the Dust Bowl can be seen as being tied to "a culture that deliberately, self-consciously set itself [the] task of dominating and exploiting the land for all it was worth". The culture he was talking about was capitalism, "which regarded the natural world as something to be used, exploited to the maximum in yielding ever greater returns, and to which no reciprocal obligation was owed".[12] Once again, I want to encourage you to hold on to his comments—we will come back to them a bit later.

World War II: impact and effects

As the U.S. was coming out of the Great Depression in the late 1930s, its leaders were primarily focused on improving the economy. While America and its leaders had experienced a lot during the previous 50 or so years leading up to the beginning of the 1940s, it was not enough to keep the rest of the world or the U.S. from falling into the same crisis—a second world war. By the time 1938 arrived, Hitler was making threats towards Czechoslovakia and had begun laying out his plans for

---

12 Allitt, Patrick. 2014. *A Climate of Crisis: America in the Age of Environmentalism*. New York: Penguin, p. 203.

war across Europe. As the year progressed, his threats grew. By September, both England and France agreed to meet with Hitler in Munich in an effort to appease him. The result of this meeting was the signing of the Munich Agreement or Pact that facilitated Germany's annexation of the Sudetenland—a section of Czechoslovakia along its border with Germany that was largely inhabited by ethnic Germans. This was the beginning of what was to become the Second World War.

For the next three years, while war had broken out in Europe, the U.S. stayed neutral. The country was not going to be drawn into a second war, on the heels of World War I and the Great Depression. This is not to say that the United States had taken no actions in preparation for the possibility of being drawn into the crisis in Europe, but officially it had remained hands off. In fact in June of 1940 President Roosevelt appointed William S. Knudsen, who had been a Sr. Executive at both Ford and GM, to develop and execute a plan that would leverage U.S. manufacturing expertise and provide the ability to build and supply the allies with many more weapons and weapon systems than the enemy could produce. To accomplish this he and his team relied on access to an almost unlimited supply of natural resources and raw materials. This allowed the U.S. to establish a multitude of manufacturing efforts led by different organizations and drawing on different resources. In addition, since the U.S. was not an active front in the war, it was able to build arms in relative peace and quiet while the other countries involved were experiencing the war on their home front making dedicated manufacturing difficult. This capability was recognized by Knudsen as why "we won because we smothered the enemy in an avalanche of production, the like of which he had never seen, nor dreamed possible".[13]

The U.S.'s desires to stay out of the European conflict changed on December 7, 1941. That is the day that Japan attacked Pearl Harbor and on December 8, the U.S. declared war on Japan. On December 11, Germany and Italy declared war on the U.S. and the Second World War escalated. Over the next four years the focus within the United States was on how and what was needed to win this war. This was the time that led to the development and growth of the economic engine that would carry the United States into a leadership position among the world's economic powers. A lot of the responsibility for the ascension of the U.S. to this position can be traced to the tools, technology, and practices it had developed within its manufacturing sector during this time. It is the development and expansion of these capabilities that is the primary focus of this section. What did the U.S. do and how did this contribute to the growth and development of the economic engine that led the world during the last half of the twentieth century?

In early 1941, the U.S. Maritime Commission placed an order for 260 Liberty ships. Sixty of these ships were initially bound for the UK and the rest to assist the U.S. in transporting cargo to Europe. Following Pearl Harbor and the U.S.

---

13 Parker, Dana T. 2013. *Building Victory: Aircraft Manufacturing in the Los Angeles Area in World War II*. Cypress, CA: Dana T. Parker Books, pp. 5, 7.

engagement in war with Japan, there was a massive need for cargo ships both to the east—to transport cargo to Europe—and to the west—to ship cargo and troops to support the Pacific fighting. Over the next four years 2,751 of these ships were constructed. During this time there were 16 different shipyards involved in the construction of these ships. The Kaiser shipyards located in Vancouver, Washington, borrowed a number of practices commonly used in the production of commercial goods—purchasing sub-assemblies, prefabricating components, and focusing on the assembly of parts into the finished goods. Kaiser became so good at this it could assemble and complete a Liberty ship every two weeks. To demonstrate the effectiveness of its processes and build support for its approach it completed one in less than five days. It was this ability to continually build and expand the number of cargo and transport ships faster than they could be destroyed that aided in the war effort and provided the foundation for the future expansion of manufacturing.

As the demand for munitions continued to grow, more of the existing factories and a number of new factories were constructed to meet the demand. In addition the military was actively seeking ways to increase the reliability of their munitions. In response, the government enacted the American War Standards Z1.1, Z1.2, and Z1.3 in 1941 and 1942, which included the adoption and use of statistical process control (SPC) tools as part of any munitions manufacturing contracts. As a result, the quality and reliability of U.S. munitions greatly exceeded those produced by any other country. The adoption and use of SPC was a result of the work done in the 1920s and 1930s at Bell Telephone Laboratories in Cicero, IL. It was here that Walter Shewhart introduced the idea and process of SPC. Prior to his work, quality was accomplished by inspecting the finished product and accepting or rejecting it based on its ability to do what it was designed to do. Shewhart took a different perspective; he recognized that production processes are like any other process and their output has a range of variation. When he began looking at the variations within a process, he realized that some of the variation in a process is common to the process and he called this "chance or common cause" variation which cannot be removed without actually making a change in the process. The other category of variation exists because something outside the process itself has caused it. He called this "assignable or special cause" variation. To effectively apply this understanding of process variation to improve the quality of manufactured parts, one has to begin monitoring all the manufacturing processes and measuring the level of variation over time, say once every hour. By tracking the variation within a process, the operator will notice when there is a shift in the variation and that is a signal that the process needs to be readjusted to remove the special causes of variation and bring it back into control (producing output with only common cause variation). This tracking is accomplished with what is called a control chart. Figure 5 provides an example of how SPC works.

Figure 5 **Example of a control chart**

Source: http://moodle.oakland.k12.mi.us/os/mod/book/tool/print/index.php?id=25499

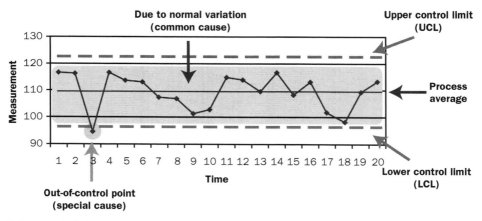

Using a control chart

Control charts provide the user with a graphic representation of all the variation (common cause and special cause) in the process. As long as the averages stay within the control limits, things are probably Ok. When one of the following occurs the operator should begin to take a look at the process:

- 1 data point falling outside the control limits
- 6 or more points in a row steadily increasing or decreasing
- 8 or more points in a row on one side of the centerline
- 14 or more points alternating up and down

As we look back at the growth and development of business and business practices during WW II, many things from Rosie the Riveter to savings bonds, to rationing of resources critical to the war effort come to mind. Dealing with the large increase in output as demanded by the war effort, manufacturing firms developed systems that addressed the procurement and management of materials required by their factories. Most of these systems were based on the development and use of what is commonly referred to as the EOQ (economic order quantity) model for establishing the proper inventory levels by balancing the costs associated with holding inventory against the costs associated with placing an order. This model, which was developed in the 1930s works really well when trading off the costs associated with the production of a single or a few end products. In addition, at this point in time America was the only country that had any real mass-production manufacturing expertise.

In addition to the aforementioned manufacturing expertise, the war effort was able to draw on all the latest technologies in addition to developing new ones to make the munitions more effective and accurate. One of these was the development of radar and sonar, which contributed to locating and removing both aircraft and U-boats, making the air and the oceans safer for the allied forces. The proximity fuse was another new technology that contributed to the successful outcome of the war. This type of fuse detonates the explosive device it is attached to when the distance to the target becomes smaller than a predetermined value. This new approach to detonating devices gave them a great advantage over the traditionally fused explosives. They were so much better that General George S. Patton said they "won the Battle of the Bulge for us".[14]

American manufacturing was able to leverage what were considered state-of-the-art practices when the war escalated to a new level. This not only included the development of proven management practices for overseeing mass production; it also included the ability to focus their research efforts on the military's needs to develop new products that helped bring the war to a close. This growth in production also caused a real shift in the employment of those not involved in the actual fighting of the war. Women and minorities were welcomed into the workforce to fill the labor shortages that existed in the factories. As a result of the increase in labor needed to meet the war demands, the average unemployment of the total population during the 6 years (1940–1945) was less than 3%. A level not seen since then. Given that the war effort for the U.S. was split between the European and Pacific theaters, there was a need for a good portion of the war munitions to be located on the west coast. As a result, many manufacturing companies opened and or expanded their facilities in the three west-coast states. This was a shift from the north-central part of the country that up to this point had been the primary manufacturing region. This shift in manufacturing to the west-coast resulted in an increase in the population of the three coastal states by 33%—from 9.8 to 13.1 million people.

With a vision towards world peace

As the war wound down, the focus turned to how and what needed to be put in place to reduce the possibility of this type of war happening again. The League of Nations, which had been established in 1920 after WWI with a goal of maintaining world peace through collective security, disarmament, and arbitration, had failed to stop the Axis powers and prevent WWII. So it was time to try again and on April 20, 1946 the United Nations was founded. This is an intergovernmental organization to promote international cooperation and prevent major conflicts. It started with the 51 members from the League of Nations and today has 193 members. As to its relative importance when it comes to maintaining world peace and supporting human development around the world, it depends on who you ask. After all, if you are busy dealing with large, politically diverse issues, the evaluation of your efforts will be strongly tied to the assumptions and beliefs of those you ask.

---

14 Baldwin, Ralph B. 1980. *The Deadly Fuze: Secret Weapon of World War II.* San Rafael, CA: Presidio Press, p. 4.

After WWII came to a close in 1946 and all the agreements were signed, there began to surface a disagreement between two of the Allied forces: the USSR, which was a Marxist-Leninist state and the U.S., a capitalist state. By 1947 this conflict was turning into what is commonly called the Cold War. For the next 34 years the level of tension between these two superpowers moved between the two extremes of being on the verge of a nuclear war to passive acceptance of one another. As a result of the growing tension between the superpowers and the fear of nationalism returning, 12 countries (Belgium, Netherlands, Luxembourg, France, UK, U.S., Canada, Portugal, Italy, Norway, Denmark, and Iceland) came together and formed NATO (North Atlantic Treaty Organization) in April 1949. Since the formation of NATO, the U.S., because of its status as a superpower, has located numerous military bases in the European countries to ensure that its troops and munitions are close at hand should the need arise. In 1955, the USSR, in an attempt to counteract the formation of NATO, brought together eight eastern bloc countries (Bulgaria, Czechoslovakia, East Germany, Hungary, Poland, Romania, Albania, and USSR) to form the Warsaw Pact. Over the next 36 years, until the Warsaw Pact was disbanded, these organizations were part of the tensions that existed between the U.S. and USSR.

Another activity that came out of WWII was a recognition that economic activities across national boundaries and around the world would become more and more important and as such something needed to be established to help deal with this increasing globalization in the future. Enter the Bretton Woods Conference in July of 1944. The focus behind this gathering was to establish and develop the mechanisms necessary to help move the world towards the idea of "open markets". As part of that it was recognized that the industrial democratic nations would have to lower their trade barriers and allow more open movement of capital. As a result of this conference two organizations were established: the International Monetary Fund (IMF) and the World Bank (WB). Let's take a quick look at their objectives.

The IMF's Articles of Agreement state that it is to promote international economic cooperation, international trade, employment, and the stability of exchange rates which would include providing financial resources to member countries to meet balance-of-payment needs. To this end it provides economic policy advice and financing to member countries while helping developing nations move towards macroeconomic stability and reducing poverty.

The official goal of the World Bank is to reduce poverty around the world. It does this by providing loans to developing countries for large capital programs. It is through these loans that are focused on providing improved infrastructure and accessibility that the attractiveness to foreign investment and new international trade will be enhanced. Both of these organizations are focused on improving the global economic condition by providing access to funds and projects that would otherwise be unattainable for the developing countries.

The post-war boom

The question to be answered at this point is: what impact did the postwar boom have on the way businesses and organizations behaved and saw themselves? At this point in time, the U.S. and its Allies had just won the Second World War. One of the major contributors to this victory was the U.S. industrial base. Throughout the war the industrial machine across the U.S. continued to: expand its capacity (the number and variety of products produced); improve its productivity (reducing the amount of labor and materials needed to produce them); increase the quality level (number of defects and reliability); and develop and integrate new technologies into its war munitions. All four of these attributes contributed to the successful transformation of the U.S. economy from one focused on war munitions to one focused on producing and delivering consumer goods for the U.S. and the rest of the world.

As the soldiers began returning from Europe and the Pacific front, there was a sizable pent-up demand here and around the world for commercial products. Given that the United States was the only world economy at the time that had not experienced some form of fighting and destruction on its soil, it was initially obliged to assist the other parts of the world to recover from the devastation they had experienced in the war. This led to the massive transformation of the industrial base from military to commercial products. According to my father, who was a chemist for Firestone during the war, once the war ended the focus of industry quickly shifted to the commercial production of tires and the continued development of synthetic rubber to support the ongoing development of new commercial products. The same can be said for the auto industry, which went from trucks, tanks, and planes back to passenger cars and commercial trucks for transporting products across the country's ever-expanding highway system. The airplane industry shifted from fighters and bombers to commercial aircraft and small planes for the growing private pilot market. My father was one of the tens of thousands of individuals that became involved in owning and flying their own small aircraft. Many of the firms involved in producing military radio and radar began shifting to commercial communications (radio and soon to be TV) as well as establishing the foundations for the electronics industry of today. This was a boom time for the U.S. economy.

Let's take a brief look at the extent of this economic growth period, starting with the preparing and selling of war products to the European allies in June of 1938 to November of 1970—a period of 389 months. During that time the total number of months that the economy was moving down instead of up was 58. Put another way for every 6.6 months of economic improvement there was one month of decline. Another perspective was to look at the growth in GDP over the same time. In 1946 the GDP (in constant 2009 dollars) was $1,959 billion and by 1970 it had grown to $4,717.7 billion which is a 240% growth rate in just 24 years. Part of the boom can be attributed to the large number of returning military personnel who used the GI Bill to attend a trade school and/or college which gave them the knowledge and training they needed to re-enter the economy and contribute to the growing middle class within the country. Another part of this growth can be attributed to the latent demand for consumer goods across the country. Remember the U.S. had been involved in WWI, then nine years later came the Great Depression and just as the country was recovering, the ramp up for WWII began. So there had not been any real consumer goods offered for over 15 years. A third part of this economic growth can be attributed to the need to rebuild a vast part of Europe and Japan. As the leading economic power of the time the U.S. offered its capabilities and expertise to those countries that needed help and assistance rebuilding their economic capabilities. This also allowed the U.S. to transplant its management tools and techniques that had proven successful during the war. Another cause for this growth can be attributed to the deepening of our understanding of marketing and our application and use of it in all businesses.

Another change that happened during this boom was the cooperation between or at least recognition and working together of the three primary groups that directly affect the overall economy: government, business, and labor. Remember, Figure 4 depicted the relationship between these three segments, prior to WWI, as being almost independent. Each was focused on doing what it thought was the best for itself. In 1918 with our involvement in WWI a reality, President Woodrow Wilson enacted the National Labor War Board to arbitrate any issues between business and labor to ensure production for the war effort was not affected by any labor problems. As the labor movement grew, the relationship between the three entities became more important to the economy. In 1932 the Norris-LaGuardia Act was passed which outlawed employers from penalizing their employees for joining trade unions. Then in 1935 the National Labor Relations Act commonly referred to as the Wagner Act was signed into law. This established the foundation for labor law in the U.S. It provided guaranteed rights for private sector employees to establish and organize trade unions with which the employer must engage in collective bargaining over the conditions and terms at work. After WWII close to 25% of the U.S. workers were members of a union and their membership and power in negotiating with businesses was growing. After all, calling a strike and shutting down the production capability of a plant was a pretty strong hand to hold. In 1947, the Taft-Hartley Act was passed which imposed limits on the union's ability to strike. Unsurprisingly, this law was strongly supported by the large business lobbies of the day. In 1959 the Landrum-Griffin Act was passed to help ensure openness and democracy within labor organizations. By this time approximately 30% of the nation's wage earners were members of a union. Needless to say this was not a segment of society that could easily be ignored. At that point in time, I would like to suggest that the interdependence between the three segments can be represented as shown in Figure 6.

Figure 6 **Interdependence between government, business, and labor**

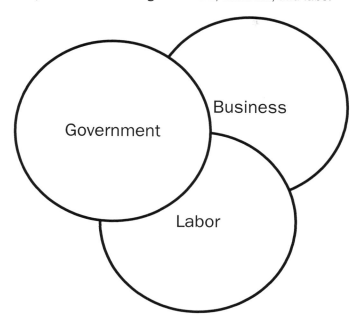

Figure 6 represents the leverage government had to bring to bear on the strained relationship between business and labor. While they both need to work together, each of them have their own set of assumptions about how that relationship should be structured. The unions were afraid of a slip back to what businesses saw as the good old days where they could hire and fire at will and be in complete control of all working terms and conditions. Conversely, organizations saw the increasingly heavy hand of the union extending its reach into what were believed to be business decisions and actions. This conflict over the proper amount of interaction between these elements and how these interactions affect the overall economy continues. Without a resolution this conflict will continue and by definition will have a nega-tive impact on all parties and the economy. More about how we might deal with this in Part III.

Transition to a consumer-based market

As has been noted, during the twentieth century leading up to and after WWII the primary focus was on increasing the efficiency of production. This shift towards the mass production model with its new technology and modern equipment ena-bled businesses to produce their products at a much lower cost than before. At the same time marketing was narrowly focused on ensuring the actual availability of a product because there were very few alternatives from which the consumer could choose. I can remember, as a young child, having both Sears & Roebuck and

Montgomery Ward's catalogs from which we wished for our birthday and Christmas presents. Not much when it comes to marketing today but it was sufficient to increase the awareness and desires of a relatively dispersed, transitioning agricultural population. By the mid-twentieth century things began to shift. As more choices were becoming available consumers were beginning to associate a quality level with certain brands. Cadillac and Kirby vacuum cleaners come to mind as being products that had a high level of quality. This led to the recognition by marketers that the brand was becoming important. If a brand was associated with high quality then the power of that brand began to reach beyond the physical product(s). The brand reputation and associated value perception could drive sales and lead to increased market share.

By the 1960s organizations began to establish and increase their focus on the function of marketing. This started with the development of market research activities focused on developing a deep understanding of the customer's likes and tastes. By knowing more information about potential customers they could develop and deliver messages and brands that were more likely to attract them. By this time advertising on television was growing. It was in this same time frame that organizations began to realize that the marketing message, providing the customer with what they are seeking, is a primary driver of profits. This shift of focus from production and efficiencies to customers, brands, and marketing brought major changes to organizations.

The last shift in marketing has been the recognition of relationship marketing—which can be best described by the phrase "customer for life". This type of marketing is not about the sale of an item today, but about building a relationship with an individual or business that will produce sales over the long term. This also is much cheaper than always having to find new customers that any of the other approaches may well have required. This is a bigger up-front expense but produces revenues over time which more than make up for the front-end load it carries.

The Interstate Highway System: the mover of people and products

Prior to the mid-1950s most long-distance moving of people or product was provided by the railroad system. While each state had its own network of roads they had been designed and put in place to facilitate and provide local/regional transportation between cities and towns. That all began to change in 1956 with the passage of the Federal Highway Act which is popularly known as the National Interstate and Defense Highways Act of 1956. While the right-of-way is owned by the states, the federal government contributed about 70% of the construction and maintenance of the interstate highways through user fees and fuel taxes. Initially conceived to take 12 years and cost about $25 billion, it ended up taking 35 years, covering over 40,000 miles at a cost of over $114 billion.

The interstate highway system led to urbanization and the establishment of sub-divisions. The first of these was called Levittown and it was located on Long Island in Nassau County. As sub-divisions began to appear around the country, not long behind them were the shopping malls which provided the residents access to shopping without having to drive miles into a neighboring town. The other phenomenon that the interstate highway system contributed to was the growth and development of inter-state trucking. Before the interstate highways existed, most cross-country movements relied on the railroad which meant loading the rail car, moving it to the final destination and unloading the car. Then the produce had to be transferred to a local truck and taken to its final location. With cross-country trucking shipping was much more flexible and could be cost effective in loads smaller than a rail car. Today, cross-country trucking accounts for approximately 25% of all the traffic miles driven on the interstate highway system. In addition, these highways have changed the way we travel and live.

The military-industrial complex

In 1958 the USSR put Sputnik I into orbit. This one achievement led to a ratcheting up of the Cold War (ever-expanding growth in military hardware and capabilities between the U.S. and USSR) and increased spending by the U.S. military and government in an effort to catch up with Russia. In January 1961 when President Dwight Eisenhower was making his farewell speech he recognized that something had changed in American life—its movement to a constant state of wartime readiness to which he had contributed—and he warned the people about the power and control within the "military-industrial complex" and how it needed to be kept in check. The warning seemed to have fallen on deaf ears. Since then, the money spent on and increased level of power within the military-industrial complex (the interdependence between the military side of government and the private industries that provided tools and technology to the military) has continued to expand to meet the ever-expanding needs and wants of the military and congressional members (Figure 7).

Figure 7 **U.S. defense budget 1946–2008**

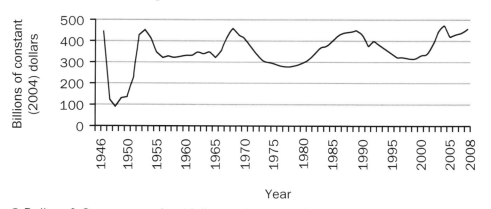

© Dollars & Sense magazine (dollarsandsense.org)

Some of the major components of this industry could be identified as traditional armaments (boats, planes, tanks, conventional weapons, etc.), while the space race, the nuclear arms race, as well as the information/intelligence race all intensified greatly during this time. While my four years in the Air Force were spent in the Security Service, which was focused on the gathering of relevant intelligence, it was in no way comparable to what the Security Service combined with NSA and other signal intelligence organizations are doing today in the name of protecting America.

Today the U.S. Department of Defense budget makes up almost 47% of all the military spending in the world. In 2009, the U.S. defense budget was in excess of $650 billion and that does not include any expenses outside the DoD budget. Imagine the benefit a politician receives from securing a defense contract for a company in his or her district? I would like you to spend a minute to contemplate what the country could do with even half that level of investment and spending if we could somehow reduce the need for armies and weapons?

Evaluation and changes in business education

As the economy continued to grow in the 1950s, many of the large companies such as Ford, General Electric, Carnegie Steel, and Standard Oil had an expanding need for professional managers to fill the empty positions in their growing organizations. These organizations were looking for employees educated with some theory and analytical techniques instead of the practical, trade school type of training that most business schools were offering. This need led to the two reports completed in 1959 that took a strong look at business education in the U.S. The Carnegie Foundation funded the work done by Frank Pierson entitled "The Education of American Businessmen: A Study of University-College Programs in Business Administration." The second was entitled "Higher Education for Business" and was co-authored by Robert Gordon and James Howell and funded by the Ford Foundation. Both reports were very critical of current business education, comparing it to a trade school instead of higher education. They talked about how most faculty tended to draw on their own real-world experiences to teach from and how most of the courses within their programs lacked any solid theory on which analytical tools and future research could be built. These reports were a real condemnation of the practices within higher education's business programs of the late 1950s.

As a result of these reports, the face of business education in the U.S. began to change. The first change was the transition among school Deans from those with senior management experience to academics with experience in quantitative research and theory building. This shift was on the assumption that, if the leadership of business schools understand quantitative methods and theory development, they can help refocus the efforts within the other departments to follow their lead. Initially, a vast majority of these new leaders came from the field of economics because it was a mathematical field focused on theory development to explain what was transpiring in the world. With this shift business schools began to focus on and reward the development and publication of theory-based research, discounting the knowledge and insights from real-world practitioners. In fact, today, many of the most respected business Ph.D. programs strongly shy away from admitting anyone with any solid real-world business experience. Twenty-five years ago, the head of the Operations Management Program at the University of Georgia had to take my application to the Dean and Provost to override the management department's disqualification of my application because of my real-world experience. To this day, I am so grateful for his willingness to go the extra mile for me. It changed my life and introduced me to what has turned out to be a career-long learning journey.

The growth of finance (1970–1990)

As we look back to the 1910s, at the beginning of what is commonly referred to as modern business, we see that initially the focus of businesses was on the product they were producing or offering to the customer. Their efforts were on being able to provide more for less and in doing this the businesses made profits and prospered. The profits were tied to the effectiveness of their production efforts. As we transitioned out of WWII we saw the beginnings of modern day marketing efforts and the focus on establishing and developing the brand and how the brand could carry customers to other products being offered. With the development of television in the late 1950s came the ever-expanding opportunity to market one's products through advertising on TV. With TV marketing, brand development and market research exploded. Organizations could no longer just depend on the product to make the sale; this had to be combined with an appropriate marketing effort.

By the 1960s we saw a shift in organizational structure. Up until that time, most organizations were focused on the production and sales of similar categories of products, for example: GM, Ford, GE, Dow Chemical, and IBM. What changed was the appearance of a conglomerate organization. These were companies that bought other dissimilar businesses through what is commonly referred to as a "leveraged buyout", using the assets and value of the company being purchased to finance the purchase. While the economy, which was going through up and down cycles at the time, helped this by facilitating buying in the down trough and selling during the high peak, this approach to corporate growth and strategy continued to expand. This shift led to the recognition by those individuals at the top of companies that the businesses they were buying were no longer necessarily valued for the products they produced but were seen as providers of "cash flow" that could cover the cost of their purchase and provide additional earnings when they were sold. It was not how good their products were or how efficient their production processes were, it was how they could use these businesses as assets to borrow against and then sell for a profit in the future.

By the time we reached the 1980s this shift in perspective—to one that sees the assortment of companies in a corporation as nothing but various streams of cash flows that can be reshuffled whenever needed—introduced the corporate takeover market. This shift was aided by the development of financial innovations such as junk bonds and a relaxation of the antitrust regulations on intra-industry mergers. As a result the era of the hostile takeover was introduced. This led to a change within organizations where the "financial performance" became the criterion of importance. As such, the focus on reducing costs, selling assets, and leveraging financial investments became much more important to corporate leadership than the products and production processes.

As the aforementioned shift within corporations was going on, another shift was taking place—the emergence of "shareholder value" as the primary measure of corporate performance. Given the growing size of corporations and their ever-expanding portfolio of businesses it was more and more difficult for anyone to understand how the various pieces individually contributed to the whole. As such, it was relatively easy to look at the corporation's stock price and see it as a valid representation of its value. Since the stock is owned by the investors it is not a big shift to seeing how increasing "price per share" and increasing "shareholder value" could be viewed as the same thing. What I find so interesting about today's use of "shareholder value" is that it forces the attention of the CEOs on to short-term objectives at the expense of long-term growth and investment, which is something that a growing economy must have if it is to continue to prosper.

Concluding thoughts on Part I

I hope this refresher course in the evolution of business in the U.S. has provided some insights and filled some holes in your knowledge about how we arrived at the situation we are in today. If your professional experiences are anything like mine, you will have encountered very few peers or subordinates that have said they thought things in business were all well. Everyone has their own ideas about the changes they would make given the opportunity. When I think about how so many of us hold that perspective, I can see only three possible explanations:

- We all worked for (employed and consulted) some poorly managed businesses

- Everybody's ego is so big that we all think we could do it better

- There are some real issues and inconsistencies within the processes and practices of business

While the first two are possible—and if they are the answer it would make everyone feel better—I believe in my heart of hearts that the third is a more supportable explanation. If we begin to contemplate the acceptance of the third alternative, then we have to start looking for the inconsistencies within the processes and practices across business. This is where some of the history lessons will come into play.

At work we see inconsistencies in how projects are evaluated and how we evaluate and make expenditure decisions. At home we know that if our check does not get bigger or our bills do not get smaller we cannot improve our financial position. At work we have seen numerous projects justified because they save labor in a department but do not increase sales or cut costs (reduce headcount). We have seen those in power make decisions based on short-term cost cutting yet we know that to improve the capabilities of our organizations to successfully compete in the future, we have to invest in improving our capabilities today. Our organizations claim that "people are important" and yet they do not provide opportunities or support for increasing their experiences or abilities.

I encourage each of you to reflect back on your careers and begin to think about those inconsistencies you have noticed in the past. As you surface these, remember the decisions were correct based on the tools and assumptions of those making them. The real issue is that these tools and techniques were developed and incorporated into business practices during the first half of the twentieth century. At that time, we understood our environment as being very linear. Since the 1960s science and more recently the social sciences have begun to acknowledge and understand the existence of the systems-based perspective, which recognizes the interdependence between and within systems. Over the last 25 years or so there has been a phenomenal growth in the development and application of systems-based tools and practices for business and organizations. Today, the real challenge facing business is how to incorporate this new understanding into processes and practices.

Part II is your introduction to systems in general and the current set of systems-based tools and practices that are available for others to use in their business. I hope you enjoy the next part of your journey.

A new way of seeing: the evolution of ecology and "seeing systems"

Part II introduces and explores the foundations and growth of "systems-thinking". This shift started about 200 years ago in the fields of biology and botany. These first researchers, who were looking into living plants and animals, came to realize that the existing research paradigm of "reductionism" did not provide a valid explanation for what they were finding as they looked deeper into the evolution of various plant and animal species. Alexander von Humboldt (1769–1859) was one of the first to see a need for an approach to science that could account for the harmony he saw in nature among the diversity that existed in the physical world. Another of the founders of this transition was Johann Wolfgang von Goethe who, in his 1831 book *Story of My Botanical Studies*, wrote:

> The ever-changing display of plant forms, which I have followed for so many years, awakens increasingly within me the notion: The plant forms which surround us were not all created at some given point in time and then locked into the given form, they have been given... a felicitous mobility and plasticity that allows them to grow and adapt themselves to many different conditions in many different places.[1]

This disconnect between the prevailing understanding of the history of plants—all created at the same time and locked into their given form—and Goethe's suggestion that plants had the ability to grow and adapt given the surrounding conditions they found themselves in, led other botanists to begin to discuss and question the currently held beliefs on plants. Their continued efforts around this question laid the foundation for Darwin and other early contributors to the history of ecology and the development that today is commonly referred to as systems thinking.

Chapter 4 will provide a brief overview of the history and development of this new perspective. Developing an understanding of both the *what* and the *how* associated with "systems thinking" should reduce the level of anxiety most people feel when being introduced to a new way of seeing or thinking.

Chapter 5 is probably the most important chapter in the book. It is here where you will be introduced to the development and growth of systems-based business tools and practices. Many of the foundational ideas can be traced back to the work of Drucker and Deming although neither of these icons actually used the term "systems" in their work. I have arranged the systems-based tools and practices by their focus and have included some "real-world" examples of the ease of use and impact these tools and processes have had.

---

1 Paris, Robert. 2016. *Goethe and Studies about Nature*. Matiè et Revolution. Retrieved November 12, 2016 (www.matierevolution.org/spip.php?article4528).

4
Evolution of systems thinking

Setting the stage

As I briefly described in the Introduction, in 1991 I had an epiphany, while sitting in a Systems Ecology class, which set me on this learning journey. The primary focus of Systems Ecology is on the interactions and transactions between the living (plant, animal, and human) and non-living components within the ecological system (a biological community of interacting organisms and their environment) being studied. A major concern of ecology is the influence humans have on the functioning of the overall ecosystem. What I came to realize in that instant is that organizations, which are composed of living and non-living components that are involved in almost constant interactions and transactions with other organizations, communities, and individuals, are involved in the same types of interdependent activities that are going on within an ecosystem. It was very evident to me that organizations are participating in the day-to-day evolution and development of what you might call an economic ecosystem (an economic community of interacting organizations, stakeholders, and the environment). Yet the models we use today to describe and analyze a business and the performance of our economic system are still based on the concept of a "machine" whose individual components can be optimized, modified, reduced, and even removed in pursuit of improved overall performance.

From that day forward I knew that the problems many of us face in our professional careers can be traced to the fact that we are still relying on a mechanistic model to guide our daily business decisions and actions while our instincts are trying to help us see that the organization is part of a larger "industrial and economic ecosystem". There are many industry subsystems within our economic ecosystem and each is composed of both primary and secondary organizations whose interactions, when taken as a whole, include all the elements and activities necessary to deliver the end products associated with that industry. As has been learned through the study of ecosystems and the environment, the only way to truly understand and be able to positively affect the performance of a system is to recognize and embrace a different lens, one that more accurately reflects the true behavior of the system being investigated. That is the perspective of **systems thinking**. My journey from business professional to understanding systems and being comfortable with this new paradigm took more than a few years—over 10 years of study and reflection.

I am not going to ask any of you to undertake the learning journey I traveled to develop an in-depth understanding of systems thinking and all of it sub-fields and elements. Most of my effort was focused on reading and digesting academic knowledge that, while interesting, may not provide you with the insights you need to move your organization forward. For those with that innate curiosity to learn, the Appendix contains a list of authors and books you might be interested in as well as a description of the various sub-topics within the broad field. All you really need to get started on this journey is a recognition of the new lens through which you see your organization and a model with which you can begin to identify and evaluate alternatives. For that you need an understanding of the basics of systems and exposure to a few proven systems-based business tools/processes that you can begin to draw on. This chapter addresses the basic systems concepts and the next chapter will introduce you to a broad spectrum of proven systems-based tools that are currently being used within and across business.

Before systems and systems theory

While many might concern themselves with the search to identify the first discussion of systems, and some say it may well have been in ancient Greece, suffice it to say, the modern-day concept is usually traced back to the field of biology. While George Perkins Marsh does not fit this description, he did study silviculture and soil conservation before becoming a lawyer and later the first U.S. minister to Italy in 1861. In his work entitled *Man and Nature* (1864), which is focused on looking at humankind's involvement and impact on nature, he says:

> There are, indeed, brute destroyers, beasts and birds and insects of prey—all animal life feeds upon, and, of course, destroys other life— but this destruction is balanced by compensations. It is, in fact, the very means by which the existence of one tribe of animals or of vegetables is secured against being smothered by the encroachments of another, and the reproductive powers of species, which serve as the food of others are always proportioned to the demand they are destined to supply.[2]

2 Marsh, George Perkins. 1864. *Man and Nature; or, Physical Geography as Modified by Human Action.* New York: Charles Schribner.

In this extract Marsh is describing the interdependence that exists within and across the various components within nature.

The level of interest in this young science continued to expand and by the end of the nineteenth century the term ecology and the foundations of what is now considered modern ecology were established. While experts may argue as to who was the founder of modern ecological theory, Haeckel or Warming, suffice it to say, the journey into seeing the study of living things had changed. Some of the most notable researchers in the early twentieth century were Frederic Clements, Arthur Tansley, and Aldo Leopold.

By the 1920s researchers across the soft sciences were beginning to look outside their narrow fields and recognize the interdependence with other fields of science. Alfred North Whitehead who was a mathematician and philosopher published a book in 1929 entitled *Process and Reality: An Essay in Cosmology.* In his book Whitehead argues that "there is urgency in coming to see the world as a web of interrelated processes of which we are integral parts, so that all of our choices and actions have consequences for the world around us."[3]

Paul A. Weiss, an Austrian biologist studying development, differentiation, and neurobiology, recognized the value and insight gained when researchers from different fields share their knowledge and insights. He had begun to notice disconnects between various fields and was looking for a new model that would encourage this integrative approach rather than the traditional model that disregarded it. This led him to begin working on developing a more systemic understanding of knowledge that was more complete and more consistently coherent. Remember, at this time, the Western world and academics within it were strongly tied to the reductionist models introduced by Bacon, Descartes, and Newton, and the work of Weiss was seen as a radical perspective.

A third individual, who became a part of the foundational work of systems thinking was Ludwig von Bertalanffy. He was an Austrian biologist who is known as one of the founders of general systems theory. He collaborated with Weiss and Whitehead, sharing insights as their efforts to develop a general theory of systems were evolving. In 1937, at a philosophy seminar at the University of Chicago, Bertalanffy first presented his idea of a "general systems theory" that eventually led to the publishing of his book of the same name 38 years later.[4]

During WWII researchers at the Servomechanisms Laboratory at MIT repurposed some work previously undertaken by Bell Telephone Laboratories in the 1920s which used negative feedback to control amplifiers, in order to develop electronic circuits to provide control systems for radar and gun mounts. This work provided the foundation for the field of cybernetics which was initially focused on the development and use of feedback as a control mechanism. The primary

3 Mesle, C. Robert. 2009. *Process-Relational Philosophy: An Introduction to Alfred North Whitehead.* West Conshohocken, PA: Templeton Foundation Press, p. 9.
4 Bertalanffy, Ludwig von. 1976. *General Systems Theory: Foundations, Development, Applications,* revised edn. New York: George Braziller.

contributors at that time were Norbert Wiener, Warren McCulloch, W. Ross Ashby, and Alan Turing. By the 1990s cybernetics had evolved from the classical focus on feedback and control mechanisms behind the steering of the agent or individual system to the decisions and actions by the system doing the steering.

In 1954, at the Palo Alto Center for Advanced Study in Behavioral Sciences four of the soon to be major contributors to systems theory met. They were: biologist Bertalanffy, mathematician Anatol Rapoport, economist Kenneth Boulding, and physiologist Ralph Gerard. One of the direct results of this meeting was the creation of the Society for the Advancement of General Systems Theory which was renamed in 1956 to Society for General Systems Research (SGSR). In 1988 it was again renamed the International Society for the Systems Sciences. This society has continued to grow and expand its reach and today it has thousands of members around the world.

I think it is critically important for all of us to recognize that this perspective of research and understanding, seeing the interconnectedness among things, has, for all practical purposes, only been around for sixty years. If you remember, in the last chapter we learned that the foundational assumptions and model for today's business practices were developed about 100 years ago. Put another way, the focus on interdependence within and across organizations is, by definition, a relatively new way of thinking about how people and organizations interact and behave. As such, our exploration will require each of you to relax your currently held assumptions and foundational beliefs about business and entertain the possibility that "there is another way".

General systems theory

In 1968 Bertalanffy published *General Systems Theory*. While he pulled the pieces together and wrote the text, it was by no means his work alone; he included insights and ideas from the other pioneers within SGSR. In addition to the four founders of the SGSR mentioned above, other well-known contributors were: William Ross Ashby, Margaret Mead, Gregory Bateson, and C. West Churchman. While I could spend pages reviewing the details and growth of systems and systems thinking, it would be of little help to you on your journey to understanding how to use this perspective to improve your organization. So let's begin by looking at the basic behavior of systems with a focus on how these behaviors affect and can be seen within organizations.

For many, a system is composed of regularly interacting or interrelating groups of activities. Put another way a system is a configuration of parts connected and joined together by a web of relationships. If you think about it, these descriptions could be describing many things, ranging from mechanical systems like a watch, a car, or a computer to human systems such as a classroom or a family. In addition, all of us can see that this definition would not apply to a pile of dirty clothes in the corner or the books in a library. From this foundation, the understanding of systems expanded to what today is commonly referred to as "complex" systems. These systems are seen as complex because they are made up of diverse components and have multiple interconnected elements. An example of a complex system might be a forest or a lake. Both of these are composed of diverse elements that have a variety of interdependent connections within and across the boundaries of both complex systems. At this point, the complex system is affected by changes within the system—the fish die because the lake freezes or a fire burns all the grasses or trees—but it cannot adapt. That is the next level.

The next step is what is commonly referred to as "complex adaptive" systems. The adaptive part of these systems refers to their ability to change and learn based on their experiences and interactions with their environment. While this does not include the forest or river because these do not adapt, it does include many of the elements within each of these that adapt to the changes in their environment and as such would be considered "complex adaptive" systems. For example, the wildlife within a forest, such as birds, carnivores, and herbivores, all adapt and change their behavior based on the changes they observe in the other wildlife within their environment. At this level, we are looking at the various living animals ranging from the single cell ameba to humans. Initially, when looking at "complex adaptive systems" it was true that all of them involved life and, as such, were always trying to adjust to the conditions they faced to facilitate their continuing evolution. Today, we have some computer-based systems that learn and adapt from their interaction with the environment that are, at times, included in this category. After all, if the complex adaptive systems do not continue to adapt relative to their environment they too will be replaced by a new and improved version. Before we leave this category, I want you to look at today's organizations—especially the one you work for. It should not be a stretch for you to see how your organization fits very comfortably into what has been described as a "complex adaptive system". How often has your organization undertaken a new initiative in response to something done by another business in your industry (part of the larger system) or in order to respond to a new regulation? It is this perspective that led me to use the term "living organization" to more effectively describe the behavior of today's businesses. After all, they are systems that are "living"—they continue to evolve—with a long-term goal of remaining viable and continuing to develop/evolve. I will address this in more detail later but, *yes*, I am saying that the true goal of an organization is not "profit" or "more profit" but its ability to continually evolve and grow.

Another aspect of systems is their permeability from the outside. This leads to them being seen as either "open" or "closed". When you think of systems from this perspective, think of them on a gradient from completely closed to completely open. On the one hand, a closed system is self-contained and shares nothing with its environment. A couple of easy examples would be a battery-powered wristwatch. It works till the battery runs out of electricity and it quits. Another almost closed system would be a space ship—it only has what it takes with it and while it may share dialog, discussions, and information with ground control and possibly some energy from its solar panels, it is completely self-contained. On the other hand, an open system interacts in a variety of ways with its environment. The human body is a prime example of such a system. We take in energy through our mouth and absorb or lose heat through the interaction of our skin with the outside environment. We take in information (audio, visual, textual, smell, taste) through a variety of senses and all of this information or feedback is processed and used by our brain to help us adapt to the current situation in our external environment.

The final important aspect of systems is that they not only have the ability to regulate themselves, but they are predisposed to maintaining a steady state. This is referred to as **homeostasis**. Once again, looking at the human body, it self-regulates the body's temperature to somewhere around 98.6 °F and when it gets hotter or colder the body, on its own, begins to adjust in order to bring it back to "normal". This behavior can also be seen in the swings in population of the predator and prey animals within a wildlife area. When there are more predators there are fewer prey animals and then the balance will move back the other way.

As you can see, a systems perspective is very different than the traditional business perspective that is focused on the individual and departmental performance while assuming any local improvement will positively affect the organization's performance. This shift to a systems-based perspective moves our understanding from: "the parts and pieces of the organization" to "the organization of parts and pieces". Such a small change in the arrangement of words leads to a completely different perspective and understanding. Thus the journey to "seeing systems".

A quick look into systems thinking

With the categories of systems identified, let's begin a deeper look into understanding systems. This next section draws from the book I would highly recommend to all of you: *Stepping in Wholes: Introduction to Complex Systems* by Ollhoff and Walcheski.[5] This book is now out of print but easily available as a used book online. The authors wrote it to introduce high school seniors to the world of complex systems and upper level college students will attest to its effectiveness in doing just that. I know it will give you a place to go to find the answers to your questions about systems.

Linear thinking vs. systems thinking

So, what is the difference between those who fall into the "traditional or linear" thinker side and those who would be referred to as "systems" thinkers? First, the

---

5 Ollhoff, Jim and Michael Walcheski. 2002. *Stepping in Wholes: Introduction to Complex Systems*. Eden Prairie, MN: Sparrow Media Group.

linear thinker sees and believes that organizations are rather predictable and somewhat orderly while the systems thinkers sees organizations as unpredictable and chaotic. That drives the linear managers to search for a way to fine-tune the predictable system and the systems managers to go with the flow and focus on making the system more robust to the unpredictable changes in the environment. Given this starting point, you would expect that the linear thinker would try to control the disorder he or she sees and bring it back to an orderly status. The systems thinker looks for patterns in the chaos to better understand what and how the system works and behaves. One other difference that really sticks out is that linear thinkers continually look for "who or what to blame" when something goes wrong—the assumption is that since the system is orderly and predictable, someone or something must have done something wrong. The systems thinker uses something going wrong as a starting point to begin looking for patterns so as to identify where within the system the disturbance is coming from and how it might be adjusted to permanently remove the disturbance.

Another difference between these two perspectives is how they perceive and respond to the existence of a symptom—a manifestation of a problem within the system. A simple example I use with my students is the existence of a pimple. While they treat this symptom with a surface treatment, the real cause of the pimple may well be what they are eating, lack of sleep, cleanliness habits, hormonal levels, etc. Symptoms are not the real problem but many times they can provide us vital information about what is the "core" problem causing the symptom. Because we have all been trained and rewarded for responding quickly and directly to problems, we see a symptom and immediately look for its "cause"—something directly associated with the symptom that is not as we expect it to be and that becomes the fix for that symptom. Simple and easy, just look for the cause. After all, the linear world is based on a cause–effect understanding. Conversely, systems thinkers, who look at the whole and understand that symptoms are caused by an underlying or "core problem", focus their efforts on identifying and fixing the problem so as to permanently remove the cause.

The term, complex systems, is used to describe the level of interdependence within and between the various elements/subsystems that make up a system. If you think about a forest or the human body it is easy to recognize the multitude of components that have an effect on the ability of the system to be "productive". Recognizing this interdependence is critical to being able to understand how "actions" will produce both intended results and unintended results. So many of today's problems are the consequences of yesterday's solutions.[6] While it is relatively easy to recognize the negative symptoms within an organization, it is much harder to identify the underlying "core problem", which may well be producing a variety of the symptoms, because the relationship between problem and symptom is not your basic "cause and effect" relationship; it goes much deeper.

6 Senge, Peter. 1990. *The Fifth Discipline: The Art and Practice of the Learning Organization.* New York, NY: Doubleday.

Like any complex system, organizations develop common and predictable patterns of behavior that can only be understood when one looks at the "whole" system and, *yes*, implementing a successful organizational change is best done with a systemic approach. Some of the symptoms might be: a reoccurring problem that never goes away, an organization that never seems to get anything done, the more it tries to change the more things stay the same (often because of a new crisis), committees made up of logical individuals continue to make illogical decisions, etc. Until these systemic patterns are recognized and effectively dealt with the organization cannot move forward. One of the biggest problems facing linear thinkers is recognizing the time delay that exists between an action and the resulting effect—it can often be years.

Below are the ten enemies of systems thinking taken from *Stepping in Wholes*. I have included them because these statements or phrases may well signal when you or someone you are talking with are about to put forth a thought based on linear thinking.

1. "*We have to fix it quick*": implies doing it before you understand what "it" is.

2. "*Oh, let's just put a band-aid on it*": this is a half-hearted attempt to fix or cover up a problem.

3. "*We must make the budget last till the end of the fiscal year*": short-term, budget-driven fixes almost always harm long-term sustainability.

4. "*We need to respond immediately*": quick knee-jerk reactions produce linear solutions.

5. "*Who cares*": lack of curiosity by definition is linear thinking and a red flag to a broader systemic problem within the organization.

6. "*We need more information*": while there is nothing wrong with more information, when this is used to search for the linear cause or answer it stifles one's ability to see the system.

7. "*Oh, you're just thinking too deeply*": the assumption behind this statement is that you are beginning to think differently than me and it is not necessary. Yet, seeing systems requires deep thinking and not everyone enjoys doing it.

8. "*To hell with the rest of the organization, we must get our needs met*": this is a prime example of the bunker mentality within organizations that pits one division or department against another. This leads to a "win–lose" perspective and the pursuit of our win.

9. "*We can't have any conflict about this*": this is a peace-at any-cost mentality meaning that individuals and organizations are not willing to look at and develop a better understanding of the situation.

10. "*You will do it this way and you will enjoy it*": an authoritarian manager is a very strong indicator of linear thinking. Expanding one's understanding is, by definition, a very collaborative experience and not supported by this type of management.

As you reflect back on these so-called enemies of systems thinking, you should try to identify how often you have heard or, more importantly, used these types of sayings. In doing this, we are beginning the journey towards a new understanding by looking within ourselves. Before we get into the tools and practices, we need to look a bit deeper into the area of "complex adaptive systems" (CAS) which we now know is the category within which organizations reside.

Complex adaptive systems

If you reflect back to Chapter 1 where I introduced economic cycles and their unpredictable behavior, or for those of you who watch the stock market and see the increased level of volatility within it, one has to ask the question: what is going on? As Peter Vaill so aptly described in his book *Learning as a Way of Being: Strategies for Survival in a World of Permanent White Water*, organizations today are behaving more and more like a boat traveling through rapids—transitioning from periods where there is no control, only chaos, to other times where there is little turbulence.[7] These changes are not so much due to what the boat and its passengers are trying to do but to the direction and exact location within the rapids providing the dynamics the boat is responding to. In that situation complete control is a myth and the same can be said for organizations. While one can, to some extent, affect the location and angle of the boat, the same is true when looking at controlling organizations; so much of the stimulus affecting both resides external to and completely out of any direct control of those charged with providing direction. Recognizing this and being able to let go of the mantra of "being in control", which our business education and organizations expect of each of us, is one of the first steps we must make to begin the transition. I can attest to the fact that this is harder than it appears because throughout our careers we have continually sought out the roles that gave us more control.

Over the last fifty years researchers have been studying *chaos* and *complexity* and their efforts have led to the realization that beneath the chaos there is always an underlying order. It is the underlying order that can provide us with valuable insights into becoming better at guiding our boat or organization through the chaos that exists external to us.

So let us take as a given that organizations are complex adaptive systems that exist in a rather chaotic economic environment within which they themselves are an active participant. That said, I would like to suggest that we adopt the term

7 Vaill, Peter. 1996. *Learning as a Way of Being: Strategies for Survival in a World of Permanent White Water*. San Francisco: Jossey Bass.

"complex adaptive economic system" (CAES) because it more effectively describes the economic world in which today's organizations are engaged. In addition, we must remember that CASs have the ability to learn and through those lessons, adapt their behavior. So, what does that mean for the CAES? First, and foremost, is that it is always changing as the organizations within this economic system learn and adapt. Yes, all organizations learn and adapt at their own rate. Some are very aware of the changes in their external environment and are open to almost constant learning and adaption, while others are much more stoic in their path forward and as such, resist the impetus to change. These are the organizations that are, like the dinosaurs, becoming extinct while those at the other extreme are always looking for how they can improve or adjust their current position.

As we begin to see and understand the economy as a CAES which includes the recognition of each business or organization as an active participant in that system, we are led to the question: *what changed* to make this the economic world we now live in and not the more stable and predictable one of the past? I believe the answer is "nothing has changed" except the expansion of our understanding of systems and how they work and finally extending that understanding to the broader economic system. So let's take another look at the evolution of economic thought over the last 240 years from this perspective and see what we find out.

In 1776, when Adam Smith published *The Wealth of Nations*, the number of businesses engaged in commerce in a region that exceeded the radius of one-day's ride was very small. This led to the existence of a number of small (local and/or regional) economic systems across a country. Because of their relative isolation and limited growth within each of these systems, changes in one area were not strongly felt in another. In addition, at the time, technology had been stable for many generations and the customer purchasing power within a region was small. The primary focus of economics at that time was on the region's comparative advantage (the ability to produce and/or sell goods and services at a lower price and realize stronger sales margins) and how it could be used to improve the region's economic performance. Additionally, any business whose reach exceeded the boundaries of its country of residence existed with the sanction and approval of the crown. Thus, within a country there was very little, if any, real economic competition to be concerned about.

If we jump forward to the mid-1800s, we can still see a somewhat similar situation. The economic regions were now much larger, and in some instances national in reach. A very limited number of organizations had a multinational reach across a common border, but businesses that reached across an ocean were almost nonexistent. During this period (1870s to 1930s) the neoclassical perspective of economics, with its belief that free markets would, in the short to medium term, automatically provide full employment, as long as workers were flexible in their wage demands, was commonly held and as such governments took a very laissez-faire or hands-off approach to business. Alfred Marshall, at Cambridge University, was one of the principal architects of this perspective. He worked to bring together the classical approach which was focused on the supply side with the marginalist theory which focused on the demand side; he did this through the introduction of the supply/demand graph. During this period the primary economic focus was on improving the short- to medium-term performance of businesses. While this is not necessarily the beginning of the "greed is good" mantra, it surely fits the behavior of the time.

By the mid-1930s a new economic understanding was emerging, developed by John Maynard Keynes. He introduced the idea of macroeconomics which positions the state as being responsible for controlling the "boom and bust" cycles of economic activity within its boundaries through its fiscal (level of investment) and monitory (adjusting interest rates) policies. Here we see the use of an economic model to inform and guide decision-makers (governments) as to what actions need to be taken to positively affect the economic conditions in their country.

By the mid-1970s the ideas of Milton Friedman were beginning to take hold. He extolled the virtues of a free market economic system with minimal intervention from government. To that end he believed that the Federal Reserve should be abolished and that the government's role in the guidance of the economy should be severely restricted. Can you see any similarities between Friedman's perspective and the neoclassical period of the previous century? He was a major advisor to both U.S. President Ronald Reagan and U.K. Prime Minister Margaret Thatcher. In a December 2012 article in the *Journal of Economic Literature*, Edward Nelson, the assistant director of the board of governors of the Federal Reserve System, stated that, "in important respects, the overall monetary and financial policy response to the crisis [2007–2008 economic crisis] can be viewed as Friedman's monetary economics in practice".[8]

As with most academic research, economics is focused on efforts to tackle the biggest problem(s) of the time. If we look back at the basic focus of the economists over the last 250 years, we see the same is true. Adam Smith's work, published in 1776, was focused on improving the small (local and regional) economic systems across independent regions. Given the time of his work, at the very beginning of the Industrial Revolution, his perspective was that of improving productivity using mechanization to improve the region's comparative advantage. The neoclassical economists (1870–1930) were focused on the issue of full employment within a country which they saw as leading to increased productivity, with export of goods and a positive inflow of foreign dollars. On the other hand, Keynes was focused on eliminating the boom and bust cycles that so dramatically affected the economic conditions across the countries of the Western world. He saw it as the responsibility of the country's government to take the necessary and appropriate actions to control these cycles and improve the economy's growth as measured by GDP. While Friedman's focus was also guided by improving the measure of GDP, his solution set was the opposite of Keynes. Friedman thought it was the role of government to step back from trying to control the country's economy and entrust it to the private sector.

---

8 Nelson, Edward. 2012. "Review." *Journal of Economic Literature* 50(4): 1106-1109.

Think about it: all three of these perspectives were developed and embraced by academics, governments, and citizens around the world and were focused on improving a single goal and measure. Their focus was like that of a mechanic whose only objective is to optimize the performance of a machine. Yet when you look at the world economics from a systems perspective—as a complex adaptive economic system—it is easy to see that none of these perspectives considered all the players, components, and elements that make up the system and are affected by the ever-changing interdependence within our world economic system. I am not an economist by any stretch of the word, but having observed the changes in the espoused solutions to the various economic issues we are facing, I am convinced that this area of research—systems and economics—is one of the most fruitful and needed research fields in the world. While I have thought about the needed shift in the field of economics for many years, my focus has always been on bringing change to businesses, because this is where my experience and education has focused. As I began researching this section of the book I was delighted to find out that others had been researching complexity and economics for some time. The following is a brief overview of their journey.

So how does the idea of a CAES and the actions of organizations or governments compare to what has previously been recommended by the economists of the past? First and foremost is a recognition that we really do not know how all the players interact and what the impact of a limited set of actions will be. In his review of the book by Eric Beinhocker entitled *The Origins of Wealth: Evolution, Complexity, and the radical Remake of Economics*, Herbert Gintis describes complexity economics as "a mirror inversion of Neoclassical theory".[9] Instead of it being about smart people in really simple situations the real world is about simple people (coping) with incredibly complex situations". If we assume this is somewhat correct, it is easy to see how ineffective our current understanding of economics is. Suffice it to say, this emerging thought and research into complexity economics is one that will expand our understanding of economics into the twenty-first century.

This perspective on economics has its roots in the Santa Fe Institute which was founded in 1984 as a nonprofit research institute focused on multidisciplinary research of complex adaptive systems, be they physical, computational, biological, or social. The founding scientists saw the need for a place where theoretical research could be supported and conducted outside the traditional disciplinary boundaries of academia and government science budgets. Their work on economics began at a 1987 conference convened by physicist Philip Anderson and economist Kenneth Arrow. A year later W. Brian Arthur was asked to lead the Institute's first research program—the Economy as an Evolving Complex System—with an initial group of twenty or so researchers. While research and understanding of the economy as a complex system has continued to grow, it remained outside the

9 Gintis, Herbert. 2006. *The Economy as a Complex Adaptive System.* Retrieved October 22, 2016 (http://www.umass.edu/preferen/Class%20Material/Readings%20in%20Market%20Dynamics/Complexity%20Economics.pdf).

mainstream economic thought until the financial meltdown of 2009. As the *Economist* magazine observed, the financial system wasn't the only thing that collapsed; standard economics had collapsed with it. So, how has this affected the field of economics? Today, many see complexity economics beginning to move towards the center of economic thought. To quote W. Brian Arthur, "There's a recognition that it is more than a new set of methods or theories: it is a different way to see the economy. It views the economy not as machine-like, perfectly rational, and essentially static, but as organic, always exploring, and always evolving—always constructing itself."[10]

I would like to introduce one last thought before we leave this introductory chapter and begin our exploration of the systems-based tools and processes that are available to organizations. That is, the recognition of how important the measures and feedback used within organizations are to the decisions and actions of those organizations. To quote Eli Goldratt, the founder of the Theory of Constraints, "Tell me how you measure me and I'll tell you how I behave".[11] If individuals and organizations are making inconsistent decisions one should first look at how these individuals and organizations are being measured and what kind of feedback they are getting. Carried a bit further one could easily see that the measures we use in organizations are responsible for the behavior we see. If we want to change the behavior or direction of the organization, we will first have to change some of the measures used within it.

10 Arthur, W. Brian. 2014. *Economic Complexity: A Different Way to Look at the Economy.* Santa Fe Institute. Retrieved December 29, 2015 (https://medium.com/sfi-30-foundations-frontiers/economic-complexity-a-different-way-to-look-at-the-economy-eae5fa2341cd?swoff=true#.mfqp72jj0).

11 Goldratt, Eli. 1995. *The Haystack Syndrome: Sifting Information out of the Data Ocean.* Great Barrington, MA: North River Press, p. 26.

5

Integration of systems and business

Setting the stage

The last chapter looked into the development of systems thinking, how the overall field has evolved over the last 75 years or so, and briefly talked about the impact it has had on our understanding of the living sciences. This chapter will look into the development and growth of systems and systems-based processes and practices from the perspective of business. This journey will pass through three interdependent parts. The first is a review of the initial incorporation of the idea of interdependence and systems within the business press which challenged the traditional mental model that business was a machine. The second part will look at how systems-based understanding was incorporated into books and research that was adopted by some businesses. The third part takes a broader look at what I would describe as the proven, ready to use systems-based tools and processes for business. These tools were built on the foundations and insight provided by those researchers that preceded them. I will draw on some of the ideas and terms introduced in Chapter 4 in order to identify and explore the various systems-based business ideas and practices.

As a side note, I believe that when introducing new ideas that may challenge an individual's currently held beliefs, it aids in their willingness to consider the new ideas when the introduction includes a logically based path showing the development of those ideas. To that end, I have structured this historical overview of systems and business to be more aligned with the needs and insights of a business executive and not as a comprehensive academic look at the journey. In addition, you will find an extensive list of research articles and books in the Appendix for those of you who are interested in a deeper exploration of this journey.

The idea without the name

In this section we will look at the foundational ideas and processes that were not specifically identify as "systems" but relied on or leveraged the interdependence between various components and functions within an organization.

Shewhart and the Hawthorne effect

In 1924 Walter Shewhart, who had a Ph.D. in Physics from UC Berkeley, was working for the Hawthorne plant of Western Electric Company which manufactured telephone equipment for Bell Telephone. At the time that plant had in excess of 30,000 employees engaged in making telephone equipment. While at Hawthorne, Shewhart worked with and provided a strong influence on both W. Edwards Deming and Joseph Juran. Today these three are often referred to as the fathers of the quality movement. Before getting into the details, let's take a quick tour of this plant, which was considered state of the art at the time, to set a common understanding for looking at the cutting-edge work of Shewhart. As we look around we see a number of different areas, each producing a unique part. A closer look would reveal that each area was composed of a large number of identical work stations which the industrial engineers had designed to be as efficient as possible. As you watch the workers in an area, you will notice that their individual movements, while not synchronized, appear to be following the exact same sequence. All of this coordinated work was brought together to produce what, at the time, would have been considered a state-of-the-art telephone.

As we continue looking around the factory we see a number of "inspectors". These are the individuals you see looking through a batch or box of completed work and pulling out what appears to be a random sample of parts and then evaluating the "level of correctness" of each part in the sample. Using a pre-established guide, which relies on the size of the batch, it identifies the appropriate sample size to be evaluated and also provides the pass or fail rate of the sample. If it has fewer than the pass/fail cut-off number the batch is accepted as good. If it has more than the cut-off number the batch is rejected. Once a batch has been rejected it is re-inspected, with a larger sample. If it fails again, the batch goes to rework to be reviewed and fixed. If it passes, it is put back into production as a "good" batch.

What Shewhart first described in 1924 was the use of a control chart to monitor and control the output of a process. As Shewhart explained, variation within a process can come from only two causes: **common or chance** variation which is normal for that process and **assignable or special** variation which is not normal. He went on to explain that bringing a process into a state of statistical control—where there is only common/chance variation—and monitoring it to keep it in control is the only way to reduce waste and improve quality. Deming and Juran were responsible for taking this foundational concept and creating what has become known today as **total quality management**. More on this later.

The importance of his efforts can be seen in the shift of people's understanding of "quality"; from it being an attribute of the production process to something that can be controlled and improved by recognizing there are identifiable causes for the variation. This shift provided management with a process to identify and control the cause of variation and is part of the transition from seeing things through reductionist eyes which are focused on the end output (result) to seeing the journey and its multitude of actions and effects that become an end product or output.

In addition, at the same time in the same location, Western Electric's Hawthorne Plant, another paradigm shifting research experiment was under way. In 1924 a committee within the National Research Council invited the Hawthorne plant to research the relationship between better lighting and increased productivity. Their quest was in response to some reports that such a relationship existed. What the Hawthorne studies found was very different. At first they found no relationship and later they found an inverse relationship—productivity went up when lights were dimmed. Further research led to the finding that the principal cause for this effect, commonly known as the Hawthorne Effect, was the attention being paid to the workers. This led to the recognition of what is now called the "informal organization" and its impact on worker productivity. This work laid the foundation for what later became known as the human relations movement in the field of business management. Up until this point the field of management was focused on improving productivity. From this perspective, the worker was seen as a commodity that was easily replaced and, as such, of no real concern to management. The beginning of the human relations movement was based on the recognition that there is an interdependent relationship between the workers and the productivity of the business. More on this later.

Total quality management

Given the foundational work on control charts associated with Walter Shewhart, the next generation of quality leaders—Deming, Juran and an engineer named Armand V. Feigenbaum—emerged in the late 1940s. These individuals independently put together the tools, techniques, and philosophy of what is now commonly referred to as total quality management. Their work continues to bring change to the way work is done across organizations.

By 1926 Joseph Juran was a part of the team of quality control pioneers at Bell Labs who brought the new quality program to its Hawthorne Plant. By 1928 Juran had put together a training pamphlet entitled "Statistical Methods Applied to Manufacturing Problems" to be used in introducing these tools to others. His efforts to train others and develop a deeper understanding of the issues associated with what at the time was referred to as "statistical quality control" (SQC), led to him becoming the Chief of Industrial Engineering for Western Electric by 1937. In this role he was charged with introducing, teaching, and training SQC to the management and engineers at Western Electric's various manufacturing plants around the U.S. After World War II, he chose to focus the remainder of his life on pursuing a deeper understanding of quality management and sharing that understanding with a wider audience. He retired in 1994 at the age of 90.

W. Edwards Deming spent time at the Hawthorne plant in late 1927, as part of his Ph.D. program at Yale. There he met and worked with Walter Shewhart, developing a solid understanding of statistical quality control. I can only assume that he also met Joseph Juran while there. The insights he developed about SQC led him to realize that this process could also be used to assist management in their role of leading an enterprise. Deming's sampling techniques were used by the census bureau in 1940 and they brought him to the attention of others in Washington.

During World War II, he was a part of the five-man Emergency Technical Committee which was charged with developing and compiling the American War Standards Z1.1-3 which contained the sampling tables needed to support the use of acceptance sampling for products used and produced for the Army Ordnance Department and the Signal Corps. The effective adoption and use of these standards required over 7,500 people to be trained in the application and use of SQC. As a result of his work with this committee and the army's successful use of SQC during the war, Deming was invited to Japan in 1950 to lecture about its use in improving quality and productivity. On July 13, he spoke with 21 of Japan's top business executives who were members of the Keidanren (Japanese Federation of Economic Organizations). It was at this meeting that Deming first introduced what has become known as the Deming chain reaction (see Figure 8).

Figure 8 **Deming chain reaction**

Source: © PQ Systems, Inc.

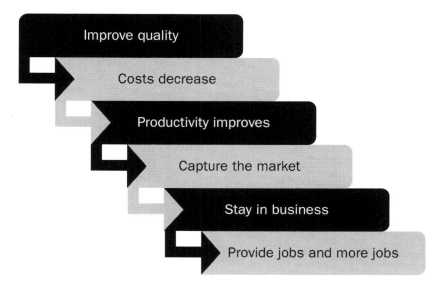

One must remember that at this point in time the quality level of Japan's manufacturing organizations was low and the only thing it was exporting was low-cost toys. The attendees embraced Deming and his lessons and the rest is history. At that meeting he also told these executives that if they followed his recommendations they would capture markets the world over in five years. They chose to follow his advice and started reaching into world markets four years later. The transition to embracing quality management led Japan towards its current status as a major actor in the world economy. While Deming did not use the term "systems" then or in later years, his use of the "chain reaction" focuses on the interdependence between improving quality and the positive and cumulative effects that would result from taking that one action. This recognition of interdependence is a foundational part of systems thinking.

The third pioneer of TQM is Armand V. Feigenbaum. He was about 20 years younger than the other two pioneers, but no less relevant. He brought with him a Ph.D. in Economics from MIT and as such had a perspective that was guided by the desire to improve organizational performance. His first book *Quality Control: Principles, Practice and Administration; an Industrial Management Tool for Improving Product Quality and Design and for Reducing Operating Costs and Losses* was published in 1945 by McGraw Hill and looked at how SQC would not only improve the product but also reduce operating costs. He was the first to make the linkage between SQC and lower operating costs and thus, increased levels of profit. His work contributed to the understanding of processes within the practices of managerial economics.[1] Indeed, all three of these individuals contributed to the foundational thinking that has given others a higher platform from which to look forward.

Socio-technical systems

In 1946 the Tavistock Institute of Human Relations was established in London, U.K. Their initial focus was to develop and combine the ideas within the behavioral sciences and systems thinking and introduce them to industry. The institute saw organizations as open systems that were pursuing primary tasks aimed at ensuring their survival and ongoing development. Given that perspective, the more aligned the organization's social, technical, and economic dimensions were the better its performance. One of the founding members of the institute was Elliott Jaques. His initial focus was developing a better understanding of the relationship between labor and management. He began by looking into what is meant by "work". His answer to this question, which he then spent the rest of his life expanding and developing into a comprehensive systems-based approach to the people side of business, was that the real difference in levels of work (roles) is the time it generally takes for your supervisor to discover your efforts have been substandard. He

---

1 Watson, Gregory. 2005. "Feigenbaum's Enduring Influence". *Quality Progress* November 2005: 52.

coined the term "time span of discretion" to describe this concept. For example; a miner in the coal mines might be able to go for a few days before his boss, the mine foreman, is able to recognize that his efforts are not producing the desired output. For the mine foreman, it might take his boss, the mine manager, a couple of months to discover that his efforts at keeping the miners productive are less than expected. As for the mine manager, it would probably take his boss (mine owner or executive overseeing a number of mines) a couple of years to discover that the manager's efforts were substandard.

As his understanding and measuring of time span of discretion developed he began asking the different levels of work what they felt was a fair wage. As he started gathering data on this question he began to realize that people had good insight into what their pay should be. This eventually turned into what he called "felt fair pay" which has been validated around the world in a variety of different economic situations. These two insights provided the foundational support for what evolved into and is commonly referred to as **requisite organization** (RO). This is a comprehensive, systems-based approach to the people side of business. RO will be explored in depth later in this chapter.

Peter Drucker

Peter Drucker was an Austrian born American educator, consultant (management), and author. His writings provided a solid part of the foundation for modern-day management practices. He is often referred to as the founder (father) of modern management. In 1954 he wrote *The Practice of Management*, which was one of the first books to consider the work and activities within the field of management. When I read this book in the early 1990s, as part of my dissertation research, it left me with three major points that I used in my work.

- First, was the definition of the goal of a business: to meet the needs of its customers. While I instinctively knew this, seeing this in one of the foundational management books helped me embrace this belief.

- Second, was his recognition that "cost accounting" (CA), which had been developed in the early 1900s, did not accurately reflect the organization's actual costs. While I had read *Relevance Lost* by Johnson and Kaplan and understood the limitations of cost accounting, it was a surprise to me that this insight had been public knowledge since 1954 while most businesses are still relying on CA as the primary criterion for their decision-making.

- Third, was his statement focused on the fact that "profits" are the results of meeting the company's goal, not the goal itself.

Up until this time, I had instinctively known that these points were correct, but I had nothing of substance to base my beliefs on. Having his words gave me a solid foundation for my beliefs and a place from which to start my learning journey. For many of you, the thought of understanding "profits" as a result of a well-run organization and not as the goal of the business, may well be a stretch, but I encourage each of you to embrace this shift. With this change, the range of alternatives is expanded greatly.

In his 1986 book entitled *Management: Tasks, Responsibilities, Practices* Drucker takes a look at the manager's role and responsibilities both within and outside of the organization. To this end he says: "in modern society there is no other leadership group but managers. If the managers of our major institutions, and especially of business, do not take responsibility for the common good, no one else can or will."[2] With this charge he is making it very clear that the role of a manager extends well past the businesses borders and into the "commons"—which is the area that we all use but no one is responsible for—such as the environment, communities, and parks.

While I do not recall seeing references to systems or systems thinking in his writings, Drucker talked about the interdependence between and among elements. In fact, in his 1993 book *The Ecological Vision* he talks about how in 1934 he was in the audience of a John Maynard Keynes lecture when he realized that all the economics students were interested in the behavior of commodities, while he was interested in the behavior of people. His focus was on how the decisions and actions of managers affect and impact the organization and the associated community.

Systems and business: the beginnings

As World War II came to a close, the United States was in a very favorable position. While a large part of the world had been damaged during the war, the U.S. and its manufacturing base had remained untouched and, as such, it became the primary provider of "things" for the rest of the world. This also put the United States in a position of world leadership that it has since maintained. The other, equally important thing to come out of the war effort was the shift in the size and complexity of the questions being asked and the research methodologies needed to understand and analyze them.

World War II brought about questions related to the development and deployment of complex weapons systems (missiles, nuclear bombs, air defense systems, etc.), which led to research focused on and understanding the possible scenarios and responses to an attack from a similar or more complex weapons system. Developing answers to these broader, more complex questions about war required a different approach than what had been used traditionally. Enter **systems engineering** (SE) and **systems analysis** (SA). Systems engineering was initially focused on the development of the complex weapons systems (Nike and Atlas missiles). Its

---

2 Drucker, Peter. 1986. *Management: Tasks, Responsibilities, Practices.* New York, NY: Truman Talley Books.

interdisciplinary approach to managing a program required all the players to be brought together to work cooperatively and coordinate their efforts to achieve the overall goals of the program. This was very different than the previous process that relied on a sequential approach to designing products and conducting research. Systems analysis, on the other hand, involves the development and use of a mathematically rigorous approach to comparing costs, benefits, and risks associated with future alternative solutions to complex problems that possess large degrees of freedom and a sizable amount of uncertainty. Another way of describing the types of problems SA was initially used for would be "a very cloudy crystal ball". This method was developed by the RAND Corporation in the 1950s to provide a suite of techniques for analyzing and assessing various wartime scenarios and thus providing a sort of "science of war". This approach combined the tools and techniques from operations research, probability and statistics, economics, game theory, and other quantitative analytic tools and paradigms. These tools were often referred to as **hard systems**. This too, required the bringing together of experts from a wide spectrum of areas to develop the appropriate tools and practices needed to address the complex questions being examined. While these tools provided success in the confines of the war and the limited scale at which they had been applied, when these tools began to be applied to the public sector in such areas as healthcare, housing, education, and poverty in the early 1960s they produced disappointing results.

One must remember that before World War II, almost all research was undertaken in what would be called Mode 1—the problem being tackled was described from the perspective of the scientific interests as defined by the academics within the scientific community. What the war effort introduced was the cross-pollination of research paradigms which led these and other researchers to begin to recognize the implicit and explicit value of cross-disciplinary collaboration on research. That said, the collaborative efforts during WWII were conducted in what is commonly referred to as Mode 2, in which the research being undertaken is to satisfy the demands of particular users—in this instance the war effort.[3] In this mode, the researchers are not limited by the narrow scientific and academic paradigm they came from; they bring their combined insights and knowledge together to develop the best understanding of the problem and to develop the best solution to it. They were all equals in this search for a viable understanding and solution. This group of researchers provided a fertile beginning for the developmental work on systems theory outside its original fields of botany and biology.

Part of the shift from the approaches used in the hard systems came out of MIT's Sloan School of Management and the work of Professor Jay Forrester. He developed and is considered the father of **systems dynamics** (SD), which is an approach to simulating the behavior of complex systems to better understand the nonlinear behavior of the various components within that system. SD looks at these

3 Gibbons, Michael, Camille Limoges, Helga Nowotny, Simon Schwartzman, Peter Scott, and Martin Trow. 1994. *The New Production of Knowledge*. Thousand Oaks, CA: Sage.

interactions as stocks and flows and incorporates feedback loops (positive and negative) along with time delays to more effectively model the system's behavior. This was a major contributor to what is now referred to as **soft systems**. His contribution was very important because until this time the primary approach to model building was quantitative and linear: A causes B. This new approach gave us the ability to see deeper into the behavior of the various components within a complex (interdependent) system.

By the early 1970s Russell Ackoff, who had been part of the operations research (hard systems) field and whose 1957 book *Introduction to Operations Research* helped define the field, had transitioned to become one of its biggest critics. What he saw was a field whose strict focus on technique-dominated research was limiting its ability to be used when addressing any issues within the "human and human behavioral systems". In 1972, Ackoff along with Frederick Emery wrote *On Purposeful Systems.*[4] From this perspective, learning and understanding the aims and goals of a purposeful system can only be gained by taking into account the various social, cultural, and psychological aspects that are active parts of the human behavioral system. Part of this shift can be linked to Ackoff's introduction of the term "mess" into the management and systems literature in reference to the human aspects within organizations. This realization led him on a 30 year journey into an ever-deepening understanding of the interdependence between humans and the organizational systems they participate in, which recognizes and includes the various elements that are internal and external to those systems. Ackoff described this shift from a mechanical perspective to a systems perspective:

> the beginning of the end of the Machine Age and the beginning of the Systems Age could be dated to the 1940s, a decade when philosophers, mathematicians, and biologists, building on developments in the interwar period, defined a new intellectual framework.[5]

By the 1980s Peter Checkland had taken Ackoff's concept of "mess" a bit further and suggested that identifying and modeling the mess was just the first of three steps. The second involved identifying and mapping the mess to identify the many factors that are limiting or keeping the system from achieving its purpose. The third step is developing a compelling story that exposes the undesirable future that is built into the current state and creating a desire to change within those who hear the story and are involved in the system under review.

In 1975 Fritjof Capra published *The Tao of Physics*. In this book he demonstrates the similarities between twentieth century physics and the mystical traditions of both Greek and Oriental traditions. Given his Ph.D. in particle physics, a book of

4 Ackoff, Russell and Frederick Emery. 1972. *On Purposeful Systems: An Interdisciplinary Analysis of Individual and Social Behavior as a System of Purposeful Events*. Chicago, IL: Aldine-Atherton.

5 Kirby, Maurice and Jonathan Rosenhead. 2005. "IFORS' Operational Research Hall of Fame: Russell L. Ackoff." *International Transactions in Operational Research* 12: 129-134.

this perspective was out of the norm to say the least. This book gave him a platform from which he published his second book, *The Turning Point*, in 1982. Here he draws on his scientific knowledge to outline the flaws associated with the reductionist paradigm (Newtonian and Cartesian thought) of science. He explains the limitations and inadequacies within them and puts forth an argument that science needs to embrace the ideas and concepts within holism and systems theory to develop solutions to society's ever-expanding set of complex problems. I was fortunate to read these books in the mid-1990s and attended a 3-day workshop where he was a primary facilitator. I came away from this event with a deeper level of insight which helped guide my search for a better understanding of the problems within business and my development of a "systems-based solution" to those problems.

One other individual I would like to introduce you to is Albert Low. In 1965 he was a manager in the fast growing Ontario Union Gas Ltd. and he was also four years into his journey into Zen Buddhism when he had his epiphany: Business is by definition "a conflict"—between costs and performance, between profits and social responsibility—and Zen teaches that fundamental conflicts exist in every individual and it is the recognition and balancing of these conflicting forces (the yin and yang) that leads to growth and progress. He shared his ideas with the organization's president and with his support Low was able to address the common source of corporate conflict: work and pay. This work led to his book *Zen and Creative Management* which was published in 1976. The book had limited initial success but in 1992 it was re-released and has since sold over 75,000 copies. In 2008 Low published a second book based on his perspective on management entitled *Conflict and Creativity at Work*. I was fortunate to spend a morning with Mr. Low about ten years ago; it was truly refreshing to share my insights with him and discuss what we both saw as the future path for business and organizations. There is a lot to be learned from his work.

The previous summaries in no way represent all of the efforts within the field of business and management relative to the recognition that businesses are systems and the inclusion of this perspective into the academic literature. However, it is my hope that the breadth and perspective contained in the preceding paragraphs paint a picture of a new paradigm beginning to appear. Part of the limitations of moving the understanding of systems into the field of business can be linked to the fact that at the time there were at least two (hard and soft systems) differing perspectives with their own sets of tools and practices. Another contributor to the lack of traction for the systems paradigm during this time is the fact that to accept the possibility of this new perspective one has to recognize that the old paradigm, the one in which business people were trained and proficient, has flaws and limitations and this is very difficult for most of us to do. By the time 1990 arrived the rate of change was increasing.

Systems and business: the big shift

Since the early 1990s there has been an explosion of books and research looking into the issues facing today's business and offering a path forward that includes a framework that is linked to some form of systems-based thinking. A few of them that I believe are important are noted below and include a few sentences outlining their content and *why* I believe you may want to add them to your reading list. The Appendix includes a list of books and authors I have accumulated over my many years of research.

In 1990, another MIT professor, Peter Senge, published *The Fifth Discipline*, which had a big impact on business thought. Indeed, in 1997 the *Harvard Business Review* identified it as one of the seminal management books of the previous 75 years. What was it about this introduction of systems into management that had not been done before? The book started by accepting the fact that organizations are systems and, as such, one has to use systems thinking—understanding how those things which may be regarded as systems influence one another within a complete entity, or larger system—to truly understand and solve the problems facing management. What Peter Senge laid out in this seminal work were the basic steps and understanding needed to transition businesses into "learning organizations". It was not about making more money for the sake of the money, it was about improving the ability of the organization to learn and resolve issues which leads to improved organizational performance and thus improved financial performance. Up until this point, the conventional mental model for businesses and organizations was that of a "machine" whose individual parts need to be optimized to improve its performance—the sum of the parts (improvements) = the improvement to the whole.

In 1992 another key book was published: *Leadership and the New Science* by Margaret Wheatley. This book goes much further than *The Fifth Discipline*. First, it focuses on identifying the limitations of the current business paradigm which had been established at a time (early 1900s) when reductionist (Newtonian) assumptions about the world were still recognized as the one true truth. Second, it asserts that the answers to today's business issues are not contained within the ideas and beliefs of the past, but located in the insights and new knowledge contained in the ever-expanding understanding of the holistic world. Our answers for today's leadership can be found in a deeper understanding of the new science fields such as chaos, systems, evolution, and quantum physics. In an article after the book was published Wheatley said that the insights that began her journey towards writing and publishing her book began when she read Capra's *The Turning Point*.

Another book published in 1992 was written by Richard Knowles: *The Leadership Dance: Pathways to Extraordinary Organizational Effectiveness*. This book presents the author's "real-world" experiences in applying a more organic and less mechanistic approach to organizational leadership while working as a plant manager for DuPont. For those of you that are seeking some applied lessons in the transitional journey, this book provides them.

In 1993, Ian Mitroff and Harold Linstone published a little book entitled *The Unbounded Mind: Breaking the Chains of Traditional Business Thinking*. Their book starts by presenting a brief overview of the U.S. growth in manufacturing during the last half of the twentieth century. This journey led to the recognition that, while at one point (mid-1940s till 1970s), bigness in itself brought and provided the organization with further strengths and advantages, today it is, in many instances, producing inefficiencies, ineffectiveness, and even weakness. To help us understand this issue Mitroff and Linstone focus on *how* we think and make decisions, which consists of four traditionally accepted ways of knowing. At this point they introduce what they call the fifth way of knowing, which is referred to as **unbounded systems thinking**. The second half of the book describes this perspective and provides the reader with guidance into how to incorporate this model in their business analysis and decision-making.

In the mid-1980s Ralph Douglas Stacey, Ph.D., joined what later became the University of Hertfordshire. From there, he has become a well-respected author and expert in the incorporation and use of complexity thinking in strategic and organizational management. Since 1991 he has published more than 12 books outlining his understanding of this perspective and provided guidance to the Complexity and Management Centre at the University of Hertfordshire. The first book of his that I read was *Complexity and Creativity in Organizations*, which was published in 1996. In this book he challenges the traditional management perspective of designing organizations and predicting outcomes which are based on the assumption that there are limited alternatives. He disagrees, and presents a solid foundation based on the understanding of complexity and its emergent characteristics as a path for more creativity in organizations. I would encourage anyone interested in this to put Stacey on their reading list.

Natural Capitalism was published in 1999 by Paul Hawken along with Amory and L. Hunter Lovins. This book should be fundamental reading for those who want to bring change to today's business. In this book the authors introduce a visionary concept that envisions business, the environment, and social interests as an integrated, interdependent system that can work together for a better world. In this book they not only identify the opportunities that can be captured through the adoption of this model they also map out the general direction and path needed to overturn the long-held assumptions the world carries about business and economic practices. They propose four central strategies associated with natural capitalism:

- Radical resource productivity
- Biomimicry
- Service and flow economy
- Investing in natural capital

There is not enough space to address these here, so I leave them along with the introduction to this book for you to contemplate.

Weaving Complexity and Business: Engaging the Soul at Work was written by Roger Lewin and Birute Regine. Lewin is the prize-winning author of *Complexity: Life at the Edge of Chaos* and Regine is a Harvard-educated developmental psychologist. In this book they espouse their position that people must become the new bottom line within organizations. They follow this claim up with a variety of examples of businesses that have taken actions to move in this direction—an eye-opening read.

Seeing the Forest for the Trees: A Manager's Guide to Applying Systems Thinking was written by Dennis Sherwood, Ph.D., who brought an educational background in systems and science and a number of years as a business consultant into this book. It provides insight into systems and how they behave as well as demonstrating how organizations can use this new paradigm and its associated tools to better identify, analyze, solve, and implement more systems-based solutions.

In 2003 Michael C. Jackson published a book entitled *Systems Thinking: Creative Holism for Managers*. What makes this book so unique is that it is designed to introduce its readers not only to the concept of systems thinking but also how its tools and perspective can be used by managers to better understand the behavior of their organizations. The first part of the book provides a basic introduction to systems. The second part of the book provides insight into the use of various systems techniques to deal with managerial issues such as goal setting, fairness, and diversity. The third part looks at how one can use what Jackson refers to as "creative holism" to address the entire organization as a system.

In 2004 Peter Senge along with co-authors Otto Scharmer, Joseph Jaworski, and Betty Sue Flowers published a book entitled **Presence: An Exploration of Profound Change in People, Organizations, and Society**. This team took an in-depth look into transformational change and how these insights might be used in a world that is dangerously out of balance. The authors discovered that many times leaders remain stuck in their old patterns of understanding and acting. Through a process that encourages deeper levels of learning, which they developed by drawing on the insight and experiences of a number of scientists and social leaders, they were able to create a larger awareness of "what is possible" or "seeing the larger whole" which led to more appropriate leadership actions targeted at shaping the envisioned future. This original work led to two more follow-on books described below and the establishment of the Presencing Institute.

In 2007 Dr. Scharmer published *Theory U: Leading from the Future as It Emerges* and this was followed in 2013 with **Leading from the Emerging Future: From Ego-System to Eco-System Economics.** In these books he continues to expand and develop the foundations developed in the initial book. By adopting the "U" methodology, which was introduced in *Presence*, we are able to see our own blind spots which allows us to pay attention in ways that enable us to experience the opening of our minds, our hearts, and our wills. This holistic approach allows us to shift our awareness and enables us to learn from the future that is emerging. In both of these books he draws on many of his personal and professional engagements and provides a number of compelling stories and examples to highlight *how* to move oneself and/or facilitate others on this journey.

In 2009 Darcy Hitchcock and Marsha Willard completed the second edition of their book: *The Business Guide to Sustainability: Practical Strategies and Tools for Organizations*. This book is targeted at the leaders, owners, and managers of organizations that aspire to improve their environmental, social, and economic performance. Instead of an academic investigation of sustainability with its complex strategies and solutions, this book focuses on identifying practical and effective actions that organizations can take to begin their sustainable journey. To that end, this user-friendly book is organized by industry sector (manufacturing, service, office operations, and government) and the most common organizational functions. For anyone in business who wants to begin demystifying the sustainability journey, this book is a good place to start.

In 2010 a book entitled *Accounting for Sustainability: Practical Insights* was published. This book is a compilation of ten case studies that capture practical "in-use" practices of firms within the UK that are part of the Accounting for Sustainability Project established in 2004 by the Prince of Wales. While Prince Charles recognized the immediate need for transitioning towards a more sustainable world, he also recognized that we needed to enhance our accounting practices so we are not trying to solve twenty-first-century issues with twentieth-century decision-making and reporting systems. This book provides some very solid insight into the issues accounting faces as it looks into providing a more sustainable organization with the most correct information on which to make decisions and take actions.

In 2011 Amory B. Lovins along with support from others at the Rocky Mountain Institute published *Reinventing Fire*. This book lays out how the use of coal and oil have built our civilization, produced fortunes for some and enriched the lives of an unknown number of people around the world. They then present a well-supported argument that we have reached the "tipping point" where alternative (clean energy) fuels have become capable of replacing the carbon-based fuels of the past. Because of its breadth of scope and depth of information it is not what I would call an "easy read" but it presents a viable path forward that is reachable by 2050. Their vision to a clean energy future relies on utilizing enhanced business models that do not require change in public policy but will be led by businesses seeking enduring profits. While this is not focused on how to transition business to a more "systems-based" model, it does include a path to changing the limited focus of business which is important to our future economic progress. To some, this may sound a bit far-fetched, but it has received strong endorsements from academics, politicians, and business executives.

The Nature of Business was published in 2012 by Giles Hutchins. In this book he combines his experiences in management, entrepreneurship, and C-Suite consulting along with a passion for applying nature's inspiration to leadership, business, and individual transformations. The book presents a new perspective to help organizations improve their ability to flourish during the more volatile times that all organizations are facing today. Hutchins makes a strong case for applying biomimicry principles to the development of a new business paradigm. His work goes past the current focus on green and responsible business and looks into the emerging new ways of operating and creating value. He does this through the use of examples and case studies. This book is a very good read for anyone wanting to develop a deeper insight into the future of organizations and business.

Sustainability: Essentials for Business was written by Professors Young and Dhanda from DePaul University and published in 2013. This was written as a textbook to introduce students to the various elements of sustainability and their effect on businesses. It focuses on what is commonly referred to as the three "Ps"—people, profit, and planet. The book addresses the costs in natural resources, waste, and pollution associated with our current business practices and behaviors. To that end it provides an overview of what options are available to businesses that will assist them to move towards sustainability in a world that is transitioning in that direction.

The final book I want to mention is *Conscious Capitalism: Liberating the Heroic Spirit of Business* written by John Mackey (co-CEO of Whole Foods) and Raj Sisodia (Professor of Global Business at Babson College) in 2013. As someone who arrived in Austin, Texas a half a dozen years before Whole Foods was started, I am well aware of its growth from the first store on North Lamar Blvd to its current position in the Fortune 500. When I read this book I began to understand the loyalty and passion displayed by its customers and employees. This book was written to challenge the business community to rethink the *why* behind the existence of businesses and to begin seeing themselves as part of the interdependent global marketplace. In the book Mackey and Sisodia introduce the four pillars of conscious capitalism:

- **Higher purpose**. While money is a necessary condition, conscious businesses focus on their purpose beyond profit

- **Conscious leadership**. Starting with the focus on "we" rather than "me", this shift inspires and fosters a transformation that brings out the best in others

- **Stakeholder orientation**. Focuses on their whole business ecosystem through the recognition that strong and engaged stakeholders provide a healthy, sustainable, and resilient business

- **Conscious culture**. As Peter Drucker said "Culture eats strategy for lunch" and this is important because it instills the common values, principles, and practices within the business

Conscious Capitalism is another must read for those of you interested in transitioning to a more sustainable organizational future.

While the aforementioned reading list is a good place to start your learning journey, it does not show anyone facing a broad set of issues within their organization what to do or where to go to get some help. The next part of this chapter contains an introduction to the various categories of centers/non-profit organizations/consulting services/processes/tools that are available to assist organizations that are interested in traveling a more systems-based path. It is my hope that the rest of this chapter will provide you with an introduction to the breadth and types of services currently available. The problem with this introduction is that it involves a truly broad spectrum of available alternatives for you, the reader, to consider but that leaves you with a big problem: which tools do I choose to move forward? The answer to that is contained in Part III which will help you develop a viable path for any organization to begin their learning journey into systems-based business solutions.

Centers and institutes focused on systems-based business processes and practices

Over the last twenty-five years numerous centers and institutes have been established to research, document, and share their insights on systems and business with an ever-growing number of individuals and organizations that are looking for a "better way" to practice business. This section introduces you to some of these organizations, provides an overview of their focus and offerings, and includes some insight into their impact on organizational performance.

Society for Organizational Learning

The first organization I want to introduce is the Center for Organizational Learning (OLC), which was established at MIT in 1991. Its founding was tied to the publication of Peter Senge's very successful book, *The Fifth Discipline*. As a result of its success and the desire of organizations, both profit and not-for-profit, to begin their transition towards becoming a learning organization, this center was established. By 1995 OLC had 19 organizational partners, ranging across the technology (Intel, HP, IBM, etc.), manufacturing (Chrysler, Shell, Harley Davidson, etc.), and service (UW West, Fed Ex, Pacific Bell) industries. These partners' involvement with the Center included training that provided participants with exposure and instruction in using the ideas and practices introduced in *The Fifth Discipline*. The Center also gave Peter Senge and his associate researchers at MIT access to these organizations and they continued to develop and improve the training and details being provided to the other member organizations. Things started to change in 1995 and in an effort led by Dee Hock, the founder and former CEO of Visa International, the Center undertook an extended reflection on itself and its future. The results of this effort led to the formation of the Society for Organizational Learning (SoL) in April of 1997.

The overall purpose of SoL is to:

> discover, integrate, and implement theories and practices of organizational learning for the interdependent development of people and their institutions and communities such that we continue to increase our capacity to collectively realize our highest aspirations and productively resolve our differences.[6]

With this focus, SoL has continued to evolve into a learning community that reaches around the world with regional groups located throughout the Americas and Europe as well as a group in India and Japan. While each of these groups is part of the whole they are independent in their ability to focus on the unique issues in their region, sharing their insights and new knowledge with the whole of SoL through conferences and their web-based sharing referred to as Virtual SoL.

During its 19 years of existence SoL's membership has continued to expand around the world. As such, it has assisted a number of organizations, both large and small (for-profit, not-for-profit, and governmental institutions), on their journey towards developing a more holistic and systems-based understanding of organizations and organizational learning. In this effort SoL continues to compile expertise in understanding what it takes for an organization to make this transition and provides access to its knowledge through training, consulting, and research activities.

The Berkana Institute

In 1991 Margaret Wheatley and Myron Kellner-Rogers were co-founders of the Berkana Institute in the U.S. which was designed to be a living experience in "self-organization". This direction can be seen in Wheatley's book *Leadership and the New Science*, which was one of the first books I read on the shift from reductionism to a systems-based approach. One of the most fundamental pieces of the Institute's theory of change is what they refer to as the two-loop model. In a nutshell this perspective sees the world as a place where the emergence and development of new ideas begins and moves forward at the same time as the system/perception that it is working to replace is still the most prevalent. As such, the individuals that are still working under the old idea (paradigm) have a tendency to challenge or delay the new idea because they fear the possibility that they may no longer be needed. Unless we are part of the change, we want stability because it is safer than the unknown within the change. Given that understanding, the Berkana Institute's overall goal is to identify, connect, nourish, and illuminate the people, ideas, and activities being developed by the "change agents" who are looking into the future.

Today the Berkana Institute is alive and well and has re-emerged from a three-year period of rest and reflection. Its first offering is to provide a catalyst for the creation and development of self-organized groups of friends who have been

6 https://www.solonline.org/?page=SoLHistory

brought together around a common understanding. It is my belief that it will continue to provide insight and assistance to individuals and organizations that have embarked on the transitional journey towards a more holistic future.

Center for Ecoliteracy

This Center was founded in 1995 in Berkeley, CA by co-founders Fritjof Capra, Peter Buckley, and Zenobia Barlow who serves as executive director. Its primary purpose is to advance the ecological education in K-12 schools (primary and secondary education). The Center has worked with educational organizations in over 200 cities around the world assisting them in their efforts to advance the teaching of sustainability. They have developed a variety of offerings, such as:

- **Academic Program Audits**. Looking at what the school is currently doing to address sustainability in its curriculum

- **Coaching**. Providing hands-on assistance to individuals and groups to improve their insight into and ability to teach sustainability

- **Curriculum development**. Assist faculty to develop lessons and projects that address sustainability

- **School Sustainability Report Card**. A broad review of the school's sustainability policies and practices to include looking at the campus, its curriculum, and the school's overall food system

- **Technical assistance** in moving forward on any school or community initiative that involves improving sustainability

In addition, the Center provides access to a variety of books, journals, essays, films, and governmental resources that schools can draw on to gain more information about Ecoliteracy and the journey towards it.

Fowler Center for Business as an Agent of World Benefit

In 2002 the Weatherhead School of Management at Case Western Reserve University launched its initiative focused on "business as an agent of world benefit". They initially were looking to identify businesses that had gone beyond their focus on "profit" and were also addressing issues in the areas of ecological sustainability and supporting social entrepreneurship. Since its establishment the Fowler Center has surely flourished. "The Fowler Center's primary focus is on for-profit organizations that use their core activities to create value for society and the environment in ways that create even more value for their customers and shareholders".[7] Their efforts to collect and document the stories of businesses engaged in this type of

7 "About the Fowler Center for Business as an Agent of World Benefit". Retrieved from https://weatherhead.case.edu/centers/fowler/about/

transformational journey has resulted in over 3,000 interviews and more than 200 cases. Their approach, which is commonly referred to as "full-spectrum flourishing", requires two major shifts in understanding. The first mental model shifts best practices in making the business case for sustainability from:

- Bolt-on strategies to **embedded strategies**
- Incremental change to **radical innovation**
- Doing less harm to **"net positive" impact**
- Serving the well-off to **socially inclusive**
- Pilot mode to scaling system change

The second mental model shift involves changing the corporate mindset, values, and culture of sustainability from:

- An exclusive left-brain analytic approach to one that embraces **emotional and spiritual intelligence**
- Treating people as fungible economic resources to creating **personal wellbeing and flourishing in the workplace**

There is no doubt that the Fowler Center advocates an extraordinary approach to business innovation and social entrepreneurship. It does this by helping the organization see how to turn the day's social and global issues into opportunities for itself. This type of shift is what Peter F. Drucker was addressing during his later years. I attended a three-day workshop on flourishing businesses at the Fowler Center in 2014 and was very impressed with the overall program.

Conscious Capitalism Inc.

Conscious Capitalism was founded in the U.S. in August 2006 and was focused on the recognition that every business has a purpose beyond the firm—something more than just profits. Two of the founding partners are John Mackey (co-CEO of Whole Foods) and Professor Raj Sisodia. Over the past nine years it has become a worldwide organization by expanding the awareness of the ideas behind Conscious Capitalism (CC) through presentations, events, publications, and social media. They have an ever-expanding number of CC Chapters (17 in the U.S. and 7 international) that provide a place for businesses and organizations to learn, discuss, and find support and guidance in their transformational journey.

Institute for the Study of Coherence and Emergence (ISCH)

ISCH was founded in Massachusetts in 1999 to facilitate and encourage the discussion of ideas and insights between practitioners and academics around the implications of complexity thinking as it applies to the management of organizations.

The research activities of ISCH are focused on social complexity theory and the use of complexity-based tools and techniques for policy analysis and decision-making. Today, the most productive applications of complexity insights are targeted on the new possibilities for innovation and growth in organizations. As with any new paradigm, it does not just happen, new models and practices have to be developed and learned. ISCH is dedicated to helping the practicing manager and today's academics examine, understand, and acquire these new models and practices. To that end they hold annual events and publish both journals and books.

Santa Fe Institute

While I introduced the Santa Fe Institute (SFI) in Chapter 4, I want to provide a deeper look into its work and offerings for those of you interested in a deeper understanding of systems, complexity, and organizations. The primary focus of SFI was and continues to be applying interdisciplinary research to today's big issues. The founding researchers had experienced first-hand the limitations when issues are investigated through the ever-narrowing academic specialization spectrum and the deeper understanding and productivity that is possible when focusing on synthesis across disciplines. To support this recognition of applying multiple perspectives, there are no permanent positions. From a staffing perspective, SFI has a few resident faculty researchers along with a number of postdoctoral researchers which rotate every year or two. They are supported by a rather large number (100+) of external faculty that frequently visit the institute to facilitate and assist in the investigative research being conducted. SFI also has established a Business Network which is composed of a group of private organizations and government agencies that are interested in complex systems research. This group participates in and receives briefings and access to the research being conducted by SFI. I have included Santa Fe Institute in this listing because they are truly at the forefront of understanding complex systems, and keeping an awareness of their developments will help organizations make better decisions about how best to direct their own transformation to a complex system-based understanding in the future.

Tools and techniques used in support of systems-based business

The following topics are what I believe to be some of the primary components an organization will have to address as it makes the transitional journey from being a traditional business towards becoming a sustainable/systems-based organization. What is important about these tools is that when they are used in combination they make the journey much less stressful because they provide an organization with a well-worn path towards their implementation and adoption. While I will examine the details of this transformational journey in Part III, you should remember that the journey, by definition, will affect the entire organization and being able to draw on proven processes and practices will make the transition easier and less resource intensive. So, let's look at some of these proven tools.

Theory of constraints

Theory of constraints (TOC) is what I would refer to as a rather comprehensive set of "systems"-based tools and philosophy for perceiving and understanding businesses. It started in the late 1970s with Dr. Eli Goldratt's involvement in the development of optimized production technology (OPT) software—an operations scheduling tool that was based on identifying and leveraging the production system's "constraint". This product was a "black-box" approach to scheduling—OPT provided the hardware, software, and oversaw the weekly development of the production schedule for its client customers. In this model, the client customer had no control over the running of OPT—the system just provided them with the schedule to follow. While OPT provided improved productivity it was not a successful business model because businesses did not understand or have any control over the scheduling of their production resources.

In the early 1980s Goldratt had established the Goldratt Institute (AGI) to provide marketing, training, and sales of **Drum-Buffer-Rope** (DBR) which is their production scheduling and control tool. Publication of *The Goal* in 1984 provided the platform upon which DBR's phenomenal growth was based. By the late 1980s the Ph.D. program in Operations Management at the University of Georgia had adopted TOC as the primary focus and began conducting cutting edge research into new applications of the TOC basics. In the very early 1990s, the program was researching some of the basics of how one would apply TOC's principles to the practice of project management. This foundational work along with efforts within the Goldratt Institute produced what has become known as **Critical Chain**. The first application of critical Chain was at the Harris Semiconductor facility that was completed in 1994. This project, which had initially been scheduled to take between 36 and 44 months, was completed in 13 months at 1% over the initial cost estimate. By 1996, commercial software for implementing Critical Chain had reached the market; the first was called ProChain.[8]

With their project management solution in place, Goldratt and the others at AGI began looking into how individuals and businesses make decisions. By the mid-1990s this group had created what is today commonly referred to as the **Thinking Processes** (TP). These tools provide a rather complete set of analytical tools. The first, called a current reality tree, is used to logically identify the "core problem" that is causing the system's "undesirable effects". The second, called an **evaporating cloud**, allows one to identify and understand the conflict that is creating the "core problem" and develop viable solution(s), called injection(s), that, when

8 https://www.prochain.com/

implemented, will remove the conflict and thus resolve the problem. The third set of tools are designed to better understand the steps and additional changes that will be needed to successfully implement the injection and bring the desired end result. This involves tools referred to as a future reality tree, a transition tree, and a prerequisite tree.

From its founding, the Goldratt Institute was the primary provider of TOC knowledge and training. To accomplish this they established a worldwide network of consultants and trainers whose efforts were focused on specific geographic areas. Every year AGI would host a conference where new insights and programs were introduced and the participants shared their experiences and successes. In 1997, Goldratt retired from AGI before his fiftieth birthday. By the early 2000s he had established Goldratt Consulting Group (GCG) which was, in some senses of the word, in direct competition with AGI. This split led to a division between the active TOC consultants around the world. Some of them stayed with AGI, some of them transitioned to be aligned with GCG and some of them chose to become independent. Thus, for those of you who might, at some time, be interested in pursuing discussions with a TOC consultant your choices are varied. The following is an abridged list of consulting firms and organizations you might contact about insight and assistance in using ToC.

- Theory of Constraints International Certification Organization (www.tocico.org)

- Goldratt Consulting (www.goldrattconsulting.com)

- Goldratt Institute (www.goldratt.com)

- Vector Consulting (www.vectorconsulting.com)

- Theory of Constraints Institute (www.tocinstitute.com)

- Science of Business (www.scienceofbusiness.com)

- QFI Healthcare (www.qficonsulting.com)

Requisite organization

Earlier in the chapter I mentioned the work of Elliott Jaques. It is now time to delve into his ideas, understandings, practices, and the various firms that offer assistance to organizations that choose to move in this direction. Today, the work of Elliott Jaques, which has been supported by others, is commonly referred to as requisite organization (RO). It is an integrated system of management that brings fairness and higher performance to the workplace through its ability to build trust and cooperation between managers and their subordinates. I like to describe RO as a systems-based approach to the management of an organization's human resources. To deliver this increased performance, it draws on a number of evidence-based tools that are used to design and align the roles and practices of individuals across and throughout an organization. When done correctly, the adoption of RO will not only improve the level of satisfaction of both the employees and customers but it will also improve the organization's financial performance.

The foundational insights for what became RO were developed by Elliott Jaques while he was at the Tavistock Institute of Human Resources, of which he was a founding member. The Institute was established in 1946 with funding from the Rockefeller Foundation and focused on developing a deeper understanding of group and organizational behavior. It was here that Wilford Brown, the young CEO of Glacier Metal Company, turned for help in his search for a better understanding of management authority—what it is and how it is perceived by workers. This led to working partnership between the two that lasted for over 15 years—Jaques' research at Glacier led to his development of solutions for the employer–employee relation problems at every level in this major manufacturing organization. Peter Drucker called the Glacier Project "the most extensive study of actual worker behavior in large-scale industry."[9] The initial work at Glacier provided Jaques and his associates with access to other businesses around the world where they could continue to develop, test, refine, and synthesize the tools and practices within RO. Today this systems-based approach to human resources management provides a complete proven package for organizations to draw upon.

The following is a list of consulting firms that provide assistance in the training, adoption, and use of the Requisite Organization model.

* Requisite Organization International Institute (www.requisite.org)

* PeopleFit (www.peoplefit.com/why-peoplefit/requisite-organization)

* Global Organization Design Society (www.globalro.org)

* The Strategic Planning Group (www.tspg-consulting.com)

Second-generation knowledge management

Knowledge management (KM) has been defined as: "the process of capturing, developing, sharing, and effectively using organizational knowledge".[10] From this perspective it has been focused on how the manipulation of data and information can be done in an efficient and supportive way to ensure everyone has access to the information they might need. Initially, its primary focus was to enhance the integration and sharing of existing organizational knowledge. This is now commonly referred to as the first generation of knowledge management. One of the aspects of second-generation knowledge management that is critically important to any organization that is contemplating a transitional journey of any kind is the changes

9 Drucker, Peter. 1974. *Management: Tasks, Responsibilities, Practices.* New York: Harper Business, p. 234.

10 Davenport, Thomas H. 1994. "Saving IT's Soul: Human Centered Information Management". *Harvard Business Review* 72(2): 119-131.

in the information it will use in its decision-making processes. New information means the use of new and different data presented it in new and unique ways to produce the information needed in the new decision-making processes and practices. To effectively accomplish this, the knowledge management resources will not only need excess capacity and time to reprogram and realign the KM tools and programs to the new and evolving managerial paradigm, it will also need to realign the goals and measures used to oversee and direct the knowledge management activities so that they support and encourage the ongoing evolution of the information systems within the organization.

Academic institutions offering degrees in sustainable business

In 2002, while I was an Associate Professor of Management within the School of Business at St. Edwards University (SEU) in Austin, Texas, I collaborated with Dr. Oscar Mink, Professor of Curriculum Studies from the University of Texas, to develop a proposal for what I believed to be the first systems-based MBA programs in the country. While the forecasted numbers made the program look viable, its content, the introduction and use of systems-based tools as a foundational paradigm for business management, was ahead of its time for the administration at SEU. This proposal still sits on my hard drive.

Unbeknownst to me, **Bainbridge Graduate Institute** opened that same year with what is recognized as the nation's first MBA in Sustainable Business (a systems-based perspective). Today this school, which offers its program in a hybrid model (one weekend a month and online learning), draws students from across the country and its metro model (evening and online) targets students from the Seattle area. It has graduated over 700 students with a focus on and understanding of sustainable business. It is considered by many as the leading graduate business program in sustainable business education. In 2015 it changed its name to Pinchot University.

There are a number of schools around the world that have begun to include some segment of "sustainable business" in their curriculum. The following list of schools, which in no way is intended to be complete, is included to provide a place to start for those of you interested in what programs are available. The first list of schools identifies sustainable business programs that were developed from the ground up—as a new program.

- Green Mountain College
- New College of California
- Persidio School of Management
- The New School, New York

The second list identifies ten major universities that have all added an emphasis on sustainability to their traditional MBA programs.

- University of Michigan

- University of North Carolina

- Cornell University

- Massachusetts Institute of Technology

- University of California, Berkeley

- Notre Dame

- Yale University

- Carnegie Mellon

- Erasmus (Rotterdam)

- George Washington University

Once again, I want to reiterate that this is not meant to be an exhaustive list—it is just an initial list of schools that have, in some form, recognized the ongoing shift in education and our understanding of the world around us. This is the transition from the traditional model of education, learning, and understanding, which can be traced back to Sir Isaac Newton and the reductionist model of learning, to what I refer to as the systems-based understanding of the world. As our learning has evolved over the last century we have begun to recognize that ideas and system components are interconnected and as such we need a new perspective to better understand these interrelationships. Enter complexity science and the transition that all learning and understanding is moving through. For some, this shift into a new paradigm is fraught with fear of the unknown. For others this shift will be seen as an opportunity for a new and better beginning. Welcome to the future.

Part III
Putting the pieces together

The final segment of this book is focused on helping the reader embrace the shift in thinking required to begin understanding the Interdependent Organization and its relationship with the other organizations and elements within the larger complex adaptive economic system (CAES) which was introduced in Chapter 4. So, what is an interdependent organization? What is it composed of (its internal environment—how is it constructed and how do the internal parts communicate and work together)? How does it interact and compete with other organizations and members of the external environment? What are its goals and how does it measure and evaluate its performance? All of these and other questions must be answered as we begin to look into this new perspective for business.

As was mentioned earlier, over the last 350 years there have been two major shifts in the Western world's knowledge paradigm. Prior to the adoption of the work of Bacon, Descartes, and Newton the perspective of almost everyone was that "God" was the reason for the existence of life and for individuals' situation. With the introduction and acceptance of the scientific method and the reductionist pursuit of a single truth upon which knowledge could be based, people had a new path towards finding the answers to fundamental questions. This perspective led to the growth of science and its ongoing pursuit of knowledge. About 120 years ago this prevailing paradigm once again was challenged. Within physics, the finding of subatomic particles and the understanding that their behavior did not follow the rules of Newtonian physics caused real issues among physicists. Also at about the same time, the field of natural history saw some challenges to the accepted beliefs that all plants and animals had been created in their present form and did not evolve with the changing environment. These new perspectives in science led scientists to the development of the second shift—towards seeing the world as a system composed of interdependent parts. While the initial adherents of this perspective were in the hard sciences, about 50 years ago a few of the cutting-edge thinkers from the social sciences began moving in this direction. While he was not the first, Peter Senge's book, *The Fifth Discipline*, published in 1990, is now viewed as the seminal work introducing this new perspective of seeing business as part of an interdependent system.

Developing an understanding of the new paradigm of the interdependent organization, what the transformational journey means to business today, and how it will impact business in the future are discussed in the next three chapters. The first of those, Chapter 6, will draw on the foundational insights and understanding introduced in the previous chapters in order to develop and present a comprehensive description of an interdependent organization. From that point, I will look into how an interdependent organization will interact with other organizations and components of the larger CAES. Chapter 7 will introduce what I envision as the long-term "generic" transformational journey on which traditional organizations will need to embark in order to become an active part of the CAES. This chapter will start by describing the foundational assumptions I have used in the development of the journey and continue with an in-depth look into the basic steps within the transformational journey. Finally, Chapter 8 will take an in-depth look into *how* (the steps and the logic behind them) an organization will traverse the transition. The first and most important step involves establishing a solid understanding of systems and systems-based thinking within the organization. This is critical to future success because if those involved in continuing the transformation do not understand the new paradigm, when they hit a roadblock or challenge they will take the easier path of reverting to the previous perspective and tools. This section contains references to both successful and unsuccessful attempts to start the journey towards becoming an interdependent organization.

It is my sincere hope that each of you will enjoy this learning journey and, on reaching the end, will have developed a deep enough level of new knowledge and understanding to become an active participant in the transformational journey of the organization of which you are a part.

6
The interdependent organization

Introduction

Chapters 6–8 are the result of my 20-year journey on this road. There is no doubt in my mind that my work was made possible because I was able to stand on the shoulders of the giants in this field that gave me a solid foundation on which to build. I will be forever in their debt for providing me the insights and knowledge that have allowed me to continue their pursuit of a more complete understanding of this new and expanding perspective of business. Let me start this learning journey by introducing what I refer to as a systems-based business model.

A systems-based business model (S-BBM)

The purpose of developing this model is to introduce a broader, more comprehensive understanding of how business can be structured and conducted. In addition, it will highlight how today's business processes, beliefs, and inherent assumptions contribute to the inconsistent behavior and results experienced by both workers and management. It is my belief and that of an ever-growing number of others that we (in the largest collective sense) are at a point of transition, moving from a world based on the mechanistic perspective of Newtonian physics to the systemic perspective.[1] Stephen Hawking, holder of the chair of mathematics at Cambridge University, once occupied by Isaac Newton, declared in January 2000 that

1 Capra (1996); Gharajedaghi, Jamshid. 2006. *Systems Thinking: Managing Chaos and Complexity.* Oxford, UK: Butterworth-Heinemann; Jackson, Michael C. 2003. *Systems*

the twenty-first century "will be the century of complexity",[2] and it is common knowledge that complexity is a subset of the broader field of systems and systems thinking. Before jumping into the details, let's briefly review the basic elements in a living system.

Common characteristics of living systems

While systems are commonly thought to be a group of parts that function as a whole and, as such, range from natural to mechanical and through living and cosmological systems, our focus on organizations limits the area of systems to those that can be created, evolve, grow, and in many instances die. These are called living systems. By accepting the fact that businesses and organizations are living subsystems that interact within a larger economic system and the belief that there are common characteristics among all types of systems, we were able to build a new business model that will enable and support business behaving as a system. First, we needed to identify the similarities across natural and living systems to establish a framework on which we could build a new business model. Listed below are the five commonly accepted characteristics of natural, living systems:

- They are living
- They are open
- They have a purpose for their existence
- They are composed of subsystems
- Subsystems perform interdependent activities
    ○ A portion of their activities supports the subsystem's function
    ○ A portion of their activities supports the system's purpose

They are living

Since successful natural systems exist over time, they have to have the ability to reproduce (both themselves and their worn or damaged components) and adapt to their ever-changing environment.[3] While the first corporations were formed for the pursuit of actions targeting the public good and as such were not expected to exist past the life of the required effort, this limitation of corporations was removed

---

Thinking: Creative Holism for Managers. Hoboken, NJ: John Wiley & Sons; Ollhoff and Walcheski (2002).

2 Lewin, Roger and Birute Regine. 2001. *Weaving Complexity & Business: Engaging the Soul at Work.* Abingdon, MD: Texere Publishing.

3 Maturana, H. and V. Varela. 1987. *The Tree of Knowledge.* Boston, MA: Shambhala; Ollhoff and Walcheski (2002).

by the early 1900s. Today, organizations are viewed and understood to exist over time.

They are open

The second characteristic of a living system is the ability to interact and exchange with other elements and systems within their environment.[4] A tree is a good example of an open system. It absorbs carbon dioxide from its environment and draws on sunlight for energy to undergo photosynthesis, expelling oxygen as its waste from this process. Organizations rely on resources (e.g., labor, natural resources, and financial resources) and energy from their environment, and through the application of processes and controls they transform their "raw materials" into end products, some waste, and provide wages to their employees for their discretional use. In both instances (tree and organization), a variation in the inputs will have an effect on the quantity and quality of outputs from the system.

They have a purpose

The third commonality is that natural systems have a purpose for existence.[5] This could be as simple as species survival, or some broader, more philosophical goal we as humans rely on. Even the single-cell ameba will change its behavior in pursuit of the nourishment that it requires.[6] By looking within today's organizations, we can usually find an explicit or implicit statement of their primary goal. While some goals are elaborate and others are simple, all of them provide some sort of guiding light for the organization to follow. More about this characteristic shortly.

They are composed of subsystems

The fourth characteristic common to all living systems is that they are composed of subsystems that work together in an interdependent way to ensure the accomplishment of the system's goal.[7] During periods of exertion in an organic system such as the human body, the heart and lungs work together to provide enough blood and oxygen to the regions of the body under stress. Once the cause that created the need for exertion has past, these two organs will slow and allow the other organs time to catch up.

In an organization, the capability to cooperate can be seen when one looks at how operations, marketing, and logistics work together to make and deliver a product to a customer. Yet, at the same time in most organizations, the measures used to evaluate and monitor individual, departmental, and divisional performance

---

4 Bahg, C. 1985. "On the System of Systems Science". *Systems Engineering: Theory and Practice,* 2; Bertalanffy (1968).
5 Jackson (2003).
6 Jaques (2002).
7 Capra (1996); Miller, J. 1978. *Living Systems.* New York, NY: McGraw-Hill.

tend to isolate and reward the improvement of the individual at the expense of the organization. More on this later.

Their subsystems perform activities

The fifth and final common characteristic, within each of a system's subsystems, is that their activities can be classified as being either directly related to achieving the common goal of the system or directly related to performing the subsystem's unique activity or work. If we look at a single-cell ameba, we see that its cell membrane serves a couple of purposes. It separates and protects the cell's other subsystems from the external environment, while it also allows the appropriate elements in its external environment to be absorbed to provide resources to the other subsystems.[8]

When we look within organizations, some of the common practices might well be categorized as their cultural and behavioral expectations, the basics of their human resources (HR) practices, how they approach and practice intra-functional communications, and conflict resolution practices, to name a few. The unique practices within an organization's subsystems are the activities that enable its subsystems to achieve their individual responsibilities. For example, in HR these might be activities tied to evaluating the potential of future employees while in operations they might be the accepted measures of productivity.

Business as a living system: the characteristics

Having identified the set of characteristics that are common to all natural and living systems, we can begin to look at businesses and organizations from this perspective and start the journey to identify the elements of a new business model based on these system characteristics.

When we look at a business from the perspective of the first two characteristics, living (existing over time) and being open (interacting with its environment), it is easy to see these terms being used to describe an organization. That said, let's move on to the third characteristic which is "having a purpose". While it is well accepted that all living creatures (animals and plants) have a life-cycle that transitions from birth, maturation, propagation, and death, we know that not every individual of all species successfully transitions through all four of life's stages. In fact, for a large percentage of these individuals, the maturation and propagation stages are not part of their lives. So, what is the purpose or overriding goal of a business?

The purpose of organizational existence

Before we get into that answer, let's take a look at the history of businesses from this perspective. A quick review of today's business literature reveals that making

---

8 Capra (1996); Miller (1978); Ollhoff and Walcheski (2002).

a profit or maximizing stockholder value is commonly offered as the overriding goal of business.[9] This almost blind pursuit of financial returns, which some see as being driven by personal greed, has been cited by a variety of economic experts and world leaders—including President Obama, the Dalai Lama, and the Archbishop of Canterbury—as being a major contributor to the worldwide financial crisis that surfaced during the fall of 2008.[10] When we look back at the last 150 years of our economic history it is easy to identify a number of economic cycles—long periods of economic growth followed by sizable downturns. We refer to these periods with names such as: the Gilded Age (1870s–1890s), the Roaring 20s (mid-1920s–early 1930s), the Dot-Com bubble (1995–2000), and the lead up to the Great Recession (2001–2007). If we look at each of the downturns, vast amounts of economic wealth were lost while families' and individuals' lives were turned upside down.

If we focus on the last forty years, we see an ever-increasing use of sophisticated, computer-based methods for gathering data and performing financial analysis of organizational options and actions. These tools have been developed in an effort to expand management's understanding and decision-making ability over larger and more complex business opportunities. These new models provided management with the ability to conduct more complex "what if" financial scenarios and compare the results as they evaluate their alternatives. The more computer usage grew, the more important "what if" financial scenarios became in selecting corporate initiatives and providing support for the quantitative decision-making processes. If a proposal can demonstrate an expected return in excess of the organization's financial hurdle rate, it meets its financial viability test and as such supports the ongoing, but subtle, shift towards financialization. This approach to focusing organizational decision-making on financial returns, by definition, shifts the perspective of the organization from using its "value-adding capability" to provide products for its customers to seeing itself as a financial entity focused on decisions that increase short-term returns. It is my belief that these tools were a major contributor to the financialization of business during this time.

Throughout this period, the primary goal of business, stated or unstated, has been to make more money. That said, if we are serious about introducing some positive change to our overall economic and financial system we have to ask, will continuing with the same overall goal, that of making more money, and the same mental model, that our businesses are machines to be optimized, lead us to

9 Jones, G. and J. George. 2007. *Contemporary Management*. Boston, MA: McGraw-Hill Irwin.

10 Oberman, M. 2008. "Obama Vows to Fight 'Greed and Scheming' on Wall Street" press-reader.com. Retrieved November 11, 2016 (https://www.pressreader.com/canada/the-vancouver-sun/20081219/283124244752872); Singh, T. 2008. "The Dalai Lama Blames 'Greed' for Financial Crisis". The Buddhist Channel, December 8, 2008. Retrieved November 11, 2016 (www.buddhistchannel.tv/index.php?id=70,7496,0,0,1,0#.WCX-YuNUrKUk); Christian Today. 2008. "Human Greed Behind Financial Crisis, Says Archbishop". Christiantoday.com, October 16, 2008. Retrieved November 11, 2016 (www.christiantoday.com/article/human.greed.behind.financial.crisis.says.arch-bishop/21664.htm).

obtaining different results? As Albert Einstein said, *"We cannot solve our problems with the same thinking we used when we created them"*.[11] If we want to improve the ability of businesses to be part of a more sustainable global economic community, we must start this process by establishing an acceptable new goal and new mental model for business, one that is more consistent with the new systems-based paradigm. If we take a look at Figure 9, we see a depiction of the traditional business structure that identifies the focus of seeking improved profits along with the resulting effects from the actions taken. This figure provides an illustration of what today's accepted business model is producing.

Figure 9 **Traditional business structure**

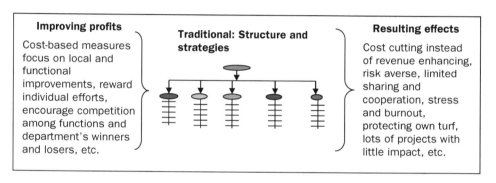

So, what is the goal of a business if it is not financial? From the organization's perspective, what lies beyond its own financial performance? How about ensuring the long-term survival of the organization, the organization's ongoing sustainability, and enhancing and expanding its ability to evolve to meet the ever-changing demands of its environment?[12] From a broader perspective, how responsible is the business for the system as a whole and what can an organization do to contribute to or enhance the long-term performance of the system of which it is a part? Remember, each independent organization is a contributing member of a larger economic system. These are examples of larger systems that a specific business must interact with:

- The industry it participates in

- The business community (suppliers and customers) it works with

- The community where it is located

By definition, the adoption of any organizational goal that is broader and looks past the organization's quarterly and annual financial performance carries with it a necessary condition of satisfactory financial performance. Without adequate

11 https://www.brainyquote.com/quotes/quotes/a/alberteins121993.html
12 Rothschild, M. 1990. *Bionomics.* New York: John Macrae Books.

financial performance, an organization will not have the needed resources (financial and human) to ensure its continued progress towards its long-term goal(s). Therefore, shifting an organization's focus from its own short-term financial performance and replacing that with something broader and more systemic, such as the organization's long-term success or its environmental adaptability, by definition, means that one of the necessary conditions for achieving the long-term goal is adequate short-term financial performance. It is not about giving up short-term financial performance, but making it subordinate to the long-term goal.

Figure 10 **Necessary conditions for increased quarterly financial performance**

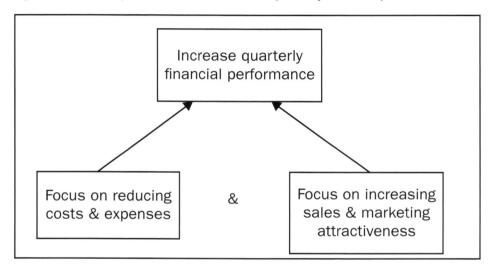

Another way to look at this is illustrated in Figures 10 and 11. Both diagrams reflect the necessary conditions to produce the desired end result. Figure 10 starts with a verbalization of what is commonly referred to as the goal of a business: "Increase quarterly financial performance". If this is the goal, then the necessary conditions are shown feeding into the end result. In this instance, the two conditions are:

- "Focus on activities that reduce costs and expenses", which ensures that its cash outflow will not be above what is expected
- "Focus on activities that increase sales and market attractiveness" ensures that the cash inflow may well be greater than expected

Given this understanding, it is easy to see that any activity that is outside the aforementioned items is less effective in producing the desired objective of "more profit".

Figure 11 **Necessary conditions for increasing long-term growth and performance**

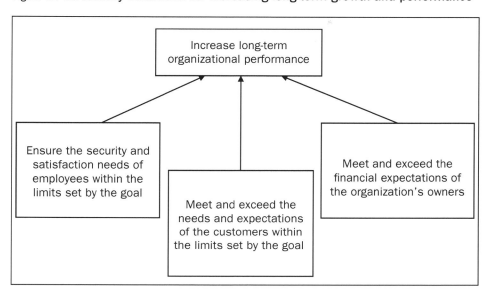

Conversely, let's take a look at Figure 11. It starts with the desired end result of "Increasing long-term organizational performance". While this goal could be seen from a number of different perspectives, one thing that is included in any of these viewpoints is that its financial performance is sufficient to accomplish everything it needs to do, which includes the necessary condition of "meeting the owners' expectations". We all know that if this cannot be accomplished, the future is very dim. The other necessary conditions ensure the organization's efforts are focused on the needs of the other two constituents, its customers and its employees. In 1954 Peter Drucker described the purpose of an organization as "meeting or exceeding the expectations of the customer".[13] After all, without a solid and expanding customer base demand will decline as will the cash flowing in. In addition, ensuring that the security and satisfaction of its employees are taken care of recognizes them as the organization's most important asset. Keeping employees satisfied ensures their focus, productivity, and ongoing contributions to the organization's needs and growth while keeping the costs associated with higher levels of turnover at a bare minimum. If either of these is neglected, sales and employee productivity will decline and the overall recruitment and training costs will increase.

In addition, if the organization wants to actively contribute to the growth and/or sustainability of the next larger system it interacts with, it must have some extra capacity and resources (i.e., dollars and labor) to undertake these efforts.

13 Drucker, P. 1954. *The Practice of Management.* New York: Harper & Row Publishing.

Organizations composed of subsystems

Since the time when the guilds and craftsmen models were being replaced with the beginning of the manufacturing model that leveraged the division of labor, there has been an ever-expanding number of departments and functions (subsystems) within these new businesses. Under the existing reductionist paradigm it was understood that increasing the efficiency of a department would improve the performance of the organization. This perspective also contributed to the excessive levels of "work in process" inventory between each operation to ensure higher levels of operational productivity. To this day, a vast majority of organizations rely on the pursuit of increased efficiency to identify and select the initiatives it will use to move the organization forward.

The difference between the aforementioned multi-departmental model and the organizational model being introduced here is that the new systems-based model focuses on how these multiple departments interact and work together, not on the pursuit of individual departmental efficiency. As I talked about earlier (Chapter 4) the shift to systems is based on a completely different perspective—one that recognizes the interdependence between the various elements (departments and divisions) as the primary focus for improving performance. More details later.

The interdependence of subsystems activities

In the mid-1980s I was manager of Industrial Engineering for Tracor Aerospace in Austin, TX. As the one responsible for developing the labor/manufacturing cost estimates for new products being designed, I would, every so often, head up the hill to the building where the engineers were located. I would make the rounds talking to some of the engineers, providing them with my manufacturing insights on the new ideas and potential products that were being considered. My goal was twofold: to see what the future might hold for us and, equally important, to provide them with some insight into manufacturing capabilities so they might in some small way make their designs a bit more manufacturable. After doing this for a few months, I was approached by my boss, the VP of Manufacturing, and told to stop making these trips—"let the engineers engineer and focus your efforts on those things within your domain". By that time I was smart enough to recognize that you "do what the boss says" or risk needing to find a new boss. I tell the story to point out how deeply rooted this perception about individual productivity contributing to organizational performance is within the average organization.

As to the impact of understanding and relying on interdependence, I want to introduce another story. In 1993, I was an Assistant Professor of Management at the University of Alabama at Birmingham. Through a couple of serendipitous events my dissertation, which introduced a new approach to the development of business planning, had made its way to the Special Assistant of the President. To cut a long story short, I was hired, along with another consultant, to train the President and all his direct subordinates in the tools and thinking processes (Theory of Constraints) I had used in my dissertation. In trying to convey the power of one of the logic-based tools, I developed a two-page cause-and-effect logic diagram that started with establishing a TOC Center in the School of Business; the following results were produced:

- Growth in reputation of our School of Business

- Increased demand for our business program graduates

- Improved effectiveness of our building efforts (lower costs and faster construction)

- Increase in our ability to solve problems

- Better ability to focus the school's limited resources

It took about 30 minutes to go through the complete diagram but, when I was done, his comment was "Let's do it". He had a complete understanding about how all the positive effects I had identified in the diagram would come to pass and these were things that he wanted to achieve. Unlike most corporate level pitches that are full of numbers and projections, this was built on the interactions between actions needed along the journey and the overall results. If you understand the interdependence between various functions and different actions, it is easy to see the path to the results. If all you have are numbers and projections, you will argue about every assumption that went into the numbers and seldom come to an agreement. More details about what this looks like in the new business model follow.

Fitting the elements together in a new business model

Given the new understanding of what a more systemic organizational goal looks like, one that is tied to long-term organizational sustainability, which includes recognition of the interdependence between the organization's subsystems and other systems within the larger business environment, a construct must be developed that is consistent with this goal and our understanding of living systems. Since even the smallest of ameba are composed of at least two different subsystems, we have a place to start. When I sit back and think about the basic types of activities that go on within an organization I can easily identify three basic types or classes. The first class involves activities that contribute directly to facilitating its transformation, production, distribution, and sale of the end-product(s) to its customers. This includes all the activities in the "value chain". I will refer to these as "value-add" subsystems. The second category is the effort involved in sharing information and the enabling of cooperation among the various "value-adding" subsystems within the larger whole (system). These will be referred to as "communications and coordination" subsystems. The third category of subsystems performs a combination of both activities and I will call them "combined" subsystems.

Value-adding subsystems

The first category of subsystems to look at are those that perform the independent functional activities within the system. Within each of the independent functional subsystems there exists an appropriate set of capabilities and capacities (e.g., tools, techniques, processes, and practices) designed to accomplish the specific activity or effort for which the subsystem is responsible. For example, our lungs are composed almost entirely of a unique membrane, the only function of which is to extract oxygen out of the air we breathe in and transfer carbon dioxide into the air we breathe out. Similarly, various functions within a business possess a unique set of machines, worker skills, and production planning and control procedures that control its value-adding activities. In both systems, our body and a business, the various functions rely on the efforts and activities of the communications and coordinating functions to enable them to work together in pursuit of the system's overall objective (life or products produced). The image I have developed to represent the concept of these functionally independent activities in the new business model is an ellipse. Figure 12 shows five different organizational functions as ellipses of various size, thickness, and color. For convenience sake, I have constructed this model around the five most common business functions.[14] Remember, each of these ellipses is made up of a number of smaller subsystems whose efforts have to be coordinated to effectively enable the function to produce its desired output to meet the organization's commitments. The more effectively these subsystems work together in a coordinated manner, the more efficient the organization's overall transformation processes become.

Communications and coordination subsystem

Higher-level living organisms rely on their nervous system to facilitate communications and cooperation among the various functions (subsystems) within their body. This ability to communicate enables the organism to deal with changes in its environment that require changes in its functions, which in turn increases its chances of achieving its overall goal of survival. I will refer to this assortment of activities and efforts as common core activities. The primary purpose of these activities is to effectively "communicate and coordinate" the actions and behaviors within and between the various functionally independent activities *within* a subsystem as well as *between* the various subsystems within the system. This communication and coordination activity must be effective enough to enable the system to learn from changes in its environment and as such, improve its ability to survive and prosper.

14   Jaques, Elliott. 1989. *Requisite Organization.* Arlington, VA: Cason Hall & Co.; Jones and George (2007).

Figure 12 **Independent organizational functions**

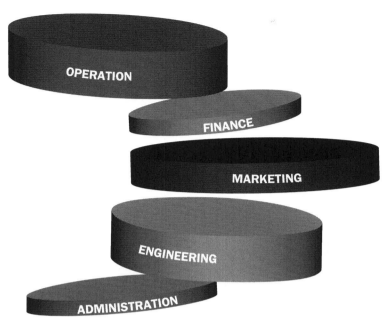

When you transfer this concept of a communications and coordination subsystem to an organization, the first question that must be answered is which set of activities should be included in this subsystem? One approach to answering the question would be to begin to develop a complete list of activities, but that would take many pages and would never be complete. Thus, I would like to provide a description of how this subsystem works and what is communicated. Each and every subsystem within an organization has at least one specific activity/function it is responsible for. Most have many such activities. For a subsystem to effectively accomplish its task(s), it needs to receive a signal (information) from outside itself that either initiates an action or response or provides the subsystem with enough information that it can make an appropriate decision and take the necessary action. This can be as simple as an automated inventory signal that triggers the purchase of more house-keeping supplies or as complex as a piece of information that, when combined with other information, initiates a complete review and possible revision of a strategic initiative. The communications and coordination subsystem is responsible for ensuring the effective collection and appropriate dissemination of all the information to ensure that the "value-adding" subsystems can continue to function in an effective manner. Yes, the overall content and structure of this subsystem can vary greatly, depending on the size of the organization and the complexity of information needed by the various subsystems within it. Included in this subsystem are the collection of chosen policies, measures and behaviors—along with the accepted norms in belief, culture, and practice—that are the necessary conditions upon which the organization relies to achieve its overall objective. Converting this requirement into a graphic representation resulted in what we call the common core column (see Figure 13).

Figure 13 **Common core of the systems-based business model**

COMMON CORE —

In addition to defining the types of activities and information flow contained within the communications and coordination subsystem, organizations also need to integrate two other elements into this information flow.

The first of these is a common set of organizational measures that will ensure all the subsystems, be they administrative or "value-adding", can evaluate the issues and alternatives from the same perspective. Let me spend a minute to explain *why* this is so important. Whether we are talking about the individual players on a sports team or the individual subsystems within an organization, if the actions of the whole are not coordinated towards achieving the "goal", be it winning for the team or long-term improvements for the business, the overall effectiveness of the group will be negatively affected. One of the primary reasons I left my professional career was this inconsistency in measures. I was given targets to work towards and yet when I proposed projects based on improving these measures many of them were rejected at the next level because they did not fit with the objectives or measures that level was using.

The solution to this dilemma is quite simple. Eli Goldratt introduced what he referred to as the TOC Measures of Performance to resolve the problem of inconsistent measures being used within business. These measures, which are nothing more than an extreme form of direct costing, are easy to use and are easily convertible to the accounting-based measures of return on investment (ROI), net profit

(NP), and cash flow (CF). The measures are defined below followed by the formulas used to calculate NP, ROI, and CF.

- **Throughput**. This is sales minus total variable expenses, which usually translates into sales minus the cost of direct materials, and perhaps commissions. Because so few costs are truly variable, throughput as a percentage of sales should be quite high.

- **Investment**. This is the amount of cash invested in order to increase the capacity of the production system to produce more units.

- **Operating expenses**. This is all expenses, not including the totally variable expenses used in the calculation of throughput. In essence, these are all of the costs required to maintain the system of production. Operating expenses may have some variable cost characteristics, but are generally fixed costs.

- Net profit = throughput – operating expenses

- Return on investment = net profit/investment

- Cash flow = throughput – operating expenses – "change in" inventory

Since its introduction in the late 1980s, the use of throughput accounting has continued to expand and has led to the publication of a few texts describing its use. At this point it is not about whether a firm adopts TOC; rather it is about recognizing the need for a "common" set of measures the entire organization can use to evaluate the financial impact of the alternatives it is considering. Until a business adopts this or something similar to ensure it has consistent measures across all levels, it will continue to pay the price of using inconsistent measures.

The second element is a consistent perspective regarding the definition of roles, the evaluation of employee performance, and the remuneration (pay and benefits) paid to employees. While there are numerous approaches and tools for addressing and managing these aspects of human resources a majority of us have biases about what works best, which we can trace to our past experiences. That said, organizations tend to become a patchwork of approaches when one looks at how these activities are performed within them. Imagine, if you can, the impact on organizational performance if every individual across the organization was working at their maximum capability, doing something that was aligned with their passions, and being evaluated on criteria that were tied to moving the organization forward.[15] Conversely, you might want to think of the impact on organizational performance from the fact that today over 70% of the employed people in the U.S. are disengaged at work. There is a path to bringing together and focusing the energies of all your employees: requisite organization. Today, there are a growing number of firms that are moving in this direction. For those of you that are interested, I would

15 Jaques, Elliott. 1998. *Requisite Organization*. 2nd ed. Gloucester, MA: Cason Hall & Co.

recommend, as a first read, Jaques's book *Social Power and the CEO* to develop a deeper understanding of requisite organization and its potential impact.

The next step

By combining the two previously described subsystems, value-adding and communications and coordination, we get a graphic representation of how these two components of the business system interact (see Figure 14). This representation shows the various functionally independent subsystems that the organization must have in order to survive and prosper. In addition, we see the communications and coordination core as the mechanism that reaches across the organization and provides the various "value-adding" subsystems with the ability to efficiently communicate, coordinate, and prioritize their work efforts. Such coordination is required to ensure the overall effectiveness of the system in making progress towards its overall goal. The amount and effectiveness of this interaction between subsystems is completely dependent on how the organization has chosen to create these subsystems and how it establishes and maintains these required relationships.

Figure 14 **General business and organizational model**

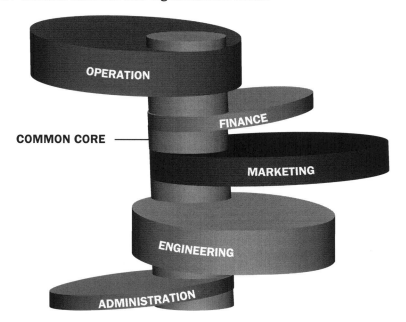

Up to this point, the model-building effort has been focused on how the various segments internal to a specific business interact with one another. Having established this general framework, we can turn our attention to how an organization interfaces with the other external entities (e.g., organizations, governmental, and NGOs) within its environment:

- Some they must cooperate with

- Others they may well have to respond to

- Others they may want to avoid

At a minimum, their interaction with the outside world involves the procurement of resources, securing employees, exchanging their output with other external entities, and communicating with governmental agencies. In Figure 15, we represent the individual organization as a circle and present the categories of external entities as ovals with bi-directional communications arrows linking them together. The openness within this type of system also means that each of the subsystems within this system is susceptible to both internal influences from other subsystems and influences from a wide variety of elements in the external environment. Examples of some of the major types of external entities that could influence the behavior of internal subsystems are actions taken by the government, the competition, or a special interest group, and changes in the economy.

Figure 15 **External forces that influence organizations**

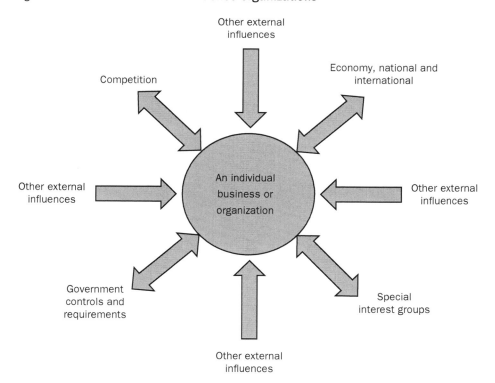

S-BBM as an integrative whole

Now that you have some understanding of the physical representation of the S-BBM, the next step is to begin looking into the transformations that will have to take place for an organization to make the journey from the traditional "command and control" perspective to the more holistic, systems-based perspective. The following provides a high-level description of the major transformations an organization will have to embrace on its journey to becoming a systems-based business. Recognize that the shifts identified below are in no way meant to be all-inclusive, but do include the major transformations that will take place as the organization replaces conflicts with cooperation, "one-upmanship" with subordination, and individual agendas with the organizational goal(s).

Becoming a learning organization

First it must recognize the need to become a learning organization that is able to absorb knowledge and lessons from its environment and experiences and adapt them into new rules and behaviors. Without this, the organization does not have the mental capabilities it needs to transition through the many learning cycles this journey will require. While this shift will have to reach across the entire organization, it does not mean that it has to happen in one fell swoop. This shift has to be led from the top and will require dedicated time and training for all. It also starts to lay the foundational understanding within the organization for "seeing systems" and the potential for their broader acceptance. The idea of organizational learning was introduced in 1990 in Peter Senge's *The Fifth Discipline*. His efforts led to the foundation of the Society for Organizational Learning.[16] In addition, a similar path has been established by the Weatherhead School of Management at Case Western Reserve University under its AIM2Flourish initiative which is focused on helping today's generation of management and the next to build a better world.[17]

Aligning the organization's "value-adding" activities

Once the organization has begun to embrace the idea of seeing the business as a system, it is ready to begin its transformational journey. One of the easiest places to introduce and build a solid understanding of these new systems-based ideas is in the production or "value-adding" activities. After all, everyone working for the VP of Operations is focused on the overall goal of getting the product out the door. The adoption and implementation of Drum-Buffer-Rope for operations and/or Critical Chain for project management can usually be done in three months or less, depending of course on the overall size of the organization. Not only is it quick and easy to put in place, but produces a bottom-line improvement that, on

16 http://www.solonline.org/
17 https://weatherhead.case.edu/centers/fowler/AIM2Flourish/

average, exceeds 30%.[18] While the increase in financial performance is good, the more important result from this first step is the fact that a larger portion of the organization will now be aware of the positive impact associated with the transformational journey and, as such, will become more open to the changes they will have to embrace. This shift in willingness to accept and participate in the coming changes is critical for moving the transformational journey past this first step.[19]

Increasing the level of trust

The primary focus of this shift is to lay the groundwork for the "communications and coordination" segment. To do that, we need to put in place changes that will improve the level of trust across the organization. Once again, this is a "top-down" shift that will encourage and support the adoption of a management model that recognizes the value of building trust and expanding open and honest communications throughout the organization. To accomplish this, management must identify, develop, and implement some rules, training, and measures that encourage and support this behavior. One of the easiest paths to this is to begin looking into the work of Elliott Jaques. One of the first changes he talks about is to make sure the managerial roles within the organization are being filled by individuals whose "complexity of mental processing" is equal to that required by the role they hold. What this means is that the manager's ability to deal with uncertainty and complexity is at the same level as the role they are holding. If these are misaligned then the manager is either in over his or her head (we have all seen this) or he or she is being under-utilized (the role does not demand enough from them) which leads to boredom and disengagement at work. With the correct manager in the correct role, the next step in building trust is to adopt RO's perspective on management where the boss is responsible for the output of the subordinate. With this one shift, the level of trust will be greatly increased because your boss is now concerned that you succeed in your role.[20] This shift is so important because so many of today's employees (around 70%) are disengaged at work.[21]

18 Kendall, G. 2005. *Viable Vision: Transforming Total Sales into Net Profits.* Ft. Lauderdale, FL: J Ross Publishing; Lang, L. 2006. *Achieving Viable Vision: The Theory of Constraints Strategic Approach to Rapid Sustainable Growth.* Throughput Publishing; Mabin, V. and S.J. Balderstone. 1999. *The World of the Theory of Constraints.* Boca Raton, FL: St. Lucie Press.

19 The following works are suggested to assist in your search for additional information on the theory of constraints: Goldratt, Eli. 2000. *Necessary but not Sufficient.* Great Barrington, MA: North River Press; Levinson, W. 2007. *Beyond the Theory of Constraints: How to Eliminate Variation and Maximize Capacity.* New York, NY: Productivity Press; Stein, R. 2003. *Re-engineering the Manufacturing System: Applying the Theory of Constraints,* 2nd edn. New York: Marcel Dekker; Woeppel, M. 2001. *Manufacturer's Guide to Implementing the Theory of Constraints.* Boca Raton, FL: St. Lucie Press.

20 Jaques (1989, 2002).

21 Adkins (2015).

Establishing a consistent set of measures

Having a consistent and commonly used set of measures to evaluate the financial contribution of alternatives brings everyone to the same page. Today, a substantial amount of managerial decisions are based on the data provided through cost accounting information; yet, since the time of its development in the early 1900s, we have known that it was only an estimate of the real costs. While organizations must continue to use cost accounting to provide the requisite information for financial reporting, they need to ensure their management has more consistent and accurate information for decision-making. An effective alternative is throughput accounting.[22] The adoption of consistent financial measures across the organization will, by definition, bring alignment to the financial aspects of decision-making across the organization and as such will reduce a large number of cross-departmental conflicts that have their roots in the use of different measures.

Reducing conflicts across the organization

Think about the time your organization wastes working to resolve conflicts within and across functions. As organizations continue to grow the number of conflicts continues to expand. In most organizations the individuals with the best conflict resolution skills, be they intellectually based or power based, are the ones that are most likely to move ahead. That does not mean that their solution was the best, only that their sponsors won the battle. Think about the positive impact on performance, increased capacity, and cooperation if an organization had a non-biased process to resolve conflicts that removed the emotion and power from the resolution process? One of the most important developments and additions to the field of management by Eli Goldratt was the conflict resolution diagram, better known as the evaporating cloud. This approach removes the reliance on forecasted data, which is always debatable because of the various assumptions used in its development. In its place the cloud relies on logic to identify the assumptions behind the alternative positions, which leads to a deeper understanding of the positions being evaluated and produces much better decisions. In addition to resolving problems, the use of the cloud and other thinking processes tools will enhance communications

22 This approach and its impact have been written about in a number of books: Bragg, S. 2007. *Throughput Accounting: A Guide to Constraint Management.* New York: John Wiley & Sons; Caspari, John A. and Pamela Caspari. 2004. *Management Dynamics: Merging Constraints Accounting to Drive Improvement.* New York: John Wiley & Sons; Noreen, E., D. Smith and M. Mackey. 1995. *Theory of Constraints and its Implications for Management Accounting.* Great Barrington, MA: North River Press; Smith, Debra. 2000. *The Measurement Nightmare.* Boca Raton, FL: St. Lucie Press; Thomas, C. 1998. *Throughput Accounting.* Boca Raton, FL: St. Lucie Press.

and cooperation within and across subsystems (functions). They are the most comprehensive set of logic-based problem solving and planning tools I am aware of.[23]

Employees valued as assets not seen as expenses

Given today's almost blind focus on the financial side—reducing costs and expenses—and the fact that employees and all of HR are categorized as expenses, there is intense pressure to improve their performance by reducing their overall costs. Yet, in the new systems-based model, employees are seen as assets and as such the focus is to protect and expand their abilities and contribution. That said, the role of HR is another area that needs a major shift. Knowing that we have the right person in the correct role and that we have an adequate succession plan is important. In addition, knowing that the organization pays all employees an equitable wage is critically important to enabling the organization to expect and receive the best of its workers every day. Ensuring our employee assets have a career path forward that will fit our future needs and their desires is also critically important to retention and as such, organizational performance. Dealing with these and other issues from a systems-based perspective was the life's work of Dr. Elliott Jaques. Requisite Organization effectively addresses the people, pay, authority, accountability, leadership, and succession issues.[24] This type of shift affects both the "value-adding" and "communications and coordination" subsystems within an organization.

Including information management in the transition

As the organization continues its transformational journey it will need to make major adjustments to its information management system that are consistent with the needs of a systems-based business. Currently, the primary focus of IT has been to provide management with the necessary information from their current enterprise resources planning (ERP) system. As with the other tools, this one is focused on providing the necessary information at the lowest possible cost. Yet, the most important thing any system needs to grow in an ever-changing environment is access to all the new information and the excess capability needed in order to process this new information in its interaction with the environment. Providing this requires an information system that has excess capacity and the capability to identify, collect, and develop new processes, and disseminate the new information as needed. This requires a new mental model for the IT system. Over the last ten years

---

23 Dettmer, H. 2007. *The Logical Thinking Process: A Systems Approach to Complex Problem Solving*. Milwaukee, WI: ASQC Quality Press; Scheinkopf, L. 1999. *Thinking for a Change*. Boca Raton, FL: St. Lucie Press; Schragenheim, Eli. 1998. *Management Dilemmas: The TOC Approach to Problem Identification and Solutions*. Boca Raton, FL: St. Lucie Press; Low, A. 2008. *Conflict and Creativity at Work: Human Roots to Corporate Life*. East Sussex, UK: Sussex Academic Press.
24 Jaques (1989, 2002).

or so the second generation of knowledge management has evolved to reflect the needs of a living, sustainable organization.[25]

While I recognize this is an incomplete list, it contains the primary transitions that an organization will move through as it makes the journey from today's model to the new systems-based business model. In addition I assume that as the subsystems within an organization begin to understand the implications of the new systems-based business paradigm, they will be able to identify the most appropriate tools and processes they will need to incorporate into their transitional journey to accomplish the function-specific work for which they are responsible.

Since both the "communications and cooperation" segment and the various subsets within the "value-adding" segment are now based on the ideas and processes within the systems-based business model, the interface between these two segments should be almost seamless. That said, Figure 16 was developed to show the results of becoming a S-BBM, which can be compared with the traditional business model previously depicted in Figure 9.

Figure 16 **New business paradigm model**

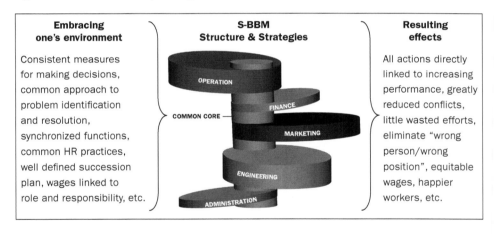

S-BBM as part of an interdependent supply chain

Organization as a subsystem within a larger system

Having previously identified the interdependence that exists between an organization and the other elements (businesses, governmental agencies, communities,

25 McElroy, M. 2002. *New Knowledge Management: Complexity, Learning, and Sustainable Innovation.* New York: Butterworth-Heinemann.

and other organizations) within its external environment (see Figure 16) we can now introduce the larger (supply-chain) system, within which a number of organizations are the subsystems that make up the supply-chain system. Given what we have learned about how the subsystems (functions) within a system (organization) should work cooperatively to improve the system's overall performance, the same is true when we look at this larger supply-chain system. This recognition carries with it an acceptance of the requirement for businesses and organizations to work together in cooperative and interdependent relationships with other organizations within the supply chain to improve the performance of the supply chain in meeting or exceeding the end consumer's expectations. In today's global economy, the relationships between the various elements (businesses as subsystems) in any value network (supply chain) are usually established independently, one business to another, without much consideration given to how they fit into the entire network. As a result, conflicts may well exist between the various network entities that hamper the effective transactions that need to take place.

The model (see Figure 17) must also look at how the various members of a value network interact as a system within the larger economic system. Since each network (supply chain) is a complete system composed of more than a single organizational entity (subsystem), and the output of this network system is a set of products and services designed to meet the needs of its customers, this new system (network) must be able to structure itself in a way that is consistent with our new systems-based view.

Figure 17 **Organizational interdependencies**

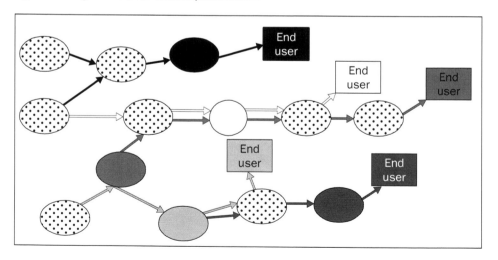

In my effort to depict the interactions between various businesses and their involvement in various value networks, I started with five squares with different types of shading which represent different customer groups (industries) that have different expectations and needs. As you move backwards from the industries, follow the similarly shaded arrows to see how many unique organizations are involved in its supply chain system. The various independent organizations are identified by a unique shade. Where you see more than one of the same-shaded circles, it represents the same organization serving the needs of more than one industry. You will also see multiple arrows associated with one circle, which means that entity is involved in more than one customer group. The interdependence depicted in the diagram is simple when compared with the real world where one business may well be a member of 10–20 different supply chains, each with their own demands and expectations. Imagine the level of complexity created within an organization that is trying to meet the unique expectations of 20 different customers. These organizations are all looking back to the time of Henry Ford, when he owned and oversaw all the manufacturing and assembly needed to produce his Model Ts, and thinking "I wish our processes and products were that simple". Some solutions for more effective management of the complexity within our organizations will be introduced in the next chapter.

S-BBM as part of a participative industry

The final perspective that needs to be introduced considers how the shift to the systems-based business model would impact the relationship between the various business competitors within any specific industry and/or the economy? First, let's look into the future to a time when an entire industry has made the transition. At that point, all the industry members embrace this systems-based perspective and see themselves as active participants in an industry which currently serves a specific need for its customers. Also, all of these members are no longer simply focused on "more profit" but have adopted a goal that, in addition to long-term financial viability and development, includes improving customer satisfaction and community stability. Notice I used the term development not growth. It is no longer about being bigger (more profits); rather it is about being better at what they do and providing an acceptable return to the owners for the level of risk being faced. Unlike in the past when businesses viewed the competition as the enemy and actions were taken in an effort to be victorious over them, today industry members are somewhat more collaborative in the way they work together to improve their ability to deliver customer satisfaction. That does not mean that they meet and share everything, but since they are focused on the same set of customers and their ability to develop, they are more willing to discuss insights and ideas that may help the industry to move forward.

I will be the first to admit that this sounds rather far-fetched, but so did the shift in physics from the purely Newtonian model in the early 1900s to quantum mechanics by the 1930s. Speaking of models, the neoclassical approach to economics, which has been the foundation of economics since the late 1800s, drew on the use of calculus from Newtonian physics to provide a mechanism for examining and analyzing patterns in the economy by modeling the equilibrium between the prices and quantities of goods consumed.[26] Since then, the assumption of equilibrium has been a foundational piece in the field of economics. By the mid-1900s the field of physics had recognized the limits of equilibrium modeling, which greatly reduced its use in this field, but economists have held strong to it. As W. Brian Arthur said in his book *Complexity and the Economy*,

> I admire the beauty of the neoclassical economy; but for me the construct is too pure, too brittle, too bled of reality. It lives in a Platonic world of order, stasis, knowableness, and perfection. Absent from it is the ambiguous, the messy, the real.[27]

To that end, he and a number of the forward thinking economists and physicists have spent over 40 years working on a new perspective of economics they call complexity economics because it is based on the recognition of systems and interdependence between and among elements and organizations. I offer this as an insight into the future of our understanding of economics and suggest that this shift in thinking and perspective may well provide some of the insight needed to completely achieve the S-BBM and the systems-based economic system I mentioned earlier.

I am the first to admit that this journey will be long and will involve a continual evolution of the answers to some of the aforementioned questions that organizations, industries, and the economy will face. I wish I had all the answers and a complete vision into the future but I do not. What I do know is that this shift from deterministic to holistic is necessary and upon us. That said, let's take a look at Chapter 7 which provides what I believe is the basic path for this transitional journey. While some of the long-term details are a bit fuzzy, I am convinced that the foundation and understanding outlined with the initial steps will provide organizations with the knowledge and insight they need to deal with some of the questions that will surely arise on their journey into the future.

26 Arthur, W. Brian. 2014. *Complexity and the Economy.* New York: Oxford University Press, p. 3.
27 *Ibid.*, p. 4.

7
A model for the transitional journey

The foundational elements

When you look into today's literature around organizational change you find a broad spectrum of thoughts and techniques about how best to formulate and implement change across an organization. Organizations, if you include governments and armies, have been around for thousands of years and we can identify exemplar individuals when it comes to organizational leadership and strategy—from Sun Tzu (*c.* 500 BC) and Alexander the Great (*c.* 300 BC) to Machiavelli (*c.* AD 1500) and modern-day generals such as Patton (1945). However, we are still seeking to better understand the elements of a more effective approach to managing organizations. So, let's take a brief review of the evolution of this topic before delving deeper into *how* and *why* the shift within the interdependent organization is so important.

In Chapters 2 and 3 about the history of business and the evolution of its modern-day practices, I mentioned that until the 1930s workers were, as a rule, viewed as "cogs in the wheel of manufacturing" and, as such, they were as replaceable as a tire on a car—if one does not work, just get another one. This mental model of workers "being replaceable" also contributed to the growth and expansion of labor unions which provided a voice for the multitude of "replaceable workers" in the ever-expanding number of factories around the U.S. This perception can, in large part, be attributed to three interrelated phenomena:

- The beginning and expansion of consumer markets which led to the ever-increasing need for new "stuff" to sell in the expanding network of stores

- The migration of a large number of agricultural workers to the growing cities in search of a better life, which created an overabundance of available workers for employment in the growing number of factories

- The validation and adoption of "scientific management", which provided "scientific proof" that relying on the "one best way to do work" as defined through industrial engineering, was more productive and provided a more consistent output

Given this perception and the exponential growth of industrialization across the U.S., it is quite understandable why researchers within the field of sociology would begin looking into the social interactions within these large factories. The Hawthorne studies, which were conducted in large Bell Labs factories around Chicago in the 1930s, provided the foundation for the emerging field of human resources (HR). These and other studies helped researchers realize that the structure and managerial practices being used in these factories affected the behavior and motivation of the workers. From this foundational research the various sub-fields of HR, organizational behavior, organizational development, organizational change, etc., have evolved. Today, one would be hard pressed to find a business college that did not have an HR major or concentration within its BA program. In addition, there are thousands and thousands of experts and consultants offering their variation on what an organization can do to get the best out of its workers. Yet most of today's workers are disengaged at work. I would like to suggest that perhaps we do not have a complete understanding of what it takes to bring together and channel the energies and insights of our employees in an effort that is focused and aligned with moving the organization forward. That said, let's look a bit deeper.

Foundational understanding, insights, and assumptions

As a trained academic, I understand the evolutionary process of theory development. You start with the existing position and enhance it by adding newly developed insight and/or removing a certain piece of the existing knowledge because of a conflict with some aspect of the new knowledge. While all research is undertaken in a search for "truth and a better understanding", when it is applied to a topic outside the hard sciences, one that does not have a physical or chemical make-up that can be accurately measured to determine the true impact, the effect of change is much harder to quantify. One of the questions faced by researchers in this field (organizational change) is "how do you measure the impact or effect of the change when you are looking at an organization"? Do you look for a direct shift in how people interact and/or how they work together, or do you look for an increase in organizational performance? Another part of that question is "how long does it take for the change to produce the effect?" The longer time lag between the implementation of the change (A) and observing the desired result (B) the less confidence one has in saying B is directly caused by A. As you can see, the journey for an academic researcher, especially those in the soft sciences is fraught with a number of issues and questions. Since this book is targeted towards those individuals working in the real world who have a desire to bring transformational change to their organization, it is not constrained by the limitations of academic research.

In putting together these last two chapters I have ensured that they provide real-world practitioners with enough insight and understanding for them to be willing and able to begin their transformational journey, knowing full well it will involve an ongoing learning process that is focused on developing more detailed answers to the ever-evolving questions they will face. Let us begin this journey by taking a deeper look into "change" itself before we delve into the basic steps needed to transform an organization.

The first thing we all need to recognize is that, for the vast majority of us, change is not an easy thing. We have, from the beginning, sought some form of stability in our life because it reduces the level of uncertainty and fear about an unknown and uncertain future. As we mature we continue to place a value on our ability to maintain some stability. Whether it is in our personal relationships, our careers, or even the type of car we drive, most of us have established and continue to seek stability in our life because it provides us a foundation to hold on to. Most of us have known at least a few individuals that have stayed in a poor relationship because the negatives associated with the "known" were much easier for them to accept than the uncertainty associated with leaving. I have a friend that spent more than 25 years working for the same organization in a few different roles that were, in his words "rather boring", but from his perspective, staying there was safer than looking for another position. I, on the other hand, have always embraced change. In the last 31 years I have had 11 different addresses in 9 different cities. Moving, new friends, and learning are things I am quite comfortable with. I am not saying to those who stay in bad relationships or boring jobs that they are wrong, only that the assumptions they hold and the fear they produce about the possible future limits their ability to even explore the alternatives.

The same can be said for many professionals—the fear associated with introducing change or a new way of seeing or understanding the world in which one works keeps most of them from looking outside the accepted norm for possible solutions. Another effect of modern-day management that effectively limits change within our organizations is the ongoing pursuit of increasing productivity (in search of more financial performance). This practice of continually squeezing more work out of everyone effectively removes any extra time that could have been used to reflect on or reconsider the processes, practices, and assumptions associated with our daily work routine.

Another perspective that is important for us to recognize is that each of us always make the best decision we can, given the knowledge, insights, and assumptions we possess and the pressures we feel. None of us gets up in the morning and says, I am going to make bad decisions today, yet, in hind sight, there is no doubt that sometimes we do. When looking backwards from a point of time in the future, things look very different and many times we recognize the errors of our insights or assumptions that led to poor or regrettable decisions and actions. Remember, our decision-making process relies on the knowledge and insight we carry with us to evaluate the alternatives and come to the "best decision" we are capable of. I can remember when I was asked by my best man a few hours before my first wedding, "how do you feel?" At that point, I realized that I probably should not go through with it (pre-wedding jitters), but there was no way I could act on that feeling because I was not willing to bring so much disappointment and anger to everyone there including my soon-to-be wife. In this situation, it was my fear (pressure) of the expected ramifications that would be immediate if I chose to walk away from the wedding. That said, I swallowed those thoughts and proceeded with the wedding because it was the "correct choice" at that exact time. Two and a half years later we got divorced, which, you might say, was just a postponement of the action I should have taken before the wedding. While that might have been true, she and I have become the best of friends, I am the godfather to her children, and my current wife and I have a close relationship with her and her family. There is no doubt that change, both personal and organizational, is difficult. That said, it is my desire to provide you with enough insights and links to new resources that a vast majority of you will feel empowered with enough *new* knowledge to begin your transformational journey.

So how do these insights on change play out at work? For the vast majority of us, doing what we did yesterday, having the predictability in the work we do, how we do it, and who we work with, provides stability in the assumptions and understanding we use in our role, in the performance measures we are evaluated with, the organizational goals we are pursuing, and the external environment we interact with. All of these provide us with some form of comfort and predictability because we know how to use and evaluate them. While this comfort can be tied to "knowing what to expect", the predictability allows all of us to develop and rely on rules of thumb, past practices, and standardized processes that have become our "proven solutions" associated with the relatively stable environment we have become accustomed to. Having these accepted practices to draw on improves our productivity because we do not have to think about or evaluate a vast majority of our daily tasks, we just rely on what has worked in similar situations in the past. Today, the world and environment we work in are much less stable than they used to be and are always in some form of flux. If you think about the actions of soldiers in active combat, they are always revisiting and evaluating their decisions because in an ever-changing environment that is the only way to ensure good (safe) decision-making. While today's business is not exactly a war environment, as the increased level of change across the business paradigm continues to grow, we need to increase the rate at which we challenge the basic assumptions we carry and revisit the practices we have relied on in the past to ensure they are still providing us with good results.

This look into our need for stability which provides us with the ability to predict results and our need for flexibility to adapt to the ever-changing environment of business, places us in a conflict—wanting two things that are in direct opposition of each other. Perhaps the solution to this conflict lies within a shift which recognizes the world we live in is something other than a machine that must be optimized. Yes, the transition to becoming an interdependent organization is based on this shift. After all, we are talking about transitioning from the mechanistic organization of the past to becoming a living organization that by its very nature and culture is an ever-evolving state that can adapt to changes in its internal and external environment. The transformational journey outlined below includes a recognition of how this shift will lead to improved performance because it is focused on leveraging the interdependence within the living system and letting go of the old machine-based model which has been the foundation on which our understanding of business has been based.

The journey towards more organizational sustainability is a long-term process that involves at least three stages and relies on a self-reinforcing process to sustain these major shifts. That said, I must warn you that the first step is always the hardest, because it is the step that requires those involved to "let go of" the well-known practices and assumptions of the past and put their trust in something they have very little experience, exposure to, and faith in. Therefore, the first step in the first stage must be well thought out and introduced in a non-threatening way with more than a couple of stage-gates that allow for review, revision, and bailing out. Once the organization has some experience and trust in the process, the steps can become bigger because there will be a deeper understanding of the mental model and processes being used. Welcome to the journey towards the new business paradigm.

The three stage model (systems-based business model)

This section addresses the three basic stages involved in the implementation of the S-BBM and the recommended sequence of implementation for each stage. First, I will introduce and discuss the graphic model depicting the implementation. This will be followed with a more in-depth look at the logic behind the suggested approach offered within each stage. Within the discussion for each stage will be an overview of the currently available tools and a brief review of the impact these approaches have had when adopted in the real world.

One of the major hurdles to adopting a model such as the one contained in this book is the magnitude of change the organization will experience on its journey to complete implementation. The journey is not for those that lack stamina. While each of the stages focuses on a different aspect of the organization and could theoretically be implemented in any sequence, the one presented here starts with the easiest to implement and, by the way, it also provides a sizable improvement to the organization's profitability. Each of the next two stages involves higher levels of complexity and, as such, requires more time and effort to successfully implement the changes.

The first stage is what I call the "tools and techniques" stage. The focus of this stage is on the individual functional activities within the organization's value-adding process. The primary focus of this stage is to change how the organization plans, develops, and executes its value-adding efforts. For the last 100 years or so the primary focus has been on increasing the performance of the individual activities within the stream of value-adding activities. This practice can be traced to two new ideas that were introduced in the early 1900s:

- **Scientific management** which established the belief that "the one correct (engineered) way" was the most efficient

- **Cost accounting** which looks at the "costs" of the individual activities and summarizes these into the overall costs (performance)

Both of these tools were based on the belief that the sum of the parts equals the whole. While this may well be true for an assortment of independent pieces, it is not valid when the focus of your efforts is an interdependent system. Conversely, the theory of constraints-based tools for production (Drum-Buffer-Rope) and project management (Critical Chain) view all the activities within the overall transformation process as an interdependent system whose overall performance is determined by the constraints within that system. Over the last 30 years, the firms that have adopted TOC have seen their bottom line improve by 35–40%.[1]

The second stage is the "common goals and measures" stage. This stage addresses the development and implementation of the requisite measures and practices that link the organization's various divisions and functions, together with consistent measures that allow everyone's efforts to be directly linked to the organization's goal. If you look within your organization and begin to identify the goals and measures used within various departments you will find that they are all different. One of the primary reasons for this is the reliance on cost accounting and its foundational assumption that each of the departments and divisions is an independent element with its own objectives and performance measures. The first step would be to expand the use of the measures now being used within the "value-adding" departments across the rest of the organization. With the use of consistent measures in place, the next step would be to address the organization's information management system (IMS). Since the IMS provides the vehicle through which the interdependent parts of the organization align, coordinate, and continually evolve, it has to be designed to have the capacity to effectively provide all of this. Like the "value-adding" segment, the IMS needs to recognize itself as an interdependent system and manage itself in that manner. The third step in this stage is beginning the shift within the organization's approach to human resources management. The organization should ensure that it uses a common approach to evaluating the "size" of its various roles and that it has the ability to match an individual's "capabilities" to the "size" of the role using the same criteria. This would

---

1   Mabin and Balderstone (1999).

ensure everyone, across the organization, is in a role that fits their capabilities and provides a mechanism to develop a valid succession planning document that is tied to the capabilities of the individual.

I refer to the third stage as the "people and skills" stage. This stage focuses on putting in place a common set of HR procedures and training that will ensure all the management practices and processes across the organization are consistent and aligned with the overall goal of the organization and the adoption of a comprehensive systems-based visioning process to guide and facilitate the organization's future development and growth. This stage builds on two foundational pieces of understanding. The first is having a solid systems-based management system (human resources management) in place. This is accomplished by adopting the additional components of requisite organization which was introduced in stage two. The second is truly the biggest shift for the organization because it entails the transition of all the elements and activities within the organization from the traditional "mechanistic" perspective to the new "systems-based" paradigm. Peter Senge refers to this as becoming a learning organization while the Fowler Center at the Weatherhead School of Management at Case Western Reserve refers to this as Flourishing, and other consultants and researchers have developed their own unique terms to describe this shift. More on this later.

Now that I have described the three stages, let's take a look at the implementation model itself. Figure 18 depicts this implementation sequence.

Figure 18 **Implementation plan for the new business paradigm**

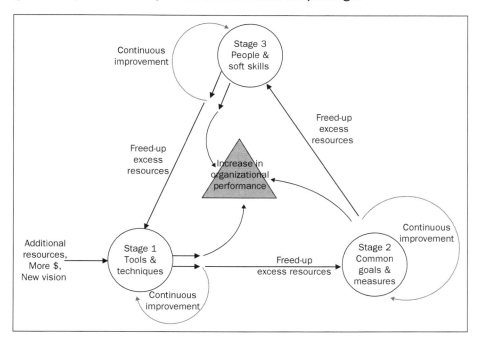

Let's start by looking at the lower left of the figure. You notice that the input arrow identifies that there is an initial investment of some additional resources, some dollars, and a beginning commitment to the new vision for the organization. The additional resources represent the acceptance that this journey will require an additional commitment of time and energy from a wide variety of organizational members as it moves forward. The additional dollars are targeted at securing outside support, in the form of consultants, content experts, software, and so on, that will be needed to bring focus and guidance to the initial efforts and ensure the knowledge and learning needed to continually facilitate the organization's learning journey is ready and available. There is no doubt that these outside experts will be part of the efforts needed to establish the organization's new vision.

You will notice coming out of the first and subsequent stages (Figure 18) that there are two output arrows. These arrows represent where and how the organization has chosen to allocate the increase in performance as a result of the transformations implemented within the stage. This increase exists because the efforts in each stage are targeted at improving the focus, prioritization, and decision-making which will result in an increase in the capabilities within the functions or activities the stage addresses. The decision on how the organization chooses to split the increase in bottom-line performance between more profits or increasing its support (financial and excess resources) for the transformational journey is up to the management team. However, it is my recommendation that the funds needed for continuing the journey (continuous improvement and resources for the next stage) should be set aside first and the remaining funds used to enhance profitability. The second arrow illustrates the flow of the resources (e.g., people, time, and dollars) that have become available as the changes in the stage begin to reduce the conflicts and divergent focus that currently exists within the organization. As you can guess, this model recommends using the windfall in excess capabilities and capacity as a way to leverage the experiences gained by those actively involved in the transformation and use their expertise to seed and guide the new learning and growth that will be needed as the transition continues toward the next stage. The next two stages follow a similar pattern, the implementation of the various steps within each stage frees up more excess capacity which leads to an increase in the bottom line that is shared between improving profits and funding the next transition step.

A detailed walk

Stage one: enhancing the value-adding processes

As is commonly practiced when introducing something new, the process starts by focusing on the simplest component(s) or idea(s) while relying on the most proven processes or practices. Once this new idea is understood and established you can progress to more complex ideas and concepts. So, within an organization where or what is the "simplest or least complex" or "the most well defined and standardized set of activities"? I believe that most business people would identify "operations" (the value-adding activities) as that function. After all, in most organizations your suppliers and the cost of materials is well established, the process routings and times are well-defined and predictable, the logistics links and costs are known, and the quality level is easily managed. When this level of predictability is compared with the other major functions in a business, such as finance, marketing, and sales, where you are not in control of all the resources, it is easy to see the increased level of complexity and uncertainty in these activities.

By focusing the first stage of the transformational journey on the organization's value-adding activities through the implementation of the proven systems-based tool, the theory of constraints (TOC), the organization will very quickly experience a sizable improvement to its bottom line. The primary requirement for making this type of shift is a willingness to change the mental model and decision-making practices used in managing the operations function. This requires those involved in the operations function to begin seeing their function as a "system" of interdependent components instead of a machine composed of a variety of independent elements that are to be optimized.

As TOC was evolving through the 1980s and 1990s Eli Goldratt, its founder, and his partners developed applications for production (Drum-Buffer-Rope, DBR), distribution (Replenishment), and project management (Critical Chain) in addition to a comprehensive set of Thinking Processes. The unique contribution of TOC in these areas was its recognition that the steps within these processes are all part of an interdependent system of events where one feeds the next. Like any flow process, the constraint within the system limits the system's output. Since its development, TOC has been adopted by thousands and thousands of organizations around the world to schedule and control their production processes. By synchronizing the activities of all the resources in the organization's value-adding efforts, a large percentage of the current conflicts and disagreements between the various operations management functions and departments are eliminated. The results from converting an organization's value-adding efforts to TOC will be a sizable increase in its profits and a large reduction in the number and size of conflicts within the organization.[2] In addition, this change will also free up a sizable amount of management's time, which, in the past, was spent resolving conflicts and disagreements and can now be used on other more important issues which include the organization's ongoing transformational journey.

So let's take a quick look at the basic steps an organization might take to implement DBR (the production planning and control tool).

---

2 Levinson (2007); Ricketts, J. 2007. *Reaching the Goal: How Managers Improve a Service Business Using Goldratt's Theory of Constraints*. Indianapolis, IN: IBM Press; Woeppel (2001).

- The first is getting the buy-in of the VP of Operations and at least a tentative buy-in from the President. This is needed because its overall adoption will change the perspective and measures used within operations to plan and make decisions which will be out of sync with the rest of the organization. It is better to cross this bridge ahead of time.

- With support, the next step is to get buy-in and build support from those individuals who are making decisions, both on the production floor and in planning, along with a solid representation of the production workers within the division. This training session is usually two days in length and it provides enough knowledge that everyone understands the basics of DBR and is comfortable with the terms and approach to using it. I also use this training to develop the steps needed to implement the shift.

- Preparing for the change-over is the next step. This involves smaller meetings with groups of workers, not previously involved, to introduce them to the shift in how things will be managed and the timing of the shift.

- Execution day is the day when DBR becomes the new planning and control process. Like anything new, be it a job, car, or computer, there is a learning curve in becoming comfortable with it. The first week is full of questions and a few miscues, but by the end of the first week everyone should be on board and the system should be functioning well.

- The last step is fine-tuning of the system as everyone becomes more comfortable with the transition.

While there are many examples that highlight the successful adoption of TOC in the value-adding activities, I want to take a brief look at two that document the timing and impact of DBR in the real world. At Bal Seal Engineering, Inc. in California, the champion of TOC was the production manager. Five individuals, chosen to become new supervisors under TOC, went through the training program and adopted the DBR production tool to fit the specific needs of Bal Seal. Within the first week of implementation, Bal Seal reduced the work in process (WIP) inventory, which represented in excess of two weeks' worth of work, by over 90%. This caused some real concerns among the workers because they had worked fifty to sixty hours a week for the last couple of years and they depended on the overtime. The solution was to maintain their pay level as associated with the plant's level of output. In other words, the workers were now earning in forty hours what they used to have to work sixty hours to earn. By the end of the first month, the complete DBR system was in place and working smoothly. The reduction of WIP greatly improved the lead-time of their products, a positive factor for their customers, and has improved their market share. Their transition from traditional methods to DBR was smooth and produced positive bottom line results within the first month.

Since then, they have continued to expand the application of TOC to other aspects of their business.[3]

In the fall of 2001, Texwood Furniture, a small manufacturer of school library furniture in Texas, started their journey. The company had piles and piles of WIP and no real planning and control processes except for expediting and "hot sheet" (late orders) meetings. Their lead-time was six to eight weeks, and they worked very long hours during their busy season, June through September. For 2002, they focused on identifying their constraint, which turned out to be the large circular saw that performed the final "to size" cuts, and then began to synchronize the work of the other departments with the pace of the constraint. As a result, they reduced their lead-time to three weeks and eliminated most of their WIP. Over the fall and winter of 2002, they continued to work on their synchronizing efforts, and, by 2003, they were producing about 10% more volume with 15% fewer people and no extra hours. In 2001 they had 1,600 late shipments. For the same period in 2002 this was down to 800 and, for 2003, this dropped further to 200 without the expenditure of capital on any new equipment. These results were produced by changing the way the management and workers thought about and measured their work. By 2003, everyone at Texwood saw their processes as a series of interdependent activities with very few critical control points. As long as the control points are working, they know the system is working. Their CEO said it is a lot like being a heart surgeon who, in the middle of open-heart surgery, notices a boil on the patient's elbow. Do you divert your attention to take care of the boil or keep focused on the heart? For surgeons it is a "no-brainer"; they know where to focus. On the other hand, most managers spend their days chasing boils because they do not know how to stay focused on the very few critical activities needed to improve their performance.

In summary, the overall objective of this stage is to continually expand the breadth and scope of the use of TOC and other systems-based tools within the value-adding domain to eventually include all of the support activities as well. As this stage continues to expand, more and more resources are freed-up because of the synchronization of resources and the reduction in conflicts within and among the various functional activities. Once a majority of the pieces within the value-adding activities, both direct and support, have embraced the change and are comfortable with the shift in how they view the operations function and the perspective they take when making decisions, the organization is ready to build on this solid foundation and transition into the second stage.

One note of caution: during the first stage, those working in the operations function will be working with two unique sets of measures. While they will rely on the ones associated with TOC to analyze and guide their decision-making, when they have to communicate with any individual or function outside of operations, they have to translate the TOC-based measures into the traditional set of measures that

---

3 The production manager at Bal Seal presented this success story at the 1996 Jonah Upgrade Conference organized by the A. Goldratt Institute for their certified members. The conference was held in Colorado Springs, CO, October 21–24, 1996.

are being used throughout the remainder of the organization. While this is usually not a problem, management must be aware of this additional burden being placed on those in the operations division.

Stage two: ensuring the use of consistent measures and information

Stage two consists of three distinct steps or phases. The first of these is focused on establishing a consistent set of measures across the organization for guiding decisions and actions. In most organizations today, each department, each function, and in many cases each individual has their own measures of performance against which their efforts are evaluated. The second step is focused on our IT systems and what changes we need in them to support the shift to a systems-based understanding. After all, the foundational assumption for IT was the optimization of individual and departmental performance and not the effective management of a system. The third step looks at having a method to align the breadth and capability needed to effectively handle the organization's various managerial roles and a way to align that with the capability of those individuals in managerial roles. If these are misaligned we will have some managers who are in way over their head and some that are bored and lack a challenge in their current roles. If you look back, all of these steps are about bringing consistency to how the organization does things by removing or revising the practices that produce this inconsistency.

An integral part of being able to establish, adopt, and monitor activities across all the organization's functions is to have a consistent and reflective set of measures as well as a comprehensive information/knowledge management system that effectively supports the organization's need for accurate and timely information while providing it with the capability to develop new knowledge as needed. A foundational item that must be in place before work on either the measurements or the information/knowledge system can be undertaken is an awareness of and agreement on the "goal" of the organization. Given the understanding that was presented earlier, in Chapter 5, that addressed the conflict between the traditional goal of "more profit" and the systems-based goal that is, in some form, focused on the "long-term", this shift is a necessary condition that must be included in this stage. Until the goal of "more money now and in the future" is replaced there will be conflicts and disruptions within and between the organization's various elements.

One of the easiest approaches to ensuring a consistent set of reflective measures is the adoption and use of the TOC measures of throughput, inventory, and operating expenses along with what is referred to as throughput accounting—an extreme form of direct costing. The purpose of relying on this approach to the collection and categorization of costs and revenue is to provide the organization's management with a consistent set of measures that better reflects the real costs and contribution of each product and its impact on the organization's overall performance. While the use of traditional cost accounting and Generally Accepted Accounting Principles are still required to report revenues and costs for taxing purposes, they distort the information management needs to make good decisions.[4] A number of books offer general guidance and direction for adopting this approach (Corbett 1998; Smith 1999).[5]

In addition to providing a consistent set of measures across the organization, this stage also includes the need for a new approach to managing the organization's knowledge and information. Before the advent of computers the knowledge associated with the how's and why's within an organization resided in its older employees and it was through their mentoring of younger employees that the knowledge was transitioned. With the advent of computers, and more specifically, the ongoing development of software designed to collect and capture data, analyze it through a set of predefined algorithms and programs, and then produce reports based on the assumptions used in the development of those algorithms, the reliance on past knowledge contained within an individual has been almost eliminated. Today these computer-based tools collect and monitor the relative progress of organizational activities along with maintaining an almost real-time connection to the flow of dollars, which provides management with an almost up-to-date synopsis of how the various functional pieces are performing. As a result of this shift to computer-based collection of information and creation of knowledge, more and more of management's analysis and decision-making is tied to the outputs provided by the information management software systems. After all, such a system is unaffected by personal bias, it is computationally much more accurate, and it provides built-in insights with its next to real-time presentation of information.

Who could ask for anything more? "Yet analyst estimates suggest that the companies in the *Fortune* 500 still lose a combined $31.5 billion per year from employees failing to share knowledge effectively".[6] That said, it behooves us to not only take a look into the practices of how an organization manages the collection, storage, and sharing of its information, but I would suggest even more importantly, to consider how it fosters and supports the efforts to generate "new knowledge" that will ensure its practices, analysis, and decision-making are based on the newest and most appropriate understanding of its business model.

4 Bell, J., M. Swain, J. Bell, and S. Ansari. 1998. *Management Accounting: The Theory of Constraints and Throughput Accounting.* New York: Irwin McGraw Hill; Bragg (2007); Drucker (1954); Johnson, H.T. and R. Kaplan. 1991. *Relevance Lost: The Rise and Fall of Cost Accounting.* Boston, MA: Harvard Business School Press; Noreen *et al.* (1995); Smith (2000).

5 Bragg (2007); Caspari and Caspari (2004); Eden, Yoram and Boaz Ronen. 2007. *Approximately Right, Not Precisely Wrong: Cost Accounting, Pricing, & Decision Making.* Great Barrington, MA: North River Press; Smith, Debra. 1999. *The Measurement Nightmare.* Boca Raton, FL, St. Lucie Press; Corbett, T. 1998. *Throughput Accounting.* Boca Raton, FL, St. Lucie Press.

6 Myers, Christopher G. 2015. "Is Your Company Encouraging Employees to Share What They Know?" *Harvard Business Review*, November 2015. Retrieved October 20, 2016 (https://hbr.org/2015/11/is-your-company-encouraging-employees-to-share-what-they-know).

Figure 19 General model for information systems/knowledge management

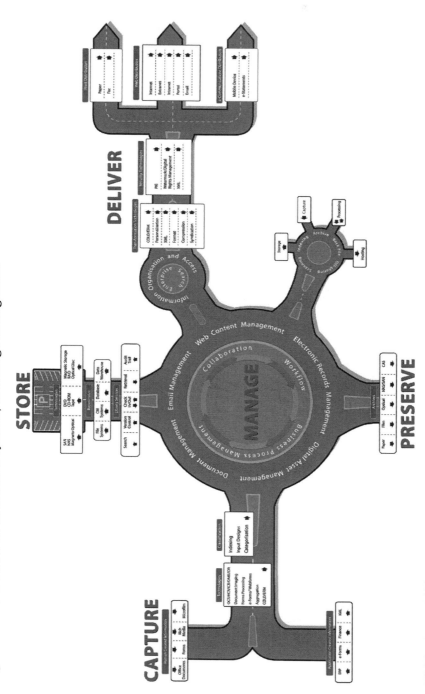

ECM Roadmap. (c) 2007 AIIM International ("http://www.aiim.org." http://www.aiim.org)

The first step is to take a look at the focus of what is an accepted Management Information System (MIS). Figure 19, which was developed by AIIM (The Global Community of Information Professionals) and is a well-known representation of the information management process, includes the various activities of: collection, storage, processing, preserving, and sharing of information. If you look a bit deeper at the figure, you will notice the absence of any activity that addresses the need to develop new knowledge and improve the current processes. This limited focus makes sense when one looks at MISs from the "traditional" mind-set whose primary focus is on increasing the performance or output of the current system rather than the ongoing development and evolution of the system.

From your new systems-based perspective, there are two critical shifts that are part of this new paradigm. The first is the recognition of interdependence between the various entities within the organization and its external environment. The second is the need to evaluate and update the internal information system to keep it aligned with changes in the external environment. In other words, this means that an up-to-date information system is consistently in flux because it is continually seeking out and including the "new knowledge" it finds into its ongoing processes and practices. So what does this new perspective of MIS or, more accurately, knowledge management look like?

In 2002, Mark McElroy introduced a systemic approach to managing an organization's knowledge, which he referred to as "second-generation knowledge management".[7] Having looked briefly at the traditional approach to MIS, the primary question becomes: what does the second generation of knowledge management provide an organization that a good MIS/ERP system does not? The important distinction this approach makes over traditional knowledge management paradigms is the recognition that an organization is a living system and in order for it to thrive and continually evolve it must have the capability to look at, evaluate, select, develop, and implement alterations and adjustments to its assumptions and understandings of everything that affects its ongoing development. That includes the internal activities under its control as well as an awareness and understanding of the external environment it interacts with. This is no different than what we, as individuals, have to do. After all, our decisions and actions are only as good as the knowledge and assumptions we rely on. No matter whether we are talking about an individual or an organization, without the ongoing creation and incorporation of new knowledge and insight into its decision-making processes, its analysis and decisions are being based on old data and assumptions, sometimes with catastrophic results. So let's take a look at what this enhanced perspective of knowledge management provides.

This approach reconsiders two major activities. The first is providing the requisite environment to encourage and support the development and formalization of new knowledge. The second is the collection, maintenance, and distribution of the organization's current knowledge. Figure 20 presents the overall approach to knowledge management.

---

7 McElroy (2002).

Figure 20 **Second-generation knowledge management model**

Source: © 2003 by Executive Information Systems, Inc. and Mark W. McElroy

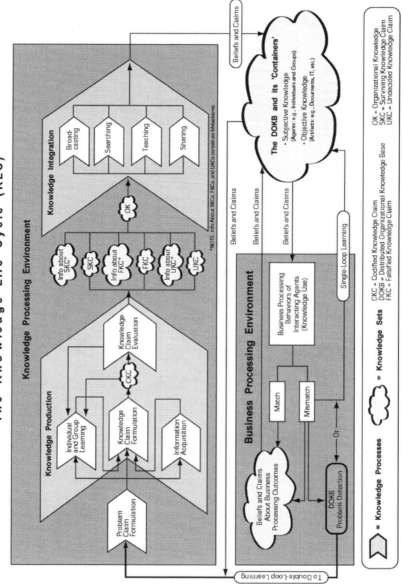

While the previous elements of Stage Two have addressed the need for and adoption of consistent measures of performance and the ongoing development of knowledge and sharing of information across the organization, there is another area where the adoption and use of consistent measures will have a strong positive impact on the organization's cohesiveness and engagement. That is having a consistent approach to measuring and categorizing the various roles across an organization and being able to effectively rely on the same criteria to identify and select the most appropriate individual to fill these roles. Today, throughout most organizations, the criterion for promotion is based on the technical capabilities of an individual. Yet, we have all seen technically competent individuals that are complete failures as they move up in management. In fact, *The Peter Principle* (first published in 1968) formulated this phenomenon: Management promotes you until you hit your level of incompetence.[8] Elliott Jaques, who was a founding member of the Tavistock Institute and later established the School of Social Sciences at Brunel University in London, was one of the first researchers to focus on people and work. This focus led him to develop a very different perspective and understanding of what it takes for an individual to be successful in their role at work. These are:

- Technical expertise

- Desire for the role

- Commitment to the role

- Possession of the level of mental processing capability that is equal to the size of the role

While our traditional HR practices do an OK job of the first two and an adequate job of the third, very few organizations are aware of the fourth. Those that understand Jaques' work do not over-promote or under-utilize the abilities of their employees.[9] By identifying the level of complexity associated with the organization's various roles, and then assessing the current and future capability of its employees, the organization is able to align the capability of the employee with the size of the role. This allows everyone to be in a position that comfortably fits their abilities. As such, the number of individuals that feel good about their job greatly increases and this greatly reduces the level of employee disengagement within the organization.

Jaques uses a measure he calls "timespan of discretion" to measure the "size" (stratum) of the role as well as the capability of an individual. When looking at the size of a role within an organization, the real focus is on how long it would take the boss to recognize sub-par performance by the subordinate in the role. At the low end it might be a day or two while at the high end it might be 15–20 years. When you are looking at a specific role, you are trying to identify the longest task within the responsibilities for that role. Figure 21 identifies the various stratums and the associated time span.

---

8 Peter, L. 1993. *The Peter Principle.* Cutchogue, NY: Buccaneer Books.
9 Jaques (1989, 2002).

Figure 21 **Basic managerial layering and information processing chart**

Source: Jaques, Elliott. 2002. *Social Power and the CEO*. Santa Barbara, CA: Praeger, p. 137.

	Time-span of role	Stratum	Information process	Industry	Army
4th Order	50 YRS —	Str-VIII	Parallel	Super Corporation CEO	5-Star General
	20 YRS —	Str-VII	Serial	Corporate CEO	Army (4-Star General)
	10 YRS —	Str-VI	Cumulative	Corporate EVP	Corps (3-Star LTG)
	5 YRS	Str-V	Declarative	VP	Division (3-Star MG)
3rd Order	2 YRS —	Str-IV	Parallel	Dept. Manager	Brigade (1-Star BG Col.)
	1 YR —	Str-III	Serial	Unit Manager	Battalion (Lt. Col. Major)
	3 Mths —	Str-II	Cumulative	Section Manager	Company (Cpt./Lt.)
		Str-I	Declarative	Operator	Pvt & NCO (E7-E1)

For example, in my role as the Director of Advanced Manufacturing Technology for a major defense industry subcontractor, I was responsible for a number of management tasks that were performed on a monthly or quarterly basis; but when it came to identifying, selecting, piloting, implementing, and verifying the success of a new manufacturing technology, this could take between 4 and 8 years. In order for anyone to be successful in a role of this type, they must have the capability to deal with a lot of future uncertainty. After all, the success of these new technology projects or any long-term project is, by definition, based on a number of assumptions that are unproven at the start and other issues that you are simply not even aware of at the time.

Having identified the stratum associated with the various roles, the next step is to identify the Applied Capability (Mode) of the employees. The easiest way to establish the level at which employees are working is to have a trained consultant interview their boss and, through focused questions and answers, they can identify the size (duration and level of complexity) of the tasks the boss thinks the person has / can successfully complete. This is accomplished by identifying the time horizon (duration) of the tasks the individual in question has accomplished and if he or she has had problems completing certain types / sizes of tasks. This collection of data is used to develop the Applied Capability (AC) of the individual. With both the stratum of the role and the AC of individual evaluated, the organization can be sure that the individual's assigned role is aligned with their capability. Jaques's continued research in this area led to the recognition that we all mature / develop our capability at a predetermined rate. Thus if you are at stratum 3 (1–2 years) at the age of 30 it will show you progressing to stratum 5 (10–15 years) over the next 15 years. Being able to identify the growth / maturation of the Potential Capability of your employees, provides an organization with a solid foundation for developing a detailed succession plan that provides both individuals and the organization with a look into the future—regarding the capabilities they will have and the roles that will need to be filled. Figure 22, presents the well-documented maturation path for individuals. For example, if you are 30 years of age and working at Mode 3 you will reach Mode 6 by the time you reach age 60. Understanding this growth path gives the organization and the individual a route forward and insight into the future roles they can hold in the organization.

Figure 22 Maturation of individual potential capacity

Source: Jaques, Elliott. 2002. *Social Power and the CEO*. Santa Barbara, CA: Praeger, p. 138.

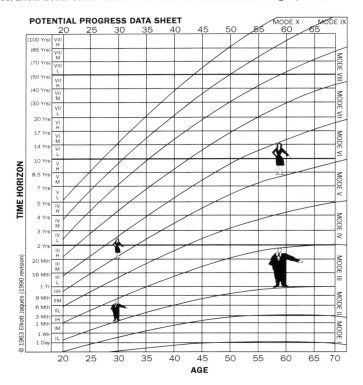

One thing I have not mentioned is that Jaques's model assumes that the individual in a role also has a commitment to the work (do their best at everything that is asked) and the skills and knowledge to accomplish it. Over the years, it has been well documented within organizations that have adopted requisite organization that the employee engagement and retention rates are much higher than the industry norms. I have purposely left the remainder of Jaques's overall systemic approach to human management for the third stage, where the other tools become the primary change.

As we review the overall changes and efforts needed to successfully complete the second stage:

- Incorporating and aligning consistent measures across the organization

- Adjusting the information system to support the organization's ongoing evolution

- Providing a consistent alignment between individual capability and role requirements

We should be aware that this is a much larger set of organizationally wide changes than were required in the first stage. Therefore, the successful completion of this stage requires a substantially larger commitment of time and resources than the first stage. While the Stage one adoption of a consistent set of measures in the operations activities is relatively easy because the overall focus of that function or division is on making more of the right thing, the adoption of a consistent set of measures across the entire organization is a much bigger issue. The following is a quick summary of the three steps within this stage.

Since all of us do what gets measured, and in the past, most of the measures used are designed to improve the local performance with no real linkage between it and the overall goal of the organization, is there any wonder *why* our departments and divisions behaved like they were in competition with each other. Let me give you an example. Valmont Industries plant in Brenham, Texas has been using TOC for over ten years. When they started bringing TOC based measures into their operations, they started to see how wrong their pricing and product mix decisions were. As a result, they changed their approach to product pricing and product mix decisions and dramatically increased their bottom line. By establishing a strategic constraint for their operations, they were able to use the measure of contribution margin per constraint unit as the single criterion for pricing and product mix decisions. As a result, everyone across the organization—sales, marketing, purchasing, production, and the rest—now rely on the same approach to establishing product priority and pricing.[10] To that end, they even use that measure as part of their approval process for capital expenditures.

---

10 Koziol, D. 1988. "How the Constraint Theory Improved a Job-Shop Operation". *Management Accounting*, May 1988: 44-49.

We all know of the problems associated with each function or division having and needing a different set of information. The adoption of the systemic approach to knowledge management ensures that everyone in the organization is getting their information from a consistent source which, when combined with a consistent set of measures, will greatly reduce the conflicts and disagreements between and within departments and divisions. A new knowledge management system will support the identification, gathering, testing, and adoption of new pieces of knowledge as they are developed. With this built into the organization, it will be able to establish a competitive advantage because it will be able to more effectively utilize the new knowledge it develops or obtains from the external world.

The final step in this stage is the use of consistent criteria to identify and classify the various roles within an organization based on the stratum or mode of the role. By using the same criteria to evaluate the capability of their employees, the organization can identify and select individuals who have the capability needed for the role. This all but eliminates the problems associated with having the wrong person in the wrong role. In addition, relying on this consistent set of measures provides a foundation upon which the organization can identify and understand future needs and its employees become more aware of their career potential.

As with the first stage, when the measures and information/knowledge become consistent, conflicts will be reduced and replaced with cooperation, which frees up more resources. These freed up resources become part of the team and experience base needed to undertake the third stage.

Stage three: ensuring the use of a consistent management system

The third stage is primarily focused on the "people" within the organization and the organization itself. This stage involves conducting an in-depth look into the organization's structure, policies, and practices as they relate to the people and the overall focus of the organization itself. After all, the people *are* the organization and the organization's overall focus provides the guidance and direction through which the people take actions and do work. Yes, this is the biggest and most difficult stage because it requires a shift within the mental models and assumptions held by all the organization's members. While most will have been exposed to some of the shifts in the first two stages, it is in this stage where the mental models and assumptions of the entire organization will become more aligned when it comes to *what* the business is and *how* it should develop. So, where does one start this stage of the journey? The answer is … it depends.

As I see it, there are two major shifts in this stage:

- Continuing the change outlined by Jaques and moving towards becoming more of a requisite organization—this shifts the understanding of the entire managerial model to one that is based on a systemic, interdependent model.

- Embracing the journey to formally recognize itself as a living system, which, by definition, means it recognizes the larger economic system as a larger living system. This shift also includes recognizing that as a living system it is also a learning organization that is continually evolving over time. This means that it must have the capability and willingness to continually review and evaluate the methods and models it uses. This also includes a recognition that its overall goal is long-term success and development. Some of the elements that would be a part of this transformational shift are listed below:

- ○ The Learning Organization
- ○ The Flourishing Organization
- ○ Conscious Capitalism

The transformational journey for both of these shifts is complex and stretches across the entire organization. As such, the planning and execution for each of them must be led from the top and have strong support from the entire senior management team. Without this, any momentum gained through the first two stages will be negatively impacted. So let's begin to look into this third stage. For discussion sake, I will address these two shifts within this stage in the order presented, but recognize that they could be undertaken in either sequence or as one large initiative.

The journey towards a more requisite organization

Given the adoption of Jaques's stratum/modes, in stage two, to identify and align the capabilities of the employees with the requirements of the roles, the organization has successfully introduced one of the foundational concepts of this transformational shift. I believe the first element to be added in this stage is a shift in understanding of the overall role of management. It is not about command and control, but much more about the facilitation and support of subordinates to ensure they successfully and satisfactorily accomplish the work associated with their roles. For those brought up in the world of command and control, this by itself is a big shift. But I ask you to imagine how your work would improve if your boss encouraged you and was there to try to understand and assist you in overcoming the hurdles you were struggling with. Imagine if you had a mentor, your boss's boss, who was concerned about your growth and progress as an employee and contributor to the organization's long-term success. This shift has to be driven from the top down and will require training along with some online support tools (schedule training and meetings, tracking questions and responses, enhancing communications, etc.) that provide guidance for both the managers and their subordinates.

Along the same line, the second element we need to take a look at is the evaluation process that charges managers to rank, identify strengths and weaknesses, and/or quantify the subordinate's performance in some form. Over the past fifty years the tools and techniques for doing this have varied greatly, yet have always ended up being used in the decision-making process about the subordinate's future employment within the organization. If we accept the fact that these processes and tools are a part of the old boss–subordinate (command and control) world and our organization is transitioning to the new holistic, systems-based world, this tool must also go by the wayside. Jaques suggests that evaluating people by their results should be replaced by the manager's judgment as to "how well" they did in achieving the results (their personal effectiveness). This form of evaluation is focused on ranking (evaluating) subordinates on how well they completed their assigned tasks compared with what the manager expected from others with the subordinates' capability level. He suggested using three levels within each stratum for this, low, medium, and high. By removing the focus on individual performance and looking at effectiveness (how well you work) the barriers between the boss and subordinate are greatly reduced, which facilitates closer communications about progress and potential problems. This contributes to a much stronger working relationship between boss and subordinate, which leads to increased engagement and productivity. Something all organizations are seeking.

Another contribution of Jaques can be found by expanding the work that began in stage two where the focus was on identifying the capability of the employees and ensuring that the roles they held were appropriately matched with their capability. The third element in this transformation process is to focus on restructuring the organization so that the size of the role (level of work) associated with each managerial level is one strata higher as you progress through the organizational structure. The first step is to look at the organization in its 'manifest' state, in other words, the way in which the organization is understood today (see Figure 23).

Figure 23 **Manifest organization diagram**

Source: Jaques, Elliott. 2002. *Social Power and the CEO: Leadership and Trust in a Sustainable Free Enterprise System*. Santa Barbara: Praeger.

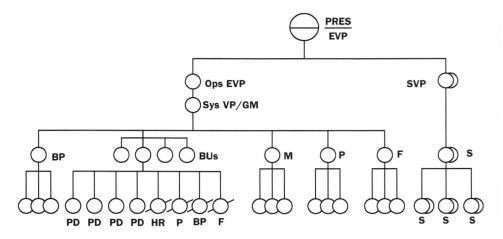

Key:
BU: BU CEOs
PD: Product Design
HR: Human Resources
P: Purchase

BP: Business Plan
F: Finance
M: Manufacturing
S: Sales

This is nothing more than a traditional Organization Chart that documents the various positions within the organization and to whom they report. In this instance, they were looking at a large manufacturing company (over 20,000 employees) that produce multiple products for a small number of customers. While this depiction was sufficient in the past, when you needed to know who to ask and who was responsible, it is insufficient in today's world. The next step is to look at what Jaques refers to as the Extant organization (see Figure 24). This is an enhancement to the traditional organization chart. Instead of just documenting what role reports to whom, this chart also includes the Applied Capability level of the individual who is currently in that role. In Figure 24, you can see the misalignment across the organization. Any time you have a boss and subordinate working with the same Applied Capability level or when there is more than one level between them, there is a substantial decrease in their ability to communicate and work together. In this example, you can see numerous instances where this gap between boss and subordinate exists.

Figure 24 **Extant organization**

Source: Jaques, Elliott. 2002. Social Power and the CEO: Leadership and Trust in a Sustainable Free Enterprise System. Santa Barbara: Praeger.

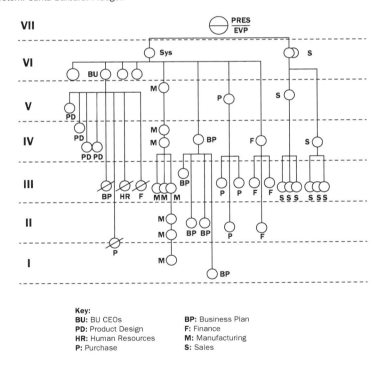

Key:
BU: BU CEOs   **BP:** Business Plan
PD: Product Design   **F:** Finance
HR: Human Resources **M:** Manufacturing
P: Purchase   **S:** Sales

Imagine if you can, that you are the senior executive of a business unit (working at stratum 6) that is responsible for all the support activities such as product design, purchasing, and business planning and your direct subordinates have an applied capability level that ranges from stratum 2 (3–12 months) to stratum 5 (5–10 years). Think about your inability to effectively communicate and engage in productive dialog or problem-solving issues because of the disparity in capabilities among your direct subordinates.

The journey from the extant perspective to one where all the roles are staffed by individuals with the appropriate level of capability is not something that can be fixed overnight. The disparities have to be identified and the viable candidates for possible new roles need to be found. A plan is required to fix the worst disconnects first and then promote or hire additional individuals for the needed roles for which there is no appropriately qualified individual—with the needed capability, knowledge, skills, and desire.

The fourth element that I would recommend in this transformation is to look into pay across the organization. One of Jaques's really important research findings has to do with what he refers to as 'felt fair' pay. His research shows that people consistently identified the same level of pay as 'fair' for each level of work (stratum) within a geographic region. That said, this now provides organizations with a pay structure that is based on the Applied Capability (the level they are currently working at) of the employee. Within each stratum, he uses the three ranges (low, medium, and high) to classify the level of effectiveness at which the individual performs. Someone at stratum 5 is carrying a greater burden of accountability, given their increased role, than someone working at stratum 3 and as such should be paid more. His research led to the development of a pay differential across the levels and stratums that in 2000 ranged from $25k for the lowest level of stratum 1 to $1.28 million for someone at the lowest level of stratum 7. While this disparity between the production worker and the CEO looks wide, it is only 51 times as much; in 2010 the highest paid CEO in the U.S. was paid in excess of 250 times the pay of the average production worker. Put in perspective, I think there is a lot that could be said for bringing CEO pay back into alignment with something that has some logic behind it.

Expanding our understanding outside our organization into our supply chain

Today, the business at the end of the supply chain, the one that sells the end product, shoulders most of the risks and, therefore, reaps most of the rewards. A deeper look at this situation shows that, in reality, no new money enters the value network (supply chain) until the end customer pays for the end product. In 2000, an effective argument was put forth by Holt and Button who suggested that if the network's members, those organizations in the supply chain, shared some of the risks associated with the production of the end product then some of the rewards associated with the sale of the product could be shared with these supply chain members. While this is a major shift from the practices of today, imagine what the adoption of this interdependent approach would do to bond and bring together, in a more cooperative arrangement, the various members of a supply chain. Of course, this shift will not occur in the short term, but by recognizing the potential benefits from such a shift, more discussions will take place around this idea and quite possibly, a new interim solution will emerge.

Embracing the journey to recognition as a living organizational system

If we look back at the previous steps and stages in this transformational journey, we see that each of the individual initiatives has been targeted at transforming a specific function or set of activities within the organization. In addition, as we have progressed on this journey, the breadth and/or depth of the changes has increased and reached across a larger segment of the organization. This final segment is focused on providing the entire organization, and by this I am referring to all the individuals that make up this entity, with a more in-depth understanding of how all aspects of the organization and its individual lives are intertwined and interconnected. It is this understanding that will empower each individual to grow and become a more active contributor to the organization's ongoing development. Said another way, this learning, understanding systems and interdependence, is how you and the organization leverage the synergy within the organization to facilitate its ongoing evolution. So let's look at the basic path an organization can take to bring this together.

While there are a variety of paths to developing and sharing this type of insight across an organization, including developing it in house, I believe the most efficient path would be to become associated with one of the universities or non-profits that are focused on supporting this level of organizational transformation. The three that come to mind are the Society for Organizational Learning (SoL), the Fowler Center for Sustainable Value at Case Western Reserve University's Weatherhead School of Management, and Conscious Capitalism which is an outgrowth of the book by the same name written by John Mackey and Dr. Rojendra Sisodia. This segment will take a look at what each of these organizations have to offer and how they can contribute to your transformational journey towards becoming an interdependent organization. Before we get into the details, there is one thing that all of you should be aware of. By being on the transformational journey outlined in this book, your understanding of the basics of systems, systems-thinking, and interdependence is well beyond that of most other organizations when they started their own journey and became associated with the support organizations mentioned above. That said, a lot of the foundational work such organizations will provide will be more of a refresher course for your organization.

A brief look at SoL

In Chapter 5 I introduced *The Fifth Discipline* which has appeared on almost every "best business book" list of the last 20 years. The uniqueness of this book is its focus on the transitional journey organizations need to take to become what Senge refers to as a learning organization. He is critical of the traditional perspective of management which relies on rather simplistic models that are used to describe the role of leaders in providing direction to an organization, which, by definition, is a very complex system. He also criticizes the perceived closeness (time) between a cause and the resulting effect. Yet, from a systems perspective we know that the proximity between these two can be anywhere from almost direct, in very simple systems, to very far apart (long delay) in large complex systems. So, what can the learning organization do to facilitate the journey towards the interdependent organization?

Dr. Senge defines a learning organization as a place: "where people continually expand their capacity to create the results they truly desire, where new and expansive patterns of thinking are nurtured, where collective aspiration is set free, and where people are continually learning to see the whole together".[11] Achieving this is based on the cornerstone of systems thinking—seeing the whole together. It is this understanding that brings together and fuses the other four disciplines he includes: personal mastery, mental models, team learning, and building shared vision. Combining these four disciplines with the understanding of systems results in an increased synergy that provides leverage to the organization and its ongoing transformational journey. It is this in-depth level of understanding of systems that will facilitate the completion of the third stage by bringing together the mental model and understanding of all the individual members of the organization and facilitate its ongoing development and growth. So, how is this shift incorporated into stage three?

Through participation in the Society for Organizational Learning (SoL), which is the outgrowth of Senge's work at MIT. The mission of SoL is to facilitate the interdependent development of people and their institutions that allows them, as a whole, to create what they cannot create alone. The focus of this was to spread and share the understanding, practices, and lessons learned by all the organizations on this transitional journey. To that end, SoL provides a variety of programs and resources that any organization on a transformational journey can draw on. While they have the usual mix of programs, consulting, and coaching, they also have a virtual presence that provides 24 hour access to their insight and knowledge. In addition this provides linkages to their network of members where sharing and assisting is available. My recommendation is that the organization should investigate SoL and its offerings to see if the fit seems to match its goals and objectives. If there is a fit, then becoming an active member of SoL is the first step. As a member, the necessary support, advice, consulting and collaboration with other members will provide the needed direction for moving forward in stage three.

A brief look at the Center for Sustainable Value

It was in 2002 when the Weatherhead School of Management (WSM) at Case Western Reserve University launched an initiative entitled the "world inquiry into business as an agent of world benefit" (BAWB). This effort was outside the norm for business schools because it was interested in seeing how businesses could become

11 Senge (1990, p. 3).

a focus for world improvement, rather than only being concerned about improving profits. Given the success of their initiative and a generous gift from the Fowler family, the WSM established the Fowler Center for Sustainable Value (FCSV) in 2009. Their goal was to "leverage the legacy and to create the finest research, education, and applied center for sustainable enterprise in the world".[12] Since its founding the FCSV has been quite busy building a well-deserved reputation for itself. Among the strongest elements in support of its overall goal of enhancing BAWB are the activities which fall under its AIM2Flourish moniker. A major portion of this work is focused on showcasing the newly developed breakthrough initiatives that demonstrate the best business practices from around the world in partnership with the 580 schools and universities involved in the UN's Principles for Responsible Management Education (PRME). Also under this AIM2Flourish initiative is the international conference for Business as an Agent of World Benefit. I attended their 2014 conference and was impressed with the knowledge and practices introduced and the wide diversity of individuals in attendance.

In alignment with its overall mission, the Fowler Center is interested in sharing its insights with businesses that are actively engaged in expanding sustainability into their business. This sharing could vary from as little as involvement in conferences and workshops to engaging their advisory services to help businesses through the uncertainties associated with becoming a more sustainable organization. For those of you on the third stage of the transitional journey towards becoming an interdependent organization, the engagement of the Weatherhead School of Management as an advisor, especially for assisting you to bring the thinking and understanding across the entire organization, would be highly recommended.

A brief look at ConsciousCapitalism.org

Since its founding in 1978, John Mackey has led Whole Foods from its first store in Austin, Texas to its current ranking of 181 in the Fortune 500 with over 76,000 employees and revenues in excess of $15 billion. Throughout this journey, Whole Foods has maintained a belief that business is about something more than making money. It has a higher purpose—it should have a positive impact on the world. In 2012 John Mackey and Rajendra Sisodia, a Professor of Marketing at Bentley University, published their book *Conscious Capitalism*, which was the foundation on which the Conscious Capitalism movement has been built. Today, this organization is composed of 28 chapters, 19 of which are located in the U.S. The purpose of these chapters is to provide a place where members of the local business community can meet, discuss, learn, share, and help each other move themselves and their organizations towards a more conscious future. In addition, this group is working to create an ever-expanding library of insights and best practices that will be easily available to those searching for a better way to do business. Since 2007, they have been holding CEO Summits where pioneering CEOs can meet, share,

12 https://weatherhead.case.edu/centers/fowler/about/cooperrider-launch

and learn from others about how to create value for all of their stakeholders—customers, employees, community, environment, and shareholders. I believe that this is another place where anyone seeking a deeper understanding about how to move forward can find support and answers.

Closing thoughts on the transformational journey

It is my hope that by the time you reach this point, you have begun to contemplate what is next. Let me elaborate a little. What I have found through the years is that, once someone sees a new and more positive perspective, they have a real hard time going back to where they were before the expansion of their insights. It is my hope that a vast majority of you fall into that category. Thus, I would like to take a minute to set the stage for the next chapter. Up to this point, you have been exposed to an in-depth look that laid out how we (business) got to our current position. We then took a look into the new paradigm of **systems**—its historical development and expansion out of science into the humanities and applications within business. In Chapters 6 and 7 I presented a model of business as an interdependent organization, which recognizes and leverages the interconnectedness within itself and between itself and the various outside constituents with which it interacts. That was followed by a solid look at what I believe is the most viable transformational journey for implementing this model in today's organizations. What I have yet to talk about is what you might do next to facilitate your ability to be an active contributor to your organization's transformational journey in the not too distant future. Welcome to the last chapter, the one that will help you build the transitional bridge to your next steps.

8

Thoughts on how to begin the journey

Introduction

In Chapter 7, I laid out what I see as the most appropriate organizational path for implementing the ideas, processes, and practices contained within an interdependent organization. As you reflect back on the last chapter, you should notice that it does not address *how* an organization moves along the transformational journey from where it is today to the point where its management team decides it is time for it to make the transition. This chapter is my take on how to fill this void. It starts by looking at how an individual might move themselves forward after reading this book and intuitively seeing its value to become someone who has developed enough insight and understanding about this new paradigm that they are looking for guidance as to *what is next?* How can they take their newly found understanding and convert that into being a founding or active member of the change initiative within their organization? This is a group of like-minded individuals who initially came together to develop a deeper level of understanding of the new paradigm and have morphed into a loosely formed team that wants to share their knowledge with others in the hope that they can bring transformational change to their organization. My thoughts and recommendations on this journey are presented below.

1. Setting the stage

2. Establishing a solid knowledge base within the organization (personal and informal working group, IWG):

   i. Expanding one's understanding—finding your passion

    ii. Building a cohesive group of like-minded peers

3. Introduction to and obtaining buy-in of senior management team (SMT):

    i. Providing SMT with foundational awareness and knowledge:

        a. Initially small, informal working and training sessions
        b. Start with "real-world" stories to establish real value
        c. Gradually expand size and depth of content being presented

    ii. Transformational process leading to SMT buy-in:

        a. More formal presentations and discussions providing more and more details and insight:

- Quantifying the impact on the future:

  - Stakeholder perspective

  - Stockholder perspective

- Identifying and quantifying the risks associated with the initiative

        b. Presentation and utilization of case based on organizational history and ending question "what next?"

- Revisit past decisions with new knowledge

- Look into the future with new knowledge

        c. Introduce proposed transformational journey, developed by IWG, to SMT:

- Identify expectations and outcomes

- Quantify risks and possible contingencies

    i. Preparation for transformational journey—under SMT guidance:

        a. Establish a new *vision* for the organization that is aligned with the new path
        b. Revisit, revise, and complete the task-level project plan for implementing Stage one: operations:

- Includes general and specific educational training that will be needed throughout the stage

- Includes processes that support continuous learning

- Includes management from all areas that will be affected by the Stage one transformation

        c. Stage two and three: update initial plan to reflect current journey

In addition to the aforementioned topics I have included a final section which contains a summary of my final thoughts and insights for each of you as you contemplate your journey forward.

Setting the stage

It is well known that introducing and bringing change to an organization is relatively easy when its back is against the wall. At that point in time, a large percentage of the organization's employees have come to recognize that continuing with a "more of the same" strategy will not work and some sort of *change* is needed. This does not mean they necessarily know "what to change" or "what to change to" but they do recognize the need for it. Conversely, when an organization sees itself as being successful, most of its employees are not open to making anything more than some minimal refinements to its current processes and practices because they carry the belief that you do not change something that is working. So, before an organization can begin talking about the *whats* and *hows* of the execution stage, it needs to have taken the transitional journey from where it is today to a point where it is ready to execute. So, let's look into the transition that needs to transpire before an organization is ready to begin taking the actions associated with its transformational journey.

I have broken this transitional journey down into three basic steps or phases. The first is focused on the journey of developing and expanding the concepts and mental models associated with the interdependent organization. This learning is first undertaken by individual(s) that have read the book and are looking to develop a deeper understanding in the hope that the new knowledge might be applicable to the organization they are associated with. This leads to the formation of what I refer to as the informal working group (IWG). This group is composed of a number of relatively like-minded individuals who have begun to see the possibilities that are available through the shift to a systems-based business perspective and are willing to take a lead in introducing these ideas and the transformational journey previously outlined within their organization. Once this group has come together, the second step involves the introduction to and "buy-in" from the organization's senior management team (SMT). Accomplishing this requires a change to the mental models currently being used by the SMT. Admittedly, this is not a small challenge, but if it is approached *logically*, from *their perspective*—bringing improvement to the overall organization—with *real-world examples* that *demonstrate* how these same changes have produced *positive results* for other organizations, there is a good chance they will see the value associated with the new perspective being introduced. After all, they carry the responsibility for the organization's overall performance and, as such, should not disregard out of hand, possible new paths. The third step is focused on the development of a detailed project plan for the transformational journey and its approval by the SMT.

Developing organizational knowledge and understanding

Given the starting point that you are part of a viable organization, one whose financial performance is satisfactory, where do you begin and what might be the initial set of activities one should undertake? The first thing that anyone should do who wishes to do more than just read this book is to recognize that the transformational journey being introduced here is a long-term effort that will involve, at its beginning, a number of like-minded individuals who are willing to look at and challenge the assumptions and beliefs they have previously relied on. It is my hope that by the time you have reached this point in the book you will have come to the realization that *you* are one of those individuals. That said, let's look at the first step in your journey. To reduce the confusion I have divided my comments into two segments—expanding your understanding and expanding the size of this initial group of participants. This does not mean they are done sequentially; in fact it might well be more effective to do them concurrently. I would encourage the early group members to develop their knowledge, instincts, and skills about how to best present these new insights and understanding since this will become more important as you move into later stages where a much broader educational effort is needed.

Expanding your understanding

There are at least three different categories of insight/new knowledge you will need to acquire as you are working through this step. The following list is in no particular order. The first is to develop a deeper understanding of systems and complexity. As your knowledge of this expands you will begin to see the interconnections between causes and effects that you probably were not aware of. The second is to expand your understanding of the limitations of today's business assumptions and models. Knowing what is wrong with a model allows you to develop a path that overcomes its limitations. The third is to develop a list of initiatives within your organization that did not produce the anticipated results. These will be used to develop real-world examples of how the limitations negatively impacted the organization's performance.

Systems and complexity

I had the good fortune to be introduced to the basics of systems through the books of Senge, Goldratt, and Lovelock that I read during my Ph.D. program. A few years later I expanded my understanding by looking into the field of chaos/complexity through the works of M. Mitchell Waldrop (*Complexity: the Emerging Science at the Border of Order and Chaos*) and Fritjof Capra (*The Web of Life: A New Scientific Understanding of Living Systems*). While this start was good for an academic who is charged with staying current with new ideas, it is not the most efficient path to beginning to understand this new paradigm. The first book you should read is: *Stepping in Wholes* by Ollhoff and Walcheski. This easy read will not only give you a basic understanding of this new world and its impact on organizations, it also has a very solid bibliography from which you can begin to expand your knowledge base. From that foundation I would start looking for additional books and websites to expand your knowledge.[1] There is no predefined path. I would suggest you start looking into books and articles that are aligned with your likes and expertise. There are many resources in this ever-expanding field and you should focus your learning on the aspects that you are drawn to. Remember, you will not be on this journey alone; as you begin to discuss and collaboratively learn with one another, the sharing of insights will enhance the breadth of each other's understanding.

Limitations in today's business models

When we reflect on the past, we see how our (human) understanding of things has changed over time. Over 200 years ago, the state of the art in medicine was focused on "blood-letting" as a way of removing the "bad blood" which caused the patient to be sick. As our understanding of the body grew, we recognized the folly of this practice. When we take a look at the field of economics prior to the beginnings of the Industrial Revolution its primary focus was on how countries could use their resources to gain an advantage over other countries and use tariffs to protect these advantages. Adam Smith's *The Wealth of Nations* began the shift to what is seen as free market economics. He argued that the true value of items was derived by the amount of labor used to produce them, that social good was tied to the effort of individuals, and the invisible hand within the market place. By the early 1900s the work of John Maynard Keynes was becoming popular. In his works he pointed to the need for government intervention to reduce the severity of the boom to bust cycles being experienced by the Western economies. By the 1950s Milton Friedman had begun to publish his ideas that were based on a totally free market with little to no government intervention. Since the late 1980s some of today's economists are looking at economics from the perspective of systems and complexity theory.

I mention the learning journey in medicine and economics as a reminder that just because we believe something and practice it, does not make it the ultimate and forever answer. The more we live, the more we learn, the more we realize that we do not know all the truths. Nowhere is this truer than in today's business practices, so let's look at places to begin your search.

---

1 For example, www.theinterdependentorganization.com

One of the easiest places to look is at the performance evaluation system used within your own organization. But, before I begin, let me establish a baseline—we all, regardless of our position, work for an organization whose current and future success is tied to improving its overall performance. If this is true, then the first question is: can any of the evaluation criteria used to evaluate your performance be directly tied to the overall performance of the organization? Without this direct link the assumption about the measures being used is that people with a higher evaluation rating are doing a better job and, as such, should be rewarded.

Another assumption is our reliance on cost accounting to provide us with **real costs** to analyze local or departmental performance. Remember, cost accounting was developed as a tool to allocate indirect labor (management and engineering which was about 10% of the total costs) across the two businesses owned by DuPont. It was a method to help their senior management evaluate the performance of their two business managers. Yet, today we still use the same basic approach even though the indirect labor costs are usually well over 50% of the total costs. To develop a deeper understanding read *Relevance Lost* by Johnson and Kaplan or review a variety of web links tied to the limitations of cost accounting.

Over the last 20 years there has been an ever-increasing volume of discussion and publications about what is being commonly referred to as financialization—the almost sole focus of business on making more dollars. One of the most important books on this topic is *Capitalizing on Crisis: The Political Origins of the Rise of Finance* by Greta Krippner. In this well-researched book Krippner looks deeply into the recent financial crisis from the perspective of the regulators and how a shift in regulations eventually led to the crisis of 2008. Another book that I would highly recommend regarding this focus on financialization is *Conscious Capitalism* by John Mackey. In it Mackey points out the limitations of having a purely financial focus and demonstrates the need for organizations to be concerned about their customers, employees, and community while making sure they are doing well financially. Given the insight within these books one should be able to begin calling into question a majority of the strategies and practices in place today that are only looking to improve financial performance.

Today, most of the scientific community recognizes the fact that the Earth and its resources are finite. Yet, most of our business and economic models, because of their short-term focus, do not consider this limitation or the long-term impact our production actions and waste creation have on the Earth's environment. My question to you is: how can we continue to make decisions without considering the long-term consequences of our actions?

As you can see there are a lot of business practices and models that we use on a daily basis, many without even thinking, that are incorrect. The more we use these, the further down the rabbit hole we go and the harder it will be to get out. It is our responsibility to understand these limitations and begin to correct our practices.

Developing a list of organizational initiatives

Since your effort to develop a deeper understanding is a prerequisite for what you hope to be a much larger journey—transforming your organization—beginning to prepare for that journey cannot start too soon. One of the most important tools in teaching is having real-world examples. While relying on published papers and how-to books that highlight how a business has made a change is nice, it is much more powerful to draw on familiar real-world examples. For example, I was Director of Advanced Manufacturing Technology for almost three years and in hindsight I can say that none of the projects I oversaw had any impact on the overall performance of the business. As you are developing your deeper insight into systems and the limits of today's business models, you will begin to recognize the mistakes within your organization's past improvement initiative approval processes (analysis and decision-making). By collecting these and the associated assumptions and projections you will begin to develop a nice series of short cases that can be used to clarify the ideas and concepts contained within the new paradigm. This collection effort should be continued throughout the entire transformational process to help document the need to change the foundational understanding across the organization.

Expanding the organization's base of knowledge and establishing the internal working group

Moving forward from the initial starting point, which will consist of one or a few like-minded employees, the journey within any organization can begin. But prior to the initiation of any formal introduction, educational training, or consideration of a change within any organization there is a sizable amount of foundational learning and educational work that must be completed. The primary effort of this initial group is to build a critical mass of individuals from across the organization who have, on their own volition, invested the time and energy needed to explore the new ideas, expand their understanding, develop familiarity with, and recognize the potential associated with the transitional journey outlined in the interdependent organization. This informal group of employees will become the primary group of "champions" for this transformational initiative. With the assistance of outside experts (consultants and/or educators) this group will read, research, discuss, review, and even develop what they believe are the "basics" of an implementation plan for the organization. For lack of a better term, I have chosen to call this the informal working group (IWG) to identify and describe the group of individuals from within the organization that will undertake the needed foundational work. While it is not necessary for this group to initially contain a member from the organization's senior management team (SMT), once the IWG has reached the conclusion that the new path is both viable and desirable for their organization, they must begin to introduce and obtain "buy-in" from some members of the SMT. After all, any organizational change initiative needs their support.

The following outlines what I believe are the basic steps that an IWG will need to transition in order to have the insight and information needed to present to their SMT. Once you have read the book and done some initial investigative research on your own you should begin working to bring together a group of peers (4–8 individuals to start) from across the organization's mid-level and/or SMT who have expressed concerns or questions about *why* we do things the way we do. In a smaller organization, you may well have a personal relationship with individuals within most divisions which makes creating your IWG pretty easy. Conversely in a large organization, this effort will take a couple of iterations. First you start with a few individuals you have relationships with and begin the journey. As the group starts to develop it reaches out to identify and invite a few others, from within unrepresented divisions, to participate. The efforts used to assist the new members to "catch up" should be tracked to begin identifying the things that are "important" in making them comfortable with the new ideas. These will be valuable when beginning to lay out the training content for a larger group. With the group established, the learning begins. I think the easiest place to start is by sharing the book and scheduling some informal "let's discuss" times when open and honest sharing, discussions, and questions about the organization and the ideas presented in the book can be delved into. As the group develops insight and a deeper understanding of the paradigm shift within the book, I would strongly encourage its members to expand their understanding by looking into some of the works/authors listed in the book along with articles and insights from web-based searches to develop a more solid understanding of the ideas and practices contained within. Once the group feels they have a good understanding of the limitations within the current practices and are comfortable talking about the potential opportunities presented by such a transformational shift, the focus should begin to turn to identifying "where", within the organization, is the best opportunity for expanding the group's reach. While initially this can be functions or divisions that are not currently represented in the group, it should also begin to identify who within the SMT they believe would be the most receptive to the ideas and practices contained within their work. This will be needed in the next step.

Another really important point you must keep in mind, as you move forward, is that the ultimate goal of the IWG is to prepare the ground, plant the seeds, nurture the young seedlings, and facilitate the growth of the new garden—bringing about a major transformation to the organization. To that end, you must recognize that there is not "one-best" path for accomplishing this. In fact, there are a wide number of alternative paths (sequences of individual initiatives and shifts) that an organization can take on its transformational journey. That said, do not look at disagreement over alternative paths or sequences with disdain; instead recognize these dialogs and discussions as a major contribution to the overall learning of those involved. A lot of the work undertaken by the IWG will provide the foundation on which the education and training efforts needed to complete the transitional phase and obtain the support of the SMT will be based. In the next section I have outlined the basic steps in this developmental journey that will take the IWG to a point where the new Transitional Planning and Implementation Group will begin its work focused on the planning and implementation of the organization's transformational journey.

Introduction to SMT and their buy-in

The second step is focused on the transference of the knowledge base developed by the IWG to others within the organization including the SMT with an end goal of receiving their support for the transformational journey. That said, I want to reiterate here that before beginning this step it is imperative that the IWG has been expanded to include representatives from the various departments or functions within the organization. Their membership will ensure that the various perspectives within the SMT and across the organization have and are being included in the planning and development of educational materials.

As for whom within the SMT to reach out to first, I would focus on the list developed in the preceding section as a starting point. Other considerations would be SMT members that have proven to be open to new ideas. If all else fails, I have provided a couple of guiding thoughts that might help focus your choice. First, since one of the foundational assumptions of this transformation is that business is not a machine to be optimized but instead is an interdependent system, you should avoid those individuals whose role is focused on squeezing more dollars out of the machine. I am talking about those individuals within the areas of finance, accounting, and to some extent information systems. Second, those within the fields of human resources, operations, and marketing should more easily recognize the concept of interdependence because they rely on close cooperation among people, departments, and other organizations to complete their daily responsibilities. Once the list has been agreed upon the initial out-reach should begin.

As with any effective educational effort, this one also needs to be designed to identify and demonstrate the limitations and omissions within the currently accepted practices without blaming or pointing a finger at those who have previously relied on them. The key to accomplishing this is to begin the educational effort by focusing on the identification and understanding of the **limitations** (foundational assumptions) associated with the currently accepted analysis and decision-making practices before introducing the "new knowledge" and showing how its adoption will eliminate the types of errors that have been made in the past. This approach should provide a rather "safe" (nonjudgmental) environment within which the SMT and other members of the organization can learn and come to embrace the new understanding.

You must remember that the initiation of this educational process within an organization is not about presenting and selling the perfect organizational vision and solution. It is about bringing people together to build a common understanding of the current situation and facilitating them to develop a conscious vision or solution for the future. So the first question that must be addressed is where and how this educational journey starts and what might it look like? To answer that I have put together what I believe is a basic plan for obtaining buy-in from the SMT. It contains three unique steps for this educational and transformational process.

- The first step is focused on providing the SMT with enough exposure and understanding of the current limitations and a solid introductory awareness of the new business paradigm so that they are willing to go forward and learn more. The preparation, scheduling, and delivery of this step is the responsibility of the IWG, those passionate individuals who have invested their time in building their knowledge base. Since you only have one time to make a first impression on the topic (a transformational journey for the organization), I suggest that you begin to lay out what the IWG believes would be the most appropriate structure and flow for this introductory meeting and begin preparing the support materials for it.

- The second step, which I call the transition process, involves the IWG expanding its reach and now involving the organization's SMT in its efforts. The goal of this step is to transfer the requisite knowledge and insight the IWG has developed to the SMT and obtain their agreement to move forward with a formal implementation initiative. I believe the development and use of an in-depth case that is based on their own business history and facilitates the SMT's analysis and review of past and future situations using the business they have intimate knowledge about is the most efficient and powerful way to complete this step. The end objective of this step is to get the tentative approval of the SMT, which should be a prerequisite for the third step— developing a comprehensive implementation plan with costs and risks.

- The third step is focused on developing the implementation plan that will guide the organization's transformational journey. Since the IWG had already prepared an initial high-level version of a transformational plan, this would provide a valid starting point for this effort. This will be an iterative process to ensure the plan details are aligned with the SMT's understanding of things like time, budgets, and expected results. I would highly encourage the IWG to draw on the TOC's thinking processes for the identification, definition, and sequencing of the multitude of tasks associated with this transformational plan. To that end I have provided an overview of all five of the thinking processes in the Appendix.

Introducing the new paradigm to the SMT

In the beginning, the meetings between the select SMT members and a few members of the IWG would be focused on introducing the ideas and concepts in an effort to increase their interest and desire to move forward. That said, these first few meetings should be structured around sharing documented impact of the new process or practice in similar businesses and highlighting how they reduced some of the negative effects that your organization is experiencing. As their interest is piqued, the journey into more details can expand. You must recognize that each of the SMT members will have their own favored perspective and, as such, these initial meetings will be more focused on meeting the specific needs and questions of individual SMT members. The primary objective of these introductory meetings is to provide each of the SMT members with enough knowledge that more formal lessons can be conducted. Once the more formal lessons start, the teaching can move them deeper into the details of the transformational processes and what is involved. As you begin this more formal training, you should remember that the training you will be providing to the SMT, while it is a bit deeper and more complex because of the audience, is the same type of training that will have to be provided to the other members of the organization as the transformation takes place. That said, think of these sessions as the proving grounds for further educational efforts. I would structure these more formal learning modules around the three trans-formational stages: operations, measures, and people. Within each of these, the training should focus on identifying the limitations of the current processes and practices and the potential impact the shift could produce. I would put off any detailed talk about "how do you do this" by saying "that will be addressed in the later training".

Transformational journey leading to SMT buy-in

Facilitating the tentative buy-in of the SMT will, by definition, require providing the team with a requisite level of education and understanding of the assumptions and practices contained within an interdependent organization and also reflect the adjustments in that model needed to leverage its fit into the specific business. This is a multi-step process that should be designed by the members of the IWG with some assistance from some local educators and consultants to ensure the structure and content follows best practices. To that end these lessons should draw on a variety of real-world examples to demonstrate a detailed look into the shift in thinking, a quick look into the change process, and a strong look at the proven results being obtained. Because of the breadth of the shift, I recommend that this step addresses the three stages (operations, measures, and people) independently and the educational effort, which may well take six months or more, should culminate with a comprehensive case based on the organization. This discussion will provide the SMT with a foundational example upon which they can develop some first-hand experience in understanding the new paradigm for analysis and decision-making.

Sessions on operations, which are the first ones presented, need to be very well prepared because, at this point, the SMT is still uncommitted to the journey but willing to learn and explore the possibility. That said, I would recommend working with educators and TOC consultants as to the sequence and approaches that have been successful in the past. Remember, the goal of each of these is to get the SMT's understanding and tentative acceptance of this new business perspective.

The measures session will have the biggest impact on the "bean counters" (finance and accounting) and HR (employee selection and personal evaluation), so make sure the lessons address their possible concerns. As you progress into this transitional journey you want to be very aware of the concerns brought up by the various SMT members and begin correlating which concerns are associated with which functional area so you can continually refine and develop your future training materials.

The third set of sessions focuses on the shift in management itself. The first two stages should give the SMT a solid foundation from which they see the need for these changes and the potential impact they will have on the employees and their engagement with the organization. Once again, I would encourage you to draw on outside experts in the area of organizational change and development to provide guidance and assistance on this step.

Once the SMT has a good grasp of the focus and processes/practices being recommended, the introduction of a real-world case, built on the past decisions and actions within the organization, should let them see how the new paradigm would have altered past decisions and results. The following list outlines what should go into this case and its use in the training. I would encourage you to draw on local educators that are familiar with the development and use of cases to assist in its preparation and use.

1. **Preparing the case**. In this effort the IWG will build a complete case package that contains the insight and information the SMT will need to understand the issues, risks, and expectations associated with the overall initiative.

    i. Establish a baseline against which the new alternative can be compared

        a. Detail the current situation—processes, practices, assumptions, limitations

        b. Quantify their impact on:

            • Stakeholders including customers and employees

            • Stockholders

    ii. Develop the future scenario in enough detail to provide the following:

        a. Identify the changes envisioned in the processes
        b. Identify practices, assumptions, limitations

    iii. Identify and quantify the costs and risks associated with the implementation of the initiative

        a. Develop a detailed implementation plan—including required tasks, resources needed, projected costs, and risk level of tasks

b. Identify any highly critical task(s) and associated contingency plan(s)

c. Summarize costs and risks of implementation initiative

1. **Present case to SMT**

i. Before presenting the case to the SMT, the IWG must be sure that their educational journey has provided them with the needed insights about systems, systems-based business processes and practices, and the growing use and adoption of these tools

ii. Present the completed case and highlight the important steps and concerns that have been identified

iii. Recognize this is an iterative process and be prepared for a few rounds of revisions and improvements driven by the SMT

With the tentative approval of the SMT to move forward, the last major item to be addressed is: "what are the major steps in this transformational journey and what are the risks?" These answers are presented and discussed in the third step.

Detailed implementation plan: the overall journey

This step is where the IWG introduces their initial implementation plan to the SMT and with the help of the SMT, develop a more comprehensive and detailed implementation plan that will serve as the foundation on which the project plans for each of the three stages will be built. Given the need to take a deeper look into the risks and the trade-offs associated with the possible paths forward, and the level of complexity in this transformational journey (the issues, possible solutions, and the sequence for their resolution) the successful completion of this step calls for some serious problem-solving and project management expertise. I would highly recommend that you bring in a consultant or educator who has experience using the thinking processes of the theory of constraints. This set of tools will facilitate the groups working through the highly complex issues of implementation in a structured and sequenced manner. The goal of this step is to develop enough details within the implementation plan so the SMT has a good grasp of the overall project size, scope, time, resources, risks, contingencies, etc. so they can make a decision as to their support of the proposed journey. This is the critical decision point or stage-gate for this effort. If they do not agree, then it stops and the journey forward is at least delayed. If they agree, the journey continues into the third step—preparing for implementation. Let us move forward with a look into what this step contains.

Final planning and preparation for implementation

With the SMT's complete buy-in there is a major shift in who is responsible for the remaining work. With their buy-in also comes funding and formal responsibility for the initiative's successful execution. It is here that the IWG is disbanded and a formally established group, which I have called the Transitional Planning and Implementation Group (TPIG) takes its place. While this group will, in most instances, contain a large number of the IWG members, I would suggest that it also contain some additional upper level managers and a few representatives from the SMT. Remember, the group should include individuals from across the organization's various departments and divisions to ensure their efforts and conclusions will include direct insight as to the possible impact, concerns, and benefits from the transformation. With its formal recognition and funding the group will be able to actively engage individuals and functions from across the entire organization. I would also recommend that this new group set up monthly briefing meetings with the SMT to keep them in the loop as the planning and implementation efforts move forward.

Since this is the final phase before the transformational journey begins all the necessary planning and details needed to put together a comprehensive plan for the journey must be addressed. That means that not only is this group responsible for completing the detailed project plans, which include tasks, timelines, staffing, and budgets, but they must also establish the timing and content of the formal and informal educational efforts that will be needed in support of this implementation effort.

With membership in the TPIG set, but before the real work can start, they need to initiate a set of educational sessions for those in the group that lack some of the detailed insight. The first step is to get the new members, those that were not in the IWG, introduced to the foundational assumptions, processes, and practices outlined in this book. They should draw on some of the experts they have already learned from for assistance and guidance to help them avoid any unnecessary hurdles in getting all the group members up to speed. If possible, they should use real-world examples from their own organization to make the lessons more real and impactful. As this learning begins, the new members will start to recognize some of the interdependence between the organization's functions and departments and come face to face with the need for a better set of tools for dealing with this level of complexity. Given the breadth, depth, and level of complexities (interdependence of various elements and activities) that will be part of this transformational journey, I highly recommend the TPIG develop a working knowledge of the five thinking process tools contained within the theory of constraints to help them identify, develop viable solutions, and prepare the detailed plans they will need to complete the steps within the stages (these were introduced in Chapter 5).

Once the foundational education of the group is complete, I believe the three primary tasks for the TPIG are as follows:

1. Develop a new organizational vision that resonates with the SMT and has enough detail to earn their buy-in for the first stage in this organizational transformation.

2. Integrate the aforementioned vision into a comprehensive implementation plan for the first stage that contains the necessary steps to successfully complete the first stage. Recognize that after each step the plans for the remaining steps will be reviewed and revised to reflect the lessons learned in the just completed step.

3. Develop a more explicit plan which includes identifying the tasks, their scope, and time estimates for completing the second and third stages.

The successful completion of this work will contain a substantial level of both formal and informal guidance and interaction from the SMT. In addition, as progress is being made through these tasks, especially once work begins on task #2, the level of education being provided across the organization will have to expand accordingly. After all, you must keep the organization's members aware of the changes going on and make them aware of what is coming in the future.

Developing/redeveloping an organizational vision

Before we begin, I just want to remind you of the foundational assumption I laid out at the beginning of this chapter: "you are part of a viable organization, one whose financial performance is satisfactory". Given that starting point, when we talk about developing or redeveloping an organizational vision, exactly what does this mean? The business dictionary defines vision as: "an aspirational description of what an *organization* would like to achieve or accomplish in the mid-term or long-term future. It is intended to serves as a clear guide for choosing current and future courses of action".[2] While most in business today would see the answer in terms of market share, global reach, technological superiority, or some other business focused response, it is my hope that by now each of you will begin to see other possible answers. When I read this, I see the following question(s): "what impact is this organization going to have on the future of our stakeholders (customers, employees, and owners)" or "how will our organization's success affect the larger whole (stakeholders, community, economy, and/or environment)". Please notice, my answers to these questions are not focused on how well the business does relative to its competition, after all this is the result of the day-to-day analysis and decisions it makes, but about how it goes about achieving something beyond financial returns—making a difference in something.

That said, when an ongoing business decides to establish or revisit its vision (what does it want to accomplish in the mid- to long term) it is a very serious undertaking that requires it to look deeply into *what* it is, *where* it wants to go, and *how* it will make decisions in the future. Since none of us undertakes or makes major life-changing decisions without a great deal of thought and analysis, we should expect nothing less from our organization's leadership. After all, this first charge, revision-ing the organization, requires its leadership to take a deep look into the assump-tions, behaviors, and practices within the organization and this is no easy task. This will be very difficult for many leaders because when they recognize a better way they will also recognize the mistakes they have made in past decisions and actions. Over the years, in my discussions with senior-level managers, I do not remember any of them telling me "the system did not need fixing", but what they all chose to do was become proficient at working within and leveraging the existing rules and practices. That said, let's delve into what it will take to revisit the organization's vision.

In my mind, the foundational piece of this shift can be found in Chapter 6 where I introduced the S-BBM which has a goal or vision that is something larger than just financial performance. In Figure 11, I depicted this shift by putting the necessary conditions of meeting or exceeding the needs of the customers, the employees, and the owners on an equal footing and making all of them subordinate to a larger organizational goal or vision. While I suggested a couple of ideas for that larger goal, the important thing to remember is this shift is from more dollars, which is a very short-term measure, to a goal that provides the decision-makers with a new final arbitrator for organizational decisions that has a long-term focus. This shift does not imply that financial performance is not important, what it does do is put all three of the factors that are necessary to the organization's continued and future success on equal footing.

The question is: how does the SMT with the assistance of the TPIG develop this new vision statement? The following are the basic steps they may need to take to develop and document a new vision statement. This activity may also be one in which they choose to hire an outside expert to assist them in facilitating this effort.

- Reflect back on the learning journey they have completed to date—observe the shift in recognizing and understanding the impact of the interdependence within and across the organization and the broader business community

- Take that new perspective (insight, processes, practices, and measures) and look into the future—identify the possible issues and opportunities the new perspective provides

- Select those which the SMT sees as having the most to contribute to the future success of this newly envisioned organization

- Synthesize a new vision statement for the organization based on the elements selected above

As the TPIG makes progress towards its new vision statement, it needs to begin thinking about bringing together the insight, understanding, and resources needed to develop the details of their second task: the development of the detailed implementation plan for completing the first stage.

Developing the detailed project plan for the first stage implementation

While the detailed implementation plan that the IWG and SMT put together earlier will serve as the starting point, no work can go forward until management selects the project management team for the first phase of its transformational journey. Since this first step is primarily focused on the operations (value-adding) activities within the organization the team must have someone that is very familiar with the structure and details of this function—most likely the VP of Operations. In addition, the team needs someone that is an expert in the use and adoption of the operations tools within the theory of constraints. This will, in most instances, have to come from the outside. A third element in this team is someone who can take over the responsibility for the development and delivery of the educational training that will be ongoing throughout the project. In addition, the team will need an assortment of individuals from across the various operations functions to be involved in developing, sequencing, and coordinating the detailed training and facilitation efforts that will be going on simultaneously. Once the team has been brought together, work on developing the details of the implementation plan can begin. The following are the basic steps I would follow to develop this plan.

1. Establish a common understanding among the team members of the new paradigm and vision for the organization

2. Define the boundaries, breadth of reach, for the first stage—which areas across the organization will be addressed in this stage and which ones will not

3. Develop a common understanding among the team as to what the end result of the first stage will look like—what and how has it been changed?

4. Working from the "end results" backwards begin to sequence the various changes that have been identified—asking the question: Looking back, what are the last change(s) that must be in place before this one can be achieved?

5. Once all have been sequenced, review the predecessor for each change and ask: is there anything I have overlooked?

6. From the beginning, take each change and begin to develop a detailed scope of work statement for it—include scope, resources, time, steps, etc.

7. Use this information to build the comprehensive project plan for stage one

8. Be sure to include a comprehensive continuous review process within the plan to ensure you capture "in-process" learning as the implementation

goes forward and a solid debriefing at the end to facilitate and improve the remaining stages

9. Throughout this plan-building process keep the SMT aware of the process and respond to any comments or concerns they offer

At this point the implementation of stage one can begin. I have included the following thoughts on the initial kick-off of an implementation effort as guidance to be included in the first stage plan. When I conducted what would be called the "initial education" session for a mid-sized machining business, we included all of its senior management team along with select members of mid-management, along with officers and long-term members of the union. When the 2-day training was complete everyone in attendance, which represented all areas and levels of the organization, understood the shift in the business model, the changes in processes and practices, and the new measures of performance that would be put in place. This allowed the execution phase to go smoothly, without a hitch. This is the overall objective of the initial implementation effort. It solidifies the path forward by providing in-house proof that these types of changes are doable and provide improved organizational performance.

Develop high-level outline or plan for the second and third stage

Once the project plan for the first stage implementation has been completed but before the implementation is started, I would highly recommend that the TPIG undertake a revision of the initial plan for stages two and three. This effort is focused on developing a deeper awareness of what will be involved in the latter two stages before the implementation journey kicks off. The need for this understanding is to be better prepared for dealing with the gaps and issues associated with the later two stages that will, by definition, surface during the first stage. This effort would encompass the second through fourth steps outlined in the project plan development sequence above. By providing the project team with this level of insight into the remaining two stages, they will be able to keep their eyes open for interconnections within the current stage that have linkages to efforts in the later stages. This insight will provide smoother transitions as the implementation moves into the later stages. With this more in-depth look into the details associated with the second and third stage implementation plans complete, it is time to begin the organization's transformational journey. Throughout this long journey, just like life's journey, one must remember that plans are based on what we thought given our knowledge when they were developed. As life and this project have progressed, reality and our understanding of it has continued to evolve and therefore, we must continually adjust and revise our journey. I encourage you to take a look at and understand the logic diagram shown in Figure 25 which I have patterned after the "chain reaction" that W. Edwards Deming drew on the blackboard in 1950 to explain the impact of focusing on statistical quality control (see Figure 8 in Chapter 5). This is the direction in which the transformational journey will take you and your organization.

Figure 25 **The systems chain reaction**

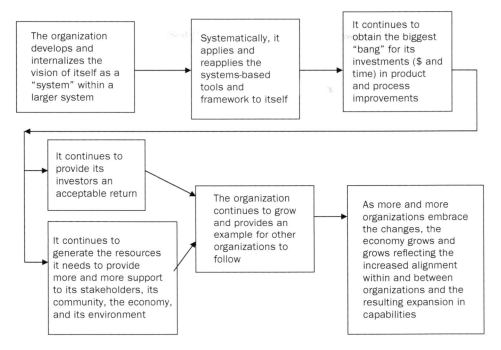

To each and every one of you who have begun your transitional journey by reading this book, I wish you continued success on your life's journey and I encourage you to continually expand your level of understanding and push back the horizons that you see.

Final thoughts and insights for your journey

In closing, I would first like to thank each of you for being curious enough to take a look into the ideas at the cutting edge of business. It was 25 years ago when I had my insight that business was not as it is taught or practiced—a machine that can be optimized—but an interdependent network of organizations which stretches from raw materials to customers. At that time, this point of view was embraced by a very small number of cutting-edge thinkers. Since then the level of insight and understanding around this perspective has grown and today there are more than a few organizations that have begun moving in this direction. It is my hope that this book will provide those already on the path and those that are considering this path in future with a clearer understanding of the magnitude of the journey and insight into how to sequence their transformation.

I know what it is like to be one of the few that see the world through a different lens. Whether it was the value of total quality management in the early 1980s, how we as employees are more focused on the progression of our careers than on improving the organization we work for, or the interdependence within and across business, seeing your world through a different lens is both a blessing and a curse. I encourage each of you to take this ability, which some might think of as a weakness, and turn it into a strength as you contribute to the transformational efforts within your organization. To all of you, I wish you the very best in your transformational journey.

Appendix 1

TOC thinking processes overview

As I look into writing an overview of the thinking processes (TP), I came to realize that others may well have done this better than I could. To that end, I searched the web and found what I believe to be a solid, concise description of them. This was taken from the website of the Center for Industrial Research and Service (CIRAS) at Iowa State University. I hope this summary helps you recognize the power and focus the TP tools provide.

> Simply stated, the Thinking Processes (TP) involve the rigorous application of cause-effect logic to solve a problem. There are 6 basic tools that make up the thinking processes. Each can be used independently or they can be used in various combinations depending on the need at the time. The TP are listed below, followed by a primary independent use.
>
> - Current Reality Tree (root cause analysis)
> - Evaporating Cloud (conflict resolution)
> - Future Reality Tree (solution testing)
> - Negative Branch (negative side-effect abatement)
> - Prerequisite Tree (reaching an ambitious target)
> - Transition Tree (fail-safe action planning)
>
> The TP can be used together when an organization is underperforming. This is done by using the TP to answer, in sequence, the following three questions:

1. What to Change?

2. To What to Change?

3. How to Cause the Change?

The first question is the most important and often the most difficult question to answer. There is usually no physical evidence to point you to the core problem in a complex environment. Instead you have to "map out" what is currently going on in your system. The logical mapping structure that is used at this point, is the "Current Reality Tree." This is not a simple task, but when it is completed successfully, you will know what to change.

That will bring you to the question, "To what to change?" There are two distinct steps to answering this question.

1. Identify a breakthrough idea, or "injection", that will overcome the problem(s) identified in the current reality tree.

2. Ensure that the "cure" that is derived will not be worse than the "disease."

The "Evaporating Cloud" is used to break through the core conflict that is currently blocking the organization from fully exploiting or subordinating to their constraint. Applying the breakthrough idea to the organization is analogous to a doctor revitalizing a patient by giving him/her an injection, and so the breakthrough idea is referred to in TOC terminology as an injection.

The "Future Reality Tree" is developed next to ensure that the undesirable affects you now are experiencing will, indeed, be changed to desirable effects by the injection. The unintended negative consequences of the proposed solution are usually identified at this point using what are called Negative Branches. If these bad things that result from a good action can be prevented, then you can be sure the "cure" (the injection) will not be worse than the "disease". Now you know what to change to.

That brings you to question 3, "How to cause the change?" The simple answer is: get the people who are going to have to live with the change to create the action plan that is needed for implementation. The Thinking Processes pro-actively involve those who are most effected by the change. These people are solicited for their vision of what obstacles might prevent the organization from moving forward on this breakthrough solution. The workers are used to generate all the additional ideas that are necessary to implement the original injection. Once these are known, a plan is mapped out. The tools used when answering question 3: the "Prerequisite Tree," and the "Transition Tree."

The following websites may be of help to you as you begin the journey into the tools of TOC:

- www.goldratt.com/ The Goldratt Institute provide business solutions in the areas of business operations, business policy and strategy, and project management

- https://www.toc-goldratt.com/ Goldratt Marketing Group provides information about TOC consultants, books, and other training materials for sale, a list of upcoming events, and a history of the Theory of Constraints

- http://www.goldrattconsulting.com/ Goldratt Consulting has decades of experience in defining and implementing TOC-based solutions across a wide spectrum of industries

- www.tocico.org/ The Theory of Constraints International Certification Organization is a not-for-profit certification organization for TOC practitioners and consultants

Appendix 2 Recommended reading

In an effort to help the reader focus their search for other supporting materials, I have divided this list of books into three categories. The first contains books that introduce, discuss, and expand our level of understanding of systems, systems-thinking, complexity, chaos, and associated new ways of thinking. These focus on the shift rather than on the adoption or use of the tools in the area of business. The second is focused on the adoption and use of the ideas and understandings presented in the first category. Here you can trace the evolution and development of the various systems-based tools, processes, and practices that have been adopted and used in business. The third category is focused on the shift in measures (financial and accounting) and economics. What I have not included is any research from the field of sustainability economics, which has been growing over the last decade. I hope some of these will find their way onto your reading list.

Understanding systems, chaos, and complexity (S, C, & C)

Bertalanffy, Ludwig von. 1968. *General Systems Theory*. New York, NY: G. Braziller.
Bateson, Gregory. 1972. *Steps to An Ecology of Mind*. Chicago, IL: University of Chicago Press.
Capra, Fritjof. 1982. *The Turning Point*, New York, NY: Bantam New Age Books.
Prigogine, Ilya and Isabelle Stengers. 1984. *Order Out of Chaos*. New York, NY: Bantam New Age Books.
Herbert, Nick. 1985. *Quantum Reality: Beyond the New Physics*. New York, NY: Anchor Books.

Campbell, Robert. 1985. *Fisherman's Guide*. Boston, MA: New Science Library.

Peat, David. 1987. *Synchronicity: The Bridge between Matter and Mind*. New York, NY: Bantam New Age Books.

Gleick, James. 1987. *Chaos: Making a New Science*. London, UK: Penguin Books.

Wallace, Alan. 1989. *Choosing Reality: A Contemplative View of Physics and the Mind*. Boston, MA: New Science Library.

Ruelle, David. 1990. *Change and Chaos*. Princeton, NJ: Princeton University Press.

Hayles, N. Katherine. 1991. *Chaos and Order: Complexity Dynamics in Literature and Science*. Chicago, IL: University of Chicago Press.

Lewin, Roger. 1992. *Life at the Edge of Complexity*. London, UK: Macmillan.

Kellert, Stephen. 1993. *In the Wake of Chaos: Unpredictable Order in Dynamical Systems*. Chicago, IL: University of Chicago Press.

Cohen, Jack and Ian Stewart. 1994. *The Collapse of Chaos: Discovering Simplicity in a Complex World*. London, UK: Penguin Books.

Sweeney, Linda and Dennis Meadows. 1995. *The Systems Thinking Playbook*. White River Falls, VT: Chelsea Green Publishing.

Capra, Fritjof. 1996. *The Web of Life: A New Scientific Understanding of Living Systems*. New York, NY: Anchor Books.

Prigogine, Ilya. 1996. *The End of Certainty: Time, Chaos and the New Laws of Nature*. New York, NY: Free Press.

Holland, John. 1998. *Emergence: From Chaos to Order*. New York, NY: Basic Books.

Termimko, John, Alla Susman, and Boris Zlotin. 1998. *Systemic Innovation: An Introduction to TRIZ*. Boca Raton, FL: St. Lucie Press.

Kaufman, Stewart. 2000. *Investigations*. New York, NY: Oxford University Press.

Capra, Fritjof. 2002. *The Hidden Connections*. New York, NY: Doubleday.

Batson, Gregory. 2002. *Mind and Nature: A Necessary Unity*. New York, NY: Hampton Press.

Gunderson, Lance and C.S. Holling. 2001. *Panarchy*. Washington, DC: Island Press.

Ollhoff, Jim and Michael Walcheski. 2002. *Stepping in Wholes: Introduction to Complex Systems*. Eden Prairie, MN: Sparrow Media Group.

Coulson, Joseph, Donald Whitfield, and Ashley Preston. 2003. *Keeping Things Whole*. Chicago, IL: Great Books Foundation.

Brown, Lester. 2006. *Plan B 2.0: Rescuing a Planet under Stress and a Civilization in Trouble*. New York, NY: W.W. Norton.

Davis, Brent and Dennis Sumara. 2006. *Complexity and Education*. Abingdon, UK: Routledge.

Meadows, Donella. 2008. *Thinking in Systems*. White River Falls, VT: Chelsea Green Publishing.

Atkisson, Alan. 2008. *The ISIS Agreement*. London, UK: Earthscan.

Norman, Donald. 2011. *Living with Complexity*. Cambridge, MA: MIT Press.

Harford, Tim. 2011. *Adapt: Why Success Always Starts with Failure*. New York, NY: Picador.

Capra, Fritjof and Pier Luisi. 2014. *A Systems View of Life*. Cambridge, UK: Cambridge University Press.

Applying S, C, & C to business and management

Low, Albert. 1976. *ZEN and Creative Management*. North Clarendon, VT: Tuttle Publishing.

Senge, Peter. 1990. *The Fifth Discipline: The Art and Practice of the Learning Organization*. New York, NY: Doubleday.

Mink, Oscar, James Schultz, and Barbara Mink. 1991. *Developing and Managing Open Organizations*. Austin, TX: Somerset Consulting Group.

Wheatley, Margaret. 1992. *Leadership and the New Science*. Oakland, CA: Berrett Koehler.

Mitroff, Ian and Harold Linstone. 1993. *The Unbounded Mind: Breaking the Chains of Traditional Business Thinking*. New York, NY: Oxford University Press.

Jaques, Elliott and Kathryn Cason. 1994. *Human Capability*. Gloucester, MA: Cason Hall & Co.

Stacy, Ralph. 1996. *Complexity and the Creativity in Organizations*. Oakland, CA: Berrett Koehler.

Wheatley, Margaret and Myron Kellner-Rodgers. 1996. *A Simpler Way*. Oakland, CA: Berrett Koehler.

Jaworski, Joseph. 1996. *Synchronicity: The Inner Path to Leadership*. Oakland, CA: Berrett Koehler.

Jaques, Elliott. 1998. *Requisite Organization*. 2nd ed. Gloucester, MA: Cason Hall & Co.

Srikanth, Mokshagundam and Michael Umble. 1997. *Synchronous Management: Profit-based Manufacturing for the 21st Century*. Wallingford, CT: Spectrum Publishing Company.

Levinson, William. 1998. *Leading the Way to Competitive Excellence*. Milwaukee, WI: ASQ Quality Press.

Mitroff, Ian. 1998. *Smart Thinking for Crazy Times*. Oakland, CA: Berrett Koehler.

Kelly, Mary and Susanne Allison. 1998. *The Complexity Advantage*. New York, NY: McGraw Hill.

Kendall, Gerald. 1998. *Securing the Future: Strategies for Exponential Growth using TOC*. Boca Raton, FL: St. Lucie Press.

Hawken, Paul, Amory Lovins, and L. Hunter Lovins. 1999. *Natural Capitalism*. New York, NY: Back Bay Books.

Savoy, Allan. 1999. *Holistic Management*. Washington, DC: Island Press.

Lepore, Domenico and Oded Cohen. 1999. *Deming & Goldratt*. Great Barrington, MA: North River Press.

Levin, Simon. 1999. *Fragile Dominion: Complexity and the Commons*. Cambridge, MA: Perseus Publishing.

Schragenheim, Eli. 1998. *Management Dilemmas: The TOC Approach to Problem Identification and Solutions*. Boca Raton, FL: St. Lucie Press.

Midgley, Gerald. 2000. *Systemic Intervention: Philosophy, Methodology, and Practice*. New York, NY: Kluwer Academic/Plenum Publishers.

Goldratt, Eli. 2000. *Necessary but Not Sufficient*. Great Barrington, MA: North River Press.

Smith, Debra. 1999. *The Measurement Nightmare*. Boca Raton, FL: St. Lucie Press.

Kilmann, Ralph. 2001. *Quantum Organizations: A New Paradigm for Achieving Organizational Success*. Mountain View, CA: Davies Black Publishing.

McCormack, Kevin and William Johnson. 2001. *Business Process Orientation*. Boca Raton, FL: St. Lucie Press.

Schragenheim, Eli and H. William Dettmer. 2001. *Manufacturing at Warp Speed*. Boca Raton, FL: St. Lucie Press.

Lewin, Roger and Birute Regine. 2001. *Weaving Complexity & Business: Engaging the Soul at Work*. Abingdon, MD: Texere Publishing.

Jaques, Elliott. 2002. *Social Power and the CEO*. Santa Barbara, CA: Praeger.

Lissack, Michael. 2002. *The Interaction of Complexity & Management*. Westport, CT: Quorum Books.

Knowles, Richard. 2002. *The Leadership Dance*. Niagara Falls, NY: Center for Self-Organizing Leadership.

Sherwood, Dennis. 2003. *Seeing the Forest for the Trees: A Manager's Guide to Applying Systems Thinking*. London, UK: Nicholas Brealey.

Jackson, Michael. 2003. *Systems Thinking: Creative Holism for Managers*. Hoboken, NJ: John Wiley & Sons.

Iansiti, Marco and Roy Levien. 2004. *The Keystone Advantage*. Cambridge, MA: Harvard Business Review Press.

Senge, Peter, Joseph Jaworski, Betty Sue Flowers, and Otto Scharmer. 2004. *Presence: An Exploration of Profound Change in People, Organizations, and Society*. New York, NY: Crown Business.

Ackoff, Russell and Fred Emery. 2006. *On Purposeful Systems*. Piscataway, NJ: Aldine Transactions.

Gharajedaghi, Jamshid. 2006. *Systems Thinking: Managing Chaos and Complexity*. Oxford, UK: Butterworth-Heinemann.

Eden, Yoram and Boaz Ronen. 2007. *Approximately Right Not Precisely Wrong: Cost Accounting, Pricing, & Decision Making*. Great Barrington, MA: North River Press.

Bebbington, Jan, Jeffrey Unerman, and Brendan O'Dwyer. 2007. *Sustainability Accounting and Accountability*. Abingdon, UK: Routledge.

Senge, Peter. 2008. *The Necessary Revolution*. New York, NY: Broadway Books.

Hitchcock, Darcy and Marsha Willard. 2009. *The Business Guide to Sustainability: Practical Strategies and Tools for Organizations*. London, UK: Earthscan.

Love, Alaina and Marc Cugnon. 2009. *The Purpose Linked Organization*. New York, NY: McGraw Hill.

Makower, Joe. 2008. *Strategies for the Green Economy*. New York, NY: McGraw Hill.

Hopewood, Anthony, Jeffrey Unerman and Jessica Fries. 2010. *Accounting for Sustainability*, London, UK: Earthscan.

Stacey, Ralph. 2010. *Complexity and Organizational Reality*. 2nd ed. Abingdon. UK: Routledge.

Wolfe, Norman. 2011. *The Living Organization*. Irvine, CA: Quantum Leaders.

Hutchins, Giles. 2012. *The Nature of Business*. Cambridge, UK: Green Books.

McElroy, Mark and J.M.L. von Engelen. 2011. *Corporate Sustainability Management*. Abingdon, UK: Routledge.

Scharmer, Otto and Katrin Kaufer. 2013. *Leading from the Emerging Future: From Ego-System to Eco-System Economics*. Oakland, CA: Berrett Koehler.

Peterson, Mark. 2012. *Sustainable Enterprise: A Macromarketing Approach*. Los Angeles, CA: Sage Books.

Young, Scott and Kanwalroop Dhanda. 2013. *Sustainability: Essentials for Business*. Los Angeles, CA: Sage Books.

Laloux, Frederic and Ken Wilber. 2014. *Reinventing Organizations*. Millis, MA: Nelson Parker.

Klein, Naomi. 2014. *This Changes Everything*. New York, NY: Simon & Schuster.

Laszlo, Chris, Judy Brown, John Ehrenfeld, Mary Gorham, Ilma Barros Pose, Linda Robson, Roger Saillant, and Dave Sherman. 2014. *Flourishing Enterprise: The New Spirit of Business*. Redwood City, CA: Stanford Business Books.

History and evolution of business processes and practices

Johnson, Thomas. 2002. *Relevance Regained*. New York, NY: Free Press.

Roth, William. 1993. *The Evolution of Management Theory, Past, Present, Future*. Great Neck, NY: Roth Publishing.

Estes, Ralph. 1996. *Tyranny of the Bottom Line*. Oakland, CA: Berrett Koehler.

Gibson, Rowan and Charles Handy. 1999. *Rethinking the Future*. London, UK: Nicholas Brealey.

Gabor, Anddrea. 2000. *The Capitalist Philosophers*. Hoboken, NJ: John Wiley & Sons.

Epstein, Gerald. 2005. *Financialization and the World Economy*. Camberley, UK: Edward Elgar.

Cooper, George. 2008. *The Origin of Financial Crisis*. New York, NY: Vintage Press.

Reinhart, Carmen and Kenneth Rogoff. 2009. *This Time it is Different*. Princeton, NJ: Princeton University Press.

Posner, Richard. 2010. *The Crisis of Capitalist Democracy*. Cambridge, MA: Harvard University Press.

Taylor, Lance. 2010. *Maynard's Revenge*. Cambridge, MA: Harvard University Press.

Mitroff, Ian and Abraham Silvers. 2010. *Dirty Rotten Strategies*. Redwood City, CA: Stanford Business Books.

Moran, Emilio. 2010. *Environmental Social Science*. Hoboken, NJ: Wiley-Blackwell.

Lovins, Amory. 2011. *Reinventing Fire*. White River Falls, VT: Chelsea Green Publishing.

Morgenson, Gretchen and Joshua Rosner. 2011. *Reckless Endangerment: How Outsized Ambition, Greed, and Corruption Led to Economic Armageddon*. New York, NY: Times Books.

Stiglitz, Joseph. 2012. *The Price of Inequality*. New York, NY: W.W. Norton.

Mackey, John and Raj Sisodia. 2013. *Conscious Capitalism: Liberating the Heroic Spirit of Business*. Cambridge, MA: Harvard Business Review Press.

About the author

Rexford H. Draman, Ph.D. started his professional career as a second shift foreman at Mohawk Tire & Rubber, while working his way through the University of Akron. Over the next 19 years he held a variety of positions, ending up as Director of Advanced Manufacturing Technology for a large defense contractor. In 1990 he entered the University of Georgia in pursuit of his PhD in Operations and Strategic Management. It was here that his search for a more sustainable approach to business began. His full-time academic career began in 1994 and, in addition to his teaching and administrative responsibilities, Rex has been actively involved in consulting, entrepreneurial initiatives, and ongoing research into systems and complexity as it applies to organizations. His consulting efforts started with the Goldratt Institute where he actively contributed to their training and program development. He is currently the TOC expert at OpEx Solutions (OpExSolutions.org). Five years ago, while Chair of the Business and Economics Division at Marymount California University, Rex developed and began teaching a new course entitled Management for Sustainability, which is also being taught at the University of Wisconsin – River Falls. Today, as a Lecturer at Texas State University, Rex continues his efforts to expand his students' awareness and understanding of the forthcoming transformational journey towards organizational sustainability.

For Product Safety Concerns and Information please contact our EU
representative GPSR@taylorandfrancis.com Taylor & Francis Verlag GmbH,
Kaufingerstraße 24, 80331 München, Germany

Printed and bound by CPI Group (UK) Ltd, Croydon, CR0 4YY
12/05/2025
01867535-0001